BLIND OWL BLUES

The Mysterious Life and Death of Blues Legend Alan Wilson

Rebecca Davis

ISBN-13: 978-0615792989
ISBN-10: 0615792987

ALAN'S TALONS

By Celeste Labadie

Sometimes getting there is the journey.

And when you get there,
you find children
fawning over naked bodies.
They complain of yesterday.

There is truth in a solution of water
inside a hummingbird's egg.
The illusion of an owl sits
atop chain link fence
haunting the propane tank
resting like a walrus in a field of poppies.

Through the small door of the mind
there are several
locks forgotten.

The key lost
the combinations of emotional restriction
like a blind guitarist
putting his minor third
in a wedding cake.

Marzipan crusted
fingers
search for a doorknob
to the soul.

The tentacles of aging angst
the dusty cobweb
in the owl's talons,

Alan's talons.

CONTENTS

ACKNOWLEDGEMENTS

Thanks to the many people who generously gave of their time and energy for Alan Wilson-related interviews, correspondence, and conversations both formal and informal. These include Mary Katherine Aldin, Marina Bokelman, Frank Cook, David Evans, the late John Fahey, the late Bill Givens, Roger Handy, Barry Hansen, Jim Horn, the late Richard Hite, Tom Hoskins, Harvey Mandel, Ed Marrow, David Maxwell, the late Claude McKee, Ed Pearl, Mike Perlowin, David Polacheck, Skip Taylor, Mike Turner, Dick Waterman, Barbara Wilson, and Martha Wynoff. Others who were kind enough to aid the author of *Blind Owl Blues* during the years of research for this book include Edward Komara and Gary and Denny Schwartz.

Special thanks goes to the late, great Alan Wilson scholar Russ Montney, who organized a groundbreaking conference in 2010 to honor Wilson and educate music fans about his legacy. We also honor the memory of Shirley Konecny, Alan's mother, who graciously received the author of *Blind Owl Blues* for a personal visit at her home, shortly before her passing in 2011. Extra thanks also to Alan's sisters, Heidi Galgowski and Lisa Konecny Lindenberg, who have been extremely kind. They honor their brother's memory by furthering his ecological goals; more information on this project can be found at AlanWilsonCannedHeat.com.

Thanks also to the many other friends, family, and colleagues, too numerous to be named here, who have provided help, support, and encouragement for *Blind Owl Blues* throughout the years.

ACKNOWLEDGMENTS

INTRODUCTION

Everyone knows the voice of Alan "Blind Owl" Wilson. They might not recall the band Canned Heat, but anyone exposed to American mass media has almost certainly heard "Going Up the Country" or "On the Road Again".

From detergent to department stores, automobiles to beer, a variety of product advertisements feature Wilson's distinctive high tenor every year. In movies about the 1960s, or those featuring free-spirited bohemian-type characters, a Canned Heat song is almost obligatory. We've all heard the band's music, even if we didn't recognize it at the time.

Everyone knows Alan Wilson's voice – but very few know who he was. In the first edition of *Blind Owl Blues*, I did my best to correct that by documenting his life and music. In the years since his passing, a number of popular tall tales had arisen, particularly surrounding his death. The book was, in part, an attempt to separate the wheat from the tares of his legend and legacy.

When I began my biographical research in the late 1990s, I quickly realized that the significance of Wilson's life, and the nature of his death, would never be resolved for everyone. Some of his friends and musical colleagues were quick to offer recollections, assistance, and even historical documentation in the form of rare pictures, recordings, and more. Others, including some people

1

associated directly with Canned Heat, were less than forthcoming with information. I was saddened to learn that a few of Wilson's family members did not want him to be memorialized in the form of a written biography.

Regardless of these obstacles, I felt that Wilson's incredible talent was worth remembering and sharing with others. Upon the 2007 publication of *Blind Owl Blues*, it became clear that I wasn't alone. Wilson fans emerged from seemingly every corner, and they weren't just the baby boomers and blues nerds I had expected. Many were youngsters, including a few teenagers; others were Deadheads and jam band aficionados of my own "Generation X" age group. I was happy to find that, almost without fail, Wilson fans were thoughtful, intelligent, and highly individualistic folks.

Blind Owl Blues had been on the market for a couple of years when I received an email from one of Wilson's half-sisters, a younger sibling through his mother Shirley Konecy. At the time of original publication I did not even know the names of all Wilson's siblings, so tight were the relatives on his father's side with basic information about his family life. Hence this sister was a new person to me. But I was excited to hear from her, and thrilled to learn that my book met with her approval.

Over the last couple of years, I've been honored to meet a few more of Wilson's family members. His mother and stepfather even granted me a personal visit in late 2011, less than a week before Shirley's passing due to old age. Though her mental abilities were hampered by Alzheimer's disease, she still remembered her talented son, and I was told that she enjoyed having portions of *Blind Owl Blues* read aloud to her.

It's been a pleasure for me to develop friendships with two of Shirley's daughters, Lisa Konecy Lindenberg and Heidi Galgowski. These thoughtful, classy ladies remember Alan Wilson as a brother who was much loved by everyone in their family. They've shown me incredible kindness through their encouragement and support of *Blind Owl Blues*, even in the face of harsh criticism from others.

Inspired by a number of conversations with Lisa and Heidi, I realized in 2010 that it was time to rework and update *Blind Owl*

Blues. No book is perfect, but I hope a second edition will provide clarification on Alan's childhood and early musical development. With the electronic publishing market in mind, my intent is also to provide a more concise book that will reach a greater number of readers.

With ecology and planetary well-being now a point of concern for many, I furthermore hope that this book can help to raise awareness about the importance of the natural world. To Alan Wilson, this was of paramount interest, almost certainly equal to music in his life. With support from other family members, his sisters Lisa and Heidi have created a fund to make his goal of old-growth forest preservation a reality.

Let us take a moment to make clear what this book is not. It is not a biography of the band Canned Heat. Wilson was a founding member and significantly influenced the Canned Heat sound; however, the other band members evolved musically after his death. Four decades later, the band continues under the leadership of drummer Fito de la Parra, who declared himself "born to play in Canned Heat" when he completed the classic-era lineup in 1968. He has documented their post-Wilson history in his memoir, *Living the Blues: Canned Heat's Story of Music, Drugs, Death, Sex and Survival*. This book is recommended to all fans.

We should remember that, just as Canned Heat should not be solely defined as "Alan Wilson's band", neither was his life defined by Canned Heat alone. This biography will attempt to balance a study of his music with a portrait of Wilson as a man. Though aspects of blues history will be presented, this is not an in-depth musicological study; rather, it is a biographical tribute.

Wilson was a master of blues tradition, but was never limited by the idiom. His greatest achievements were songs featuring his original lyrics. These often involved the selective use of blues elements, grafted onto an original sound. His remarkable abilities allowed him to comprehend the inner workings of whatever musical style caught his interest. During his life, this included New Orleans jazz, acoustic and electric blues, classical Indian music, and more.

Wilson's adaptation of various genres proved both artistically and commercially effective. He was responsible for both of Canned Heat's most popular songs, "On the Road Again" and "Going Up the Country", and served as the band's musical director from its inception to his death in 1970. Through his guitar, harmonica, and band arrangements, he was the heart and soul of Canned Heat. His vocals, extremely distinctive to listeners, made the band's hits instantly recognizable.

Canned Heat's importance cannot be neatly traced to a specific influence on any significant band or artist. They were, instead, influential in their popularization of the blues in general, particularly their collaborative album with John Lee Hooker, which expanded his audience significantly. Their songs celebrated their love of the music and have educated three generations of listeners about the bluesmen who inspired their sound.

It seems quite likely that Alan Wilson's personal creativity would have eventually diverged from the "Canned Heat sound". If they live long enough, most musicians end up parting ways with the bands of their youth, forging solo careers, or bringing other projects to the forefront. Sadly, the development of Wilson's unique musicianship was cut short with the end of his life. The best commercially available examples of his creativity are a handful of songs like "On the Road Again", "Raga Kafi", "Poor Moon", "Shake It and Break It", and "Skat". We can now only imagine what else he might have accomplished, had he been given more time.

Delve far enough into the Canned Heat story, and the subject of Alan Wilson's personal problems is inevitable. One frequently repeated tale, promulgated in part by friends who jumped to conclusions or were given misinformation, is that Wilson committed suicide. However, this is not supported by hard evidence, and his death was legally deemed an accidental overdose by the attending coroner.

When I began writing the first edition of *Blind Owl Blues*, it was obvious that such conflicting stories would have to be resolved. Clearing up the matter of Wilson's death ranked high on my list of priorities. Unfortunately, the full truth will probably never be told, due to the inconsistency between various sources as well as an apparent lack of long-term records retention and availability at the Los Angeles Coroner office.

Herein I shall present the reader with the most significant and immediate accounts of Wilson's death that were available to me. The most complete picture possible is given in this book's final chapter. Intelligent readers can then determine their own thoughts on the matter. Since nobody can - or is willing to - say that they were in Bob Hite's backyard with Wilson the night of his death, ultimately any conclusion can only be tentative at best.

Regardless of what one thinks of his death, we can come to some agreements about Wilson's life. He was known to suffer from depression, and a few friends and family members now hypothesize that he may have also been affected by some form of Asperger syndrome or autism. We'll never know for sure, but this kind of condition might have explained a lot about his intriguing combination of musical ability and social awkwardness.

This book will not pretend to psychoanalyze Wilson, but will shed some light on a few of the issues that caused him grief, as recalled by friends and colleagues. Most agree that one of his main problems throughout life was loneliness, and the inability to form and maintain a satisfying romantic relationship.

Throughout his songs, Wilson explored themes of loneliness and mistreatment, with a consistent emphasis on his dissatisfaction in life. Another frequent theme is that of escape. In various ways, his unhappiness led to drug abuse and alienation, to Bob Hite's backyard where he swallowed the red barbiturate pills that played a part in his death. Whether he actually sought to escape his personal pain in death or simply in a night's sleep, there can be little doubt that Wilson was trying to escape.

Most of the quotes herein from Alan Wilson, Bob Hite, and Henry Vestine are from interviews conducted by Marina Bokelman in 1968. Selected quotes from Alan Wilson are from letters he sent to John Fahey and David Evans. All other quotes have been collected by this author via letters, telephone, email, and in-person interviews.

Withheld from the text is information which could not be sufficiently confirmed, or which was deemed too highly personal for public consumption. If any given information is uncertain but deemed worthy of inclusion, it will be noted as such.

The various informants consulted during my research frequently gave conflicting information. Great care has been taken to establish the true nature of the facts. In some cases, of course, this was impossible. Where necessary, this is noted, and all relevant claims and viewpoints will be presented so that the reader can make his or her own conclusion.

1 THE YOUNG OWL

Alan Christie Wilson was born at 8 a.m. on July 4, 1943. His birth took place in Massachusetts Osteopathic Hospital in Arlington, Massachusetts. His mother was Shirley E. Wilson, born Shirley Brigham in Pittsfield, Massachusetts. His father was John C. Wilson, Jr., born in Everett, Massachusetts. The attending physician was J. A. Robertson.

John Wilson, commonly known as Jack, was twenty-nine years old. According to Alan's birth certificate, he was working as an electrician; at various times, he would be involved in other aspects of the construction industry including bricklaying. He and Shirley already had one child together: a daughter, Darrell, who had been born two years before. The family lived at 61 Wollaston Avenue in Arlington.

Shirley was interested in art, music, and culture, and created a number of paintings throughout her life. As an elderly woman, she retained in her collection many of the jazz records that Alan had enjoyed as a teenager. There can be no doubt that her creative sensibilities were a significant influence on him, both through genetic and environmental factors.

When Alan was three years old, Shirley and Jack divorced, and she left the house on Wollaston Avenue. Alan and Darrell Wilson were left with their father and grandparents.

Two years later, Jack Wilson married a second wife, Barbara. She was an old friend of Shirley, and was already fond of Alan and Darrell. She acted as a second mother to them both, and in later years, she and Darrell would become especially close. Barbara and Jack would have three children of their own together: David, Sharon, and Jayne.

Alan, though accepting of Barbara's presence in his life, remained close to his birth mother Shirley. He visited her often, even going on his own at times when his older sister did not accompany him.

By the time Alan Wilson started school, it was obvious that he was unlike other children. He had not yet begun immersing himself in music, but already seemed attuned to another world. An interest in nature, which would continue to develop throughout his life, had already become apparent; even as a boy he seemed as interested in trees as in people.

Many aspects of nature were fascinating to the young Wilson. As a small boy, he watched the clouds closely and regularly, learning the local meteorological patterns. His family's neighbors soon began depending on him to predict the weather. One family member recalls that with just a glance at at the sky, Alan could forecast whether the day would be cloudy, rainy, or sunny. One neighbor was reportedly unwilling to leave on a shopping trip until Alan advised her whether an umbrella would be necessary.

Trees and plants became Wilson's best friends in the natural world, a source of peace and comfort. Sometimes, however, he sensed that nature experienced pain too, just as humans did. One story recalls him as a child, walking down the street one frigid New England winter. He was holding his hands over his ears as tears streamed down his face. When his stepmother Barbara asked what was wrong, he cried, "I can hear the trees. They're *crying*."

That year, the bitter New England cold had descended upon the trees in the form of ice. This caused many branches to break with loud popping and cracking sounds. This was very upsetting to Wilson, who was keenly sensitive to every aspect of nature. Even as an adult, he would be easily upset by the idea of harm to the natural world. This extended to other natural environments including Earth's moon, to which he felt a strong connection.

Alan Wilson's vision was very poor, and before long he was fitted for eyeglasses. It's possible that his inability to see properly heightened his natural introversion. By all accounts, he was also of very high intelligence, which also probably tended to set him apart from peers of his age.

Reportedly, Wilson was academically outstanding. One of his teachers informed his stepmother that there was no need for her to attend the annual parent-teacher conferences, because there was nothing to discuss. Alan was doing so well, the teacher explained, that she had no concerns. The only issue she described was his handwriting, which was often sloppy, but apparently not so bad as to be a significant problem.

Occasionally Alan even overcame his shyness sufficiently to try his hand at public speaking. With permission from his teacher, he would stand up in class and give a presentation on whatever topic he was studying. Often he reported on some subject, such as music or an aspect of the natural world, that he had been researching independently. As Barbara Wilson found out, Alan taught the entire class, including his teacher, new and intriguing facts this way.

Unfortunately, this kind of intellectual brilliance didn't make his school career easy. Some of the other children resented Alan's intelligence, and his extreme shyness, with resulting social awkwardness, didn't help.

Later in life, Wilson would recall being teased, harassed, and tormented by his schoolmates. With the other members of Canned Heat, he once visited his family home, which was located at the top of a steep hill. To his fellow musicians, he unburdened himself, sharing memories of being chased up the hill by bullies on his way home from school. There can be little doubt that such experiences contributed to his lifelong depression and difficulty with social situations.

Alan Wilson was always an emotionally sensitive individual. His other sensitivities included hearing, a sense that for him was extremely acute. With an ability often referred to as "perfect pitch", he was able to perceive tiny graduations of pitch and tone that were inaudible to the average person. Once he began learning to play various instruments, he was also able to duplicate almost anything he heard on records, simply by hearing a song once and then picking up an appropriate instrument.

As Wilson grew from a child into a young man, music became his activity of choice. In junior high school, he became fascinated by a jazz record. The story goes that Barbara Wilson was shopping at a local supermarket which featured monthly "specials" of dishes, pots and pans, and novelties which could be purchased at discount prices by grocery buyers. One month, the special was a series of record albums. Barbara brought home a jazz record, which she gave to Alan.

In junior high school, Alan began playing the trombone. Without much formal musical training, he was able to teach himself all the instrumental parts from the jazz record Barbara had given him. Soon he was teaching the parts to his friends, and moving on to other records to learn more.

Along with participating in a school band, Alan formed his own jazz ensemble with some musically inclined friends. They called themselves the Crescent City Hot Five. Throughout his teen years, he played with other young musicians as opportunity presented itself, and began some tentative forays into the world of public entertainment.

Pianist David Maxwell played music with Alan Wilson during his high school years. Together, they rehearsed and even played a few public shows together, marking Wilson's first attempts in the music business. Along with this came other kinds of experimentation, not uncommon with youth of the time.

Together, Wilson and Maxwell formed a band which rehearsed at their drummer's house. Parental discipline was relaxed, as Maxwell recalls: "The drummer's name was David Potter. It was a rather lewd scene at David Potter's house. His parents were very laissez-faire, so we'd get messed up."

During this period, Wilson had very discriminating musical values when it came to jazz, foreshadowing his later strictness regarding the blues. "At that time," says Maxwell, "Alan was into traditional New Orleans music. He was very emphatic that it be *pure* New Orleans music — no Dixieland! We used to kid him about being a moldy fig."

Maxwell recalls Wilson as a major influence, in terms of finding new and significant music. "I used to hang out with Al a lot, because I was attracted to his musical sensibilities," says Maxwell. "He actually turned me on to different people, like Thelonious Monk and Coltrane. He'd say, 'Hey, check this out, check that out.' He really made a case for their music. I would say that he was a profound influence on my musical awareness at the time."

Together, Wilson and Maxwell played a handful of gigs as teenagers. Maxwell remembers, "We did some gigs in the combo band, while we were both in high school. They were non-union gigs, for low pay. We were under age. I used to play in bars and stuff like that when I was sixteen and seventeen."

Jazz was not the only genre of music that Wilson enjoyed. He was also interested in classical European and Indian music forms, and helped his friend Maxwell explore these genres. "We were both into East Indian music, and other Asian music as well," says Maxwell. "I think that he brought that kind of sensibility and nuance to the blues. He listened to both Northern and Southern Indian music, but seemed to relate to South Indian music more comfortably. He was a purist about the fundamental nature of South Indian music."

At that time, fans could sample music albums in local record shops before purchasing. Maxwell remembers, "We listened to a lot of that stuff together, like at music stores. At the time in record stores, there were listening booths where you could take stacks of LPs and hear them."

Along with the exotic music, Wilson was interested in Eastern philosophy. He became involved with the fringes of the cerebral Beatnik scene, and along with Hinduism and Buddhism, studied the poets and philosophers of the time. Maxwell explains, "He kind of considered himself part of the tail end of the Beatniks. He was attracted to the Beat writers, such as Alan Watts, and Buddhism. He turned me on to some of that. He particularly liked Alan Watts' books, and of course the Beatnik poets, like Allen Ginsberg."

The Buddhist standard of compassion came very naturally to the sensitive Wilson, who was acutely attuned to the suffering he perceived in the world around him. "He was always an oddball," says David Maxwell. "He was extremely intelligent and very sensitive, consumed with the suffering of the world and taking it on his shoulders in a way that would be exaggerated or extreme. He was caught up with the injustices and ills of the world."

As a teenager, Alan Wilson devoted most of his energy to music. Experimentation with the opposite sex seemed a mystery to him. One family report suggests that he did attend a prom with a female companion; however, he did not have regular girlfriends.

David Maxwell recalls, "He'd bum out, because he couldn't get anything going with girls. He liked particular girls, and he wanted to be successful with girls — but he just had no sense of appearance or presentation. No social skills."

In his adult life, Wilson would continue to struggle with intimate relationships. His lack of "presentation" is often recalled as a near-legendary lack of attention to personal cleanliness, as attested by some colleagues and band mates. Other acquaintances have suggested that his hygiene was not really so bad, but that his personal habits, were, rather, a byproduct of living in the 1960s when many hippies and counterculturalists took an "all natural" approach, eschewing deodorant, frequent bathing, and the like.

In Wilson's case, it seems likely that his cerebral nature and obsession with music simply distracted him from things like personal appearances. Looking polished was just not important to him (though he was certainly capable of putting on a suit and tie for certain occasions, as will be documented later in this book).

Wilson's love of nature also meant that he went outdoors frequently, and enjoyed collecting samples of leaves, pinecones, and other natural objects. This time spent in nature left its mark by way of physical dirt on his clothing, and the like. In this, he was similar to naturalist Henry David Thoreau, best known for his book *Walden*.

Hailing from Concord, Massachusetts, Thoreau lived from 1817 to 1862. *Walden* documented his sojourn in a rural cabin, during which he attempted to live as simply as possible. He also wrote many other essays and books including *A Week on the Concord and Merrimack Rivers*, "Civil Disobedience", and "Life Without Principle". His influence on Wilson is easily traceable.

Thoreau was well described in a biography, *The Days of Henry Thoreau*, by scholar Walter Harding. This book is good reading for Thoreau fans as well as Alan Wilson fans. Wilson was deeply inspired by Thoreau's life, and by many accounts, the two had a great deal in common in terms of interests and personal habits.

In Harding's biography, one person who encountered Thoreau recalled that his hair looked as if he had run a pine cone through it instead of a comb. His clothes were disheveled, indicating his many "tramps" through woods and swamps, and his eyes had a faraway look. It's even recalled that Thoreau smelled of campfires. Such descriptions sound uncannily similar to recollections of Wilson from his friends and colleagues.

Wilson's seeming befuddlement around the opposite sex was another thing he had in common with Thoreau, who never married. In Thoreau's case, there has been some speculation that he was gay. Though there is no evidence he actually engaged in a same-sex relationship, a 1991 article by Harding in the *Journal of Homosexuality* provides considerable evidence that Thoreau may indeed have been interested in other men.

As for Wilson, speculations about his sexuality have run the gamut. It's possible that he himself might have been uncertain about his true inclinations — though, to be sure, he wrote and performed copious songs expressing the desire for a relationship with a woman. In the 1960s, of course, exploring same-sex interests wasn't a socially acceptable option, and those who felt such desires often kept them repressed.

Ultimately Wilson's intellectual obsessions, combined with his quirky personality and lack of "presentation", made it difficult for him to explore intimate relationships in general. Had he lived longer, perhaps he would have found his way to an opportunity for an appropriate relationship of whatever persuasion.

As a youngster, Wilson also missed out on the milestone of getting his driver's license, an event typically celebrated in the life of the young American male. Legally, his vision was acceptable when he wore his glasses, but his poor vision combined with clumsiness had hindered him. One family member has mentioned that he did attempt learning to drive as a teenager, but was so poor at it that he apparently gave up. In his hometown of Boston, it's also likely that public transportation and other forms of travel were readily available, so the lack of a license might not have been a big hindrance at the time.

Instead of cruising town and hitting on girls, Wilson spent his teenage years playing music and reading books. Thoreau was a positive influence during this time. In a high school essay entitled "The Kind of Success I Want", Wilson commented, "Thoreau's ideas appeal to me greatly. ... I also think that a life such as he led at Walden is very rewarding."

In this essay, Wilson notes that he would also like to enjoy a successful music career. He was not ready to retire entirely into the solitude of the forest. Rather, he expresses a remarkable self-awareness of his music as an outlet for personal expression, as well as a means to help him relate with other people. "Playing trombone gives me a chance to express the full gamut of my emotions, and at the same time communicate with other people," he wrote.

Despite the connections he found through music, Alan Wilson still had trouble relating to people. Though there is no doubt that he was loved as a child, his difficulties included relationships with his own family members, particularly his father.

Jack and Alan Wilson were very different, and struggled to find common ground. Jack was supportive of Alan's musical endeavors, but also seemed to feel some disappointment that his first-born son did not follow in his footsteps in any activity or interest. The two were able to share an interest in sports, but Alan preferred watching ball games to actually playing them. When it came to recreation, he enjoyed cerebral activities such as chess or Scrabble.

Alan did get actively involved in sports occasionally, and in school, played tennis. At one point, as he later told his friend John Fahey, he decided to try out for football, and began obsessively studying the game. One afternoon, while falling asleep on his bed, he became immersed in thoughts of strategic game plays. The thoughts became strange half-waking dreams over which he had no control, as the plays and players took on a life of their own in his mind. Alan found this bizarre and somewhat unnerving, as he would tell Fahey.

Other strange things happened to Alan when he slept. David Maxwell remembers, "When he'd wake up, he'd have sleep paralysis. He couldn't move for twenty to thirty minutes. ... This happened to him when he was in high school. He would talk about the weird stuff that would happen while he was going to sleep, staring up at the ceiling. Then when he woke up, his muscles were without the ability to move for a long time, ten, fifteen, twenty minutes. He was kind of freaked out about it."

Sleep paralysis is a well documented phenomenon. Historically, it has been attributed to a variety of sources ranging from alien abduction to demonic oppression. From the scientific standpoint, it can be blamed on a mundane physiological occurrence known as "Rapid Eye Movement atonia", and is a variation on normal human sleep patterns. In extreme cases, sleep paralysis may indicate some pathology, but is unlikely to be a sign of paranormal or alien activity.

However, this wasn't much help to Wilson, who was tormented by the occasional paralysis he experienced upon awakening. This might have contributed to his later issues surrounding sleep. As a child and teenager, he was able to sleep easily, but suffered from insomnia later in his adult life. For this, he would attempt to medicate himself using the street drugs that eventually played a factor in his death.

Another pastime Jack Wilson enjoyed was ham radio operation. Alan got involved in this as a youngster, even obtaining an amateur license. However, ham radio didn't intrigue him as music did, and not much came of the hobby except for the attempt to connect with his father. He also became involved with the Order of De Molay, a fraternal organization for young men, but apparently did not maintain ties to the group as an adult.

Jack Wilson also hoped that Alan would follow in his trade by taking up bricklaying, or some other respectable construction work. As a teenager, Alan began efforts in this direction by assisting his father on local job sites. One family member reports that the two helped build a local church, among other projects.

This work did not come naturally to Alan, however. He learned the craft of bricklaying and even acquired his own tool set; however, his heart did not seem to be in the work. Adding to the job site tensions, he became the target of occasional jokes from some of his coworkers who felt that eyeglasses were cause for ridicule. (This was according to a later report from his friend Phil Spiro, who was interviewed for the book *Baby Let Me Follow You Down* on the Cambridge music scene.)

In an interview after Alan Wilson's death, his band mate Bob Hite recalled that when they first met, Wilson hadn't spoken to his parents in over a year. He had also stockpiled a number of unopened letters from his family. When the band began touring and booked a show in Boston, Wilson became nervous. Considering that he hadn't been reading his family's correspondence, he was uncertain of how to deal with them when he finally saw them again.

When considering this, of course, it's worth noting that Wilson had a number of relatives, and that Hite's comments might not apply to all of them. Wilson's active correspondence with some of his relatives — including his mother Shirley — is well documented. Hite's later remarks may not necessarily reflect all of Wilson's family relationships, which as with most families, were complex and involved numerous individuals.

Bob Hite also recalled encountering Alan Wilson's mother in Boston during Canned Heat's first national tour. In such recollections, Hite is actually referring to Wilson's stepmother Barbara, who was thought by many of Wilson's acquaintances to be his biological mother (most had apparently not been informed of his parents' early divorce). As Hite remembered in interview, Barbara approached him and demanded to know, "What did you do with my son?"

Baffled, Hite asked what she meant. Barbara explained that she had been trying for years to convince Alan to tidy up and wear clean clothing. These efforts were largely unsuccessful, but Alan now looked much better in her view. She attributed these good results to Hite's positive influence. When recounting this story, Hite went on to remark that his own mother had raised a "clean boy", and that while he himself often looked sloppy, he felt that body odor was unacceptable.

Years after Alan's death, Bob Hite's younger brother Richard played bass with Canned Heat, and visited the Wilson family while on tour. Richard recalled that Jack Wilson, unlike the highly sensitive Alan, seemed to be more of a traditional "man's man". Though Jack no doubt tried to understand his first-born son, the two were so different that a strained relationship should come as little surprise.

"Every time we'd go to Cambridge, we used to go to the Wilson's house for dinner and stuff like that," said Richard Hite. "Even though he was dead, still part of the family type thing. His father was the type of, old-type family-like stuff. Like, when you went to dinner there, the roast was put in front of his father and his father carved, and it was definitely the old-type family sort of situation like that."

The memoirs of Canned Heat drummer Adolfo de la Parra contain statements to the effect that Alan Wilson felt some level of estrangement from his family. Apparently, this was something he expressed to his band mates. De la Parra even claims that at one point, Wilson composed a lengthy letter to his father with the intent of "divorcing" his family. However, de la Parra provides no documentation of this, and it's uncertain what Wilson's real intent might have been with any such letter.

As with all families, there are surely multiple sides to this story, and the relationships involved are myriad and complex. Alan Wilson's surviving relatives express love for him in their own ways, and it's possible that over time, any rifts with his father or other family members might have been mended. There can be little doubt, however, that these kinds of issues contributed to Wilson's difficulties with human relationships, especially when in young adulthood when many find parent/child relationships to be especially trying.

2 CAMBRIDGE BLUES

Around the age of sixteen, Wilson's musical tastes underwent a distinct shift. Though he still loved jazz, he had become somehow dissatisfied with his trombone playing, and this had a big effect on him.

Wilson's playing ability was a significant element in his self-esteem. Years later, after his death, his mother recalled that he "became hung up on the trombone and seemed filled with self-doubt and much confusion". Specific reasons for Wilson's uncertainty with his playing are unknown, but this may help explain why, in later years, his music did not tend to show significant jazz influences.

One day, Wilson's stepmother Barbara Wilson noticed that he had returned home from school without the trombone. "I lost my lip," he said when she questioned him. In later interview, he was equally evasive, saying, "I had to put that down. I wasn't making it."

This didn't mean that he was through with music, though. The Wilson family owned a piano, and Alan played it occasionally. As John Lee Hooker has always done, Wilson kept time by stomping his feet. It's said that on occasion, he stomped so loudly while playing piano that neighbors called his stepmother to complain about the noise.

The piano did not prove to be of great long-term interest to Wilson. His friend David Evans, a musicologist, recalls his relationship with the instrument. "He could play one tune. It was Leadbelly's 'Eagle Rock Rag', which was about the only tune Leadbelly could play on piano and was apparently very easy to play. It was very simple in terms of its execution. I remember Al could play that pretty well, but he said that was about the only thing he could do. ... I don't remember him or us listening to a lot of piano. It's a very harmonic instrument, and most of the players play it very harmonically."

Before long, Wilson had developed a new fascination. Through a friend, he was exposed to blues music in the form of a Muddy Waters record. "When I was about sixteen, a friend of mine played the first blues record I ever heard," he later said. "That was the LP *The Best of Muddy Waters*. That thing was just a killer to my head. This has Little Walter on harmonica, Muddy Waters singing and playing bottleneck, Otis Spann on piano, and Freddy Below on drums. They're all at the top of their respective categories. It sounded really great."

Soon he found a new wind instrument to replace the trombone. Inspired by Little Walter, he took up harmonica. Regular visits to the music store soon ensued, to invest in various keys and replace harmonicas worn out by intense playing.

Around this time, Wilson was exposed to a John Lee Hooker record. Hooker's guitar, tuned to an open key, was unlike anything in the jazz or pop world. This motivated Wilson to pick up the acoustic guitar, and for the rest of his life, he would play mostly in open tunings with a distinctive Hooker-inspired sound.

Though John Lee Hooker was a post-World War Two artist, active in a period usually associated with ensemble playing, he was at his best when performing solo. Even when electrified, his guitar playing was an illustration of a relatively archaic blues form. He was one of the most significant influences on Wilson's musical development, and Wilson would come to be known for his mastery of Hooker's deceptively simple style. Colleague David Evans, who met Wilson in Cambridge and would become his first blues playing partner, said, "He must have been one of the first white guys to be able to play some semblance of Hooker. He really studied Hooker's guitar style, and collected his 78s pretty seriously."

Wilson wanted to hear more blues, and on the recommendation of a jazz magazine, purchased a record by Sonny Terry and Brownie McGhee. He quickly found, however, that their style of blues did not interest him. This was primarily because Brownie McGhee's guitar playing, quite unlike Hooker's modal sound, lacked appeal to him.

Throughout his life, Wilson would be dedicated primarily to the Mississippi Delta blues and the electric harmonica players of Chicago. Folk blues, exemplified by Terry and McGhee, contained harmonic progressions not to Wilson's liking. Some colleagues speculated that the folk blues style might have been too light or upbeat for his taste.

David Evans comments, "Al didn't like what were conventionally referred to as songsters. Folk songs and sort of bright, happy tunes, ragtime progressions, he didn't care for at all. People like Blind Blake, maybe even Gary Davis, would have been of a lesser rank to Al. And he didn't like ragtime; that was a bad word. Ragtime, songster, folk music... he didn't like hokum stuff or double entendre stuff in blues. He took blues very seriously."

Blues items recorded before the onset of World War Two are typically referred to as "prewar", with the classic years of prewar blues considered to be the late 1920s. In 1968, Alan WIlson recalled, "I think my first prewar LP was Robert Johnson on Columbia. That was really great when that came out." Several months later he began hearing music reissued on labels such as Origin Jazz Library. Their releases included the likes of Charley Patton, Mississippi Fred McDowell, Skip James, and other artists whose caliber surpassed nearly everything Wilson had heard before.

These early blues reissues had started as little more than fallout from the folk and jazz scenes. Now, however, it was taking on a life of its own. When the trend made its way overseas, British artists such as Jimmy Page, Eric Clapton, and the Rolling Stones embraced the blues as well. Ironically, the blues was in many ways more successful in foreign lands than in its native United States.

In 1968, Wilson would look back and say, "At the time, those releases formed like the whole of the excitement for a bunch of people. Ooohh, that was really some scene! And now it's a little different; we've heard so many of them. They're really neat. It's funny to see how so many of those sides, on those anthologies, how many of them are done on European rock and roll records. And all groups. Those songs are so well known now. It's incredible."

After graduating high school in 1961, Wilson began attending Boston University. He was funded in part by the Town of Arlington's F. E. Thompson Scholarship Fund, and planned to major in music.

Impatient to start finding his own way in life, but unsure of exactly how to do that, Wilson moved out of his family home, then moved back in. As with many college students, he was finding that finances were a hurdle. A search for a cheaper place turned up results, and soon he was back out on his own again.

After a year and a semester of college, Wilson dropped out of school. It's unclear whether money was an issue or if formal education simply did not fit him. In later interview, his father Jack Wilson would recall that he had the habit of correcting his professors, which probably did not endear him to the collegiate system.

Harvard student David Evans met Wilson in a record store around this time. Of Wilson quitting school, he conjectures, "I think he was just an early dropout. The discipline of college wasn't for him. He was kind of a free spirit; he wanted to explore things *his* way."

Evans was horrified by the cheap apartment Wilson rented at the time. "It was absolutely filthy," he says, "and Al had some heroin addicts staying there. He had taken them in, basically. I asked him, 'Why?' I was very naive, and didn't know about a lot of things that were out there in the world. This was my first contact with anything like that; it was kind of scary to me. And Al basically felt pity for them, took them in, and gave them a place to crash."

Eventually, his strung-out guests began to abuse Wilson's hospitality. "Sometimes they'd steal something from him," remembers Evans. "They'd steal a record and sell it for a dollar or two. ... But he felt real sympathy for these people, the down and out. Because I guess he considered himself down and out in a lot of ways. I'm sure that was a lot of the attraction of the blues."

Eventually, Wilson found a better apartment and arranged to share the rent with a roommate who did not use heroin. He had never tried any of the drug that the addicts had made available, and was aghast at their addiction. Evans says, "He finally got tired of being ripped off, and just pulled out of that scene. I asked him, 'Do you use that stuff?' He said he didn't, and I believe him. He wasn't into it."

However, Wilson had begun experimenting with other substances, including alcohol. Evans observed that alcohol never made Wilson lewd or violent, but only "pleasantly slobbery". Other friends recall that he was fond of beer and occasionally drank gin, but did not care for wine.

Alan Wilson and his friends formed a sort of brotherhood as they explored the music together. Already, Wilson was showing the ability to help others reach new levels of musicianship. "We became aware of the fact that we were both trying to learn music," says David Evans. "The guitar, and also the banjo but I never got anywhere with that. Al played guitar and harmonica. Al seemed to grasp some of the blues ideas a little quicker than I did. A lot of times he would show me something, and then I could pick it up. Eventually I began grasping it directly."

The two had entered the blues world from different directions. Evans says, "Al was into jazz music too. Al was less into the other range of folk music and just really more into the blues side of it. He got into blues through jazz — whereas I got into it through folk music, and later on people got into it through rock and roll. Al knew people that were a little older and that were more into the beatnik and fifties scene. Al had a little touch of influence from that crowd, which in places like Cambridge sort of blended into the sixties folk/hippie movement."

Wilson had absorbed many aspects of jazz culture. "He knew the jazz scene and jazz talk," says Evans. "He would use some phrases from jazz, like 'cool' and 'hip', and he'd say, 'I dig it,' or 'I'm hip' instead of 'I understand'. Some of this jazz jargon he'd picked up, and he liked modern jazz."

Much of Wilson's "jazz talk", from the historical slang of black jazz musicians, was already passing into the 1960s counterculture and would become popular among young white people. Those who were not fans of jazz music were mostly unaware of the origin of their newly adopted slang. However, it didn't stop the trend from spreading, and Alan wasn't the only "hip cat" to pick up on the vocabulary.

If there was one thing that made Wilson distinctive at this point in the Cambridge folk scene, it was his harmonica playing. Evans says, "I don't think there were really many people trying to play blues harmonica at the time. There were a few in the jug band scene that didn't play it very well. I don't remember any of the folkies or blues aficionados really seriously trying to take up harmonica. There was the occasional person here or there, but guitar was really the instrument of choice."

Although he was finding more opportunities to play, and even perform, with others, music wasn't yet a real source of income for Alan Wilson. He could often be found on blue-collar job sites, laying bricks with his father. He was glad to make a living, and by some family accounts his father was supportive of his music, even driving him to shows occasionally. However, the relationship — as with many father-son dynamics — was not without its painful aspects.

"Al hated bricklaying," says David Evans, "and he had a very difficult relationship with his father. I imagine he learned to be somewhat of a bricklayer. But he hated that kind of work. I mean, Al was an intellectual, and he was not meant to be just a manual laborer in his life. He couldn't see very well, for one thing; he had a vision problem. He wore thick glasses. And he was just not into being a bricklayer, probably wasn't very good at the work, and his mind was elsewhere."

Wilson was apparently a good enough bricklayer to continue finding work in the field. However, he lamented to Evans that his skills weren't up to par with his father's expectations. As Evans recalls, "He said his father used to just get on him and criticize everything he did. Apparently his father was exasperated with Al; he considered Al more or less useless. I remember Al saying one time that his father said, 'What did I do to spawn such a son as you?' or something to that effect. Al used to laugh about it, but I knew he took it very seriously. He really felt rejected by his father. I could tell that it bothered him, that he was such a disappointment to his father."

It wasn't a matter of active rebellion against his father, or anyone else. Wilson was just having a hard time fitting in with those around him. He stood out from people his own age as well as the older workers on construction job sites.

Evans says, "Al wasn't trying to create an image, like to grow a long beard and be a guru or a hippie, or wear outlandish costumes or look outlandish. He just looked kind of like your all-American nerd, I suppose you could say. He'd tape his glasses up when he'd break them, the rim, the nose, or on the side. He'd take bandage tape and tape it together."

In addition to looking like a "nerd", Wilson sometimes disregarded society's standards of hygiene. Some family members have suggested that this might have been related to his potential condition of autism or Asperger syndrome. In any event, a number of those close to Wilson have confirmed that he did have issues with cleanliness. Though his habits were not so offensive as to cause him to lose friends, it's possible this was a factor in his difficulties forming romantic relationships.

David Evans reports, "You'd kind of need to remind him to take a bath or a shower and all that. He wasn't into washing too frequently, or that kind of stuff. I don't recall being too grossed out by it when we were rooming together in California [in 1965]. I think he started taking a little more care of himself there. But I remember in Massachusetts, it was really bad."

Often, Wilson showed up at Evans' dormitory to listen to music and play blues. Occasionally he would become involved in games of Scrabble with Evans' roommate. "I had a roommate named Peter," Evans says. "Al got to know him just by visiting me. Pete wasn't into blues, but he was into playing Scrabble with some other students. I wasn't into that at all, rarely playing. But Al was, and I think he was into other games like backgammon, and some card games too. He was into those mental things, games where you have to think. Anyway, they needed four people or something to play Scrabble, and Al would play. He would come, and I remember Peter, and I believe the others too, exclaim — maybe not to Al himself — that the odor was pretty overpowering. They asked me, because I was his friend, 'Does he ever wash?'"

Apparently the other Scrabble players were able to tolerate Wilson's body odor, as the members of Canned Heat would in later years. Wilson, for his part, seemed oblivious. "You know, they liked him," says Evans, "and I guess they felt that he was up to speed as a player, but really had a hard time with his B.O. So that was Al, you know. He was not concerned with his looks, appearance, anything like that. I believe he got a little better in California, because I was certainly close enough to him where it probably would have bothered me."

Wilson was concerned first and foremost with music. While he wasn't trying to shock or offend those around him, he didn't seem to care about impressing them either. "In a lot of ways, he was just kind of the classic nerd, I guess," says Evans. "He was the guy that was just out of it. He wasn't concerned socially about things; he just wanted you to take him as he was! He didn't try to put on anything for anyone as far as how to look or present himself; he didn't think that was important. I don't know if he was aware of the fact that it was important to other people."

There was also an nervous habit that would persist throughout Wilson's life. "He used to pull at his hair," Evans says. "He had a little bald spot where he pulled his hair out so much. It was somewhere where he parted his hair. It was sort of a nervous thing." Later, Wilson documented his own habit in a song called "Pulling Hair Blues", which was featured on a live Canned Heat album.

In 1963, Wilson was living in Cambridge with roommate Phil Spiro, who was a student at the Massachusetts Institute of Technology. Spiro later recalled that Wilson cleaned the house only twice during the time they lived together, and that he had a very simple method of cleaning. Wilson brought three trash cans into the house, filled them with the detritus that had accumulated, and took them back outside. They had no phone, little food, and even less money.

However, Wilson had his records, guitar, and harmonica, and could play his music in peace. His artistic needs were being satisfied, and that was paramount in his life. Spiro was interested in music also; he played guitar occasionally, and would later host a radio show through M.I.T.

Here and there, Wilson made a few dollars by providing lessons to other aspiring musicians. He taught guitar and harmonica, specializing in the deep blues styles. This didn't bring a lot of income, but every bit helped, and this kind of job was more his style than bricklaying.

Around this time, Wilson found the ideal slide for the Mississippi bottleneck guitar style he was working so hard to perfect. The bottleneck technique involves tuning the guitar to an open chord and using some object to slide up and down the guitar neck, in addition to fingering certain notes, thus enabling one to create "blue" notes and other tonal variations. Blue notes consist of notes played or sung a microtone between the standard notes of the European scale.

On guitar, the choice of instrument to be used as a "slide" is crucial. In the rural South, musicians have used everything available, including meat bones, knives, and of course the necks of bottles, from whence the term "bottleneck" sprang. Wilson, however, wanted to capture the perfect tone and timbre. For a while, he had been seeking the perfect slide to help him achieve it.

Wilson gathered many objects for private experimentation and practice. When he finally identified the perfect slide, his friend Dick Waterman was there to witness the scene. Waterman was a local photographer and journalist whose work included a position at the folk-oriented *Broadside Magazine*. Now he was getting involved on the fringes of the growing blues scene.

Waterman recalls, "Al was looking for the perfect slide with the perfect tone, resonance, and everything. He tried copper, brass, all kinds of various things. This went on for days, weeks, whatever. He kept looking for the perfect slide. Then Spiro and I came into his apartment one day, and it was a *mess*, with all of these slides lying around everywhere — all kinds of slides! And Al said, 'I got it!'"

Wilson was in a state of euphoria. "We said, 'What?'" recalls Waterman. "Al held it up on his hand and said, 'Coricidin.' And that's what it was! It was the perfect size for the finger, the perfect tone and everything."

Coricidin was the brand name of an over-the-counter cold medication that came in small glass bottles. The containers were indeed perfect as guitar slides, and other guitarists including Duane Allman concurred with Wilson's conclusion.

Several years later, bottleneck guitarists were dismayed when the manufacturing company began bottling their pills in plastic, a material not at all acceptable for use as a guitar slide. A musical instrument company now creates glass slides identical to the original bottles, marketing to blues and rock players. However, as David Evans lamented in the 1990s, they cost more than the old ones did when sold full of pills.

Evans and Wilson had begun playing as a team. Usually, Evans sang and played guitar, and Wilson accompanied him on harmonica or second guitar. Though he had experimented with singing, Wilson hadn't yet developed his vocal style.

In 1963 and 1964, the two performed a repertoire consisting mostly of classic-era blues covers. Some of these items included

John Hurt's "Avalon Blues", Sleepy John Estes' "Special Agent" and "Down South Blues", Leadbelly's "Leaving Blues", and Big Joe Williams' "Baby Please Don't Go". The two didn't have any original songs, but tried to feature their own creativity instead of slavishly emulating their sources as some contemporary folk singers did.

Evans explains, "It was not necessarily to cover note for note, but to get within that particular style of individual player and play it *like* they did. Not like you would learn off tablature to play it note for note, or sing it with precisely the same inflections. We realized that these artists didn't do these songs the same way every time. So, why take one performance or record and make that your model? But I think we were odd in that respect. Most people *were* trying to cover those early records very literally. They were working at that, and usually not very well!"

The blues style was deceptively simple. "It's not that hard, really," says Evans. "I mean, Skip James had a lot of technique. John Hurt had a certain amount. But most of them — they had a great *feel*, but what they actually do is not terribly complex. Reverend Gary Davis, sure. But Son House — as Skip James used to say, he plays with his fist! And he more or less did. The style is very spare. But it's great, of course, and not many people could come close to that. Certainly not in that scene we were in. ... They could listen to the records; they could even see the same people we saw. But they just couldn't seem to get it!"

Wilson's increasing mastery of the blues style brought him a few opportunities for public performance. "A lot of these were free gigs," Evans says. "We didn't really have a lot of paying gigs. Our playing was at these hootenannies, these open-mike things. We had some at the Club 47, which was the big folk club in Cambridge. We'd go there occasionally, but didn't get a terribly good reception. Our music was really too heavy, probably too weird, too authentic or something. It was closer to authentic than what any of the folkies were doing."

Many folk artists just couldn't seem to grasp the rural blues, or didn't want to. Blues purists like Evans and Wilson, for their part, had something of a disdain for the popular folk singers of the day.

Evans recalls, "You had people like Tom Rush, Jackie Washington, Geoff Muldaur, Dave Van Ronk ... Just to be frank, they were terrible! And yet this is what people liked."

One performer who did have some affinity for the blues was Jim Kweskin, who ran his own band, and on the side hosted weekend hootenannies at a local club called the Café Yana. "It was a small place; sometimes just ten or twelve people were there," says Evans. "Kweskin was always very encouraging to us. He really liked us. Sometimes he would sit in and back us up with a lot of taste. He was very encouraging to a lot of aspiring people."

Kweskin was part of a circle of performers who were already established in the local coffeehouse circuit. Audiences were there mostly to see their style of folk music, which was quite different from the raw blues Wilson and Evans embraced. Not everyone was as welcoming as Kweskin.

"Most of the people that were performing in the coffeehouses were a little older, and had gotten started maybe around 1961 or 1962," says Evans. "They were a step ahead of us, and had established an audience and kind of a profile for that music. To come in with really heavy Delta blues just didn't fit the profile. If you were Mississippi John Hurt or Booker White, it was fine. But guys like us ..."

Blues was expected from older black artists, not white youngsters. "Al could really grasp that old music and figure it out," says Evans. "It was unusual for any white guy at the time to do that. It's unusual enough today, but at that time, there really weren't any others. There were others that were trying, and Al didn't think they were very good, and I didn't think they were very good. Some of them were having a lot of commercial success. We still didn't think they were very good! But Al could get that stuff, that music, and figure it out. That was pretty unusual for the time."

More and more people around them were becoming caught up in the blues, part of the slow but sure rolling stone that was later dubbed a blues revival. At this point, however, blues was marketed largely to folk and coffeehouse audiences as a subset of folk music. Those who were, like Wilson, interested only in the blues and didn't care to clothe their music in a "folk" guise, had trouble finding a dedicated listenership.

Lack of popular acceptance wasn't terribly disheartening to Wilson. It certainly didn't dissuade him and his friends from their fascination with the blues. As more dusty 78 records turned up, more LP records were released, and more tapes were passed around the local enthusiasts, each discovery was a revelation.

"We had heard a very limited amount of blues compared to what's available today," says Evans. "Surprisingly, though, we heard a lot of the very greatest, deepest country blues: Son House, Booker White, Robert Johnson, stuff like that. Early on, before we left Massachusetts, we'd heard virtually all of those recordings, many of which had still not been reissued."

Wilson was discriminating when it came to blues, going only for the deepest sounds he could find. "He was very particular about what he liked," says Evans. "He dismissed a lot of people he thought were second-rate."

One of these would be Babe Stovall, a blues singer from Tylertown, Mississippi. He was a well-accepted songster on the streets of New Orleans, and visited Cambridge in March 1965 to play some coffeehouse gigs. With humorous false modesty, he often confessed his lack of artistic preeminence. "I ain't the best in the world," he chortled, "but I'll do till the best gets here!"

When Alan Wilson and David Evans went to see Stovall play, Wilson was respectful but clearly not impressed. "I liked Babe, although I felt he wasn't the best in the world," Evans admits. "But he would even say that himself. Al had very high standards, and there was just a little bit of blues that was top-notch. The stuff that was second-rate, he didn't want to spend a lot of time listening to. But he'd listen to the great stuff over and over again very intensely, really trying to learn it. I guess he wanted to take that for his own standards and try to reach that level."

After becoming familiar with some of the most impressive blues ever recorded, Wilson and his friends began ranking the music according to their tastes. Seriously and meticulously, as only the very obsessed can, they considered the relative quality of each artist and created lists placing each bluesman at a certain level in the musical hierarchy.

The top portion of a list would typically include the likes of Robert Johnson, Son House, Skip James, Charley Patton, Tommy Johnson, and Booker White. Lesser-known performers such as Garfield Akers, whose recordings were few in number but musically impressive, might make it onto the lists. Though most of the favored artists were pre-war, a few post-war artists were considered top-caliber, including Robert Pete Williams and Fred McDowell.

"I think he [Wilson] got into the lists with Laurie Forti," says Evans. "We would make these lists, top ten lists. Who were the ten greatest blues singers, the ten greatest blues songs. We had a lot of fun making those lists and arguing over them, although we did have a pretty good deal of agreement. We'd try to come to a consensus and develop it together."

Eventually, lists of favorite artists and their best songs led to even more tightly defined standards. Evans remembers, "Finally we got to the ten greatest individual notes in the blues. We were very serious; I mean, this was not just in jest! We were really into figuring out what was the greatest, the ultimate in blues."

Many blues songs contained lyrics about intense and passionate matters of life, love, and death, all delivered in voices of unquestionable sincerity. It was natural for listeners like Wilson and Evans to speculate on what the singers were like as people. They heard songs like Son House's "My Black Mama" and Booker White's "Fixin' to Die", and concluded that blues artists were probably men of considerable depth and wisdom.

Wilson was no doubt pondering serious issues in his own life as he came to grips with his evolving adulthood. Blues themes naturally resonated with him, as part of a search for truth and artistic integrity. "He considered blues to be very serious, deep music with a lot of meaning," says Evans. "Philosophical truths about life and all that, something very profound. Which it is; it can be a lot of things."

The young white blues fans conjured up fantasies about the men behind the names on the dusty old record labels. "We were into the depth and profundity of it," Evans recalls. "We would fantasize about blues singers — what they were like, their personalities, as projected in their songs. Oftentimes we turned out to be quite wrong when they were rediscovered. But, at any rate, these were games we played, fantasies."

For Alan Wilson, his fantasies were about to come to life in forms he had never expected.

3 THE REDISCOVERIES

In 1928, songster John Hurt recorded thirteen songs for the Okeh record label. One of these, entitled "Avalon Blues", described the town of Avalon, Mississippi as Hurt's home.

Thirteen years later, a blues enthusiast named Tom Hoskins heard the record. He went to Avalon in search of Hurt, and in a stroke of fortune, found him still there. Hurt was working on a local farm, with no idea that his old records had gained a following among young white listeners.

Hoskins persuaded Hurt to come north and perform for audiences in the coffeehouse and folk circuit. There, he attained considerable popularity. His gentle voice, mild personality, and intricate guitar playing were instantly likable. Even hard-core blues fanatics like David Evans and Alan Wilson couldn't help but enjoy Hurt's music.

In February 1964, Hoskins brought his "rediscovery" star to Cambridge for a Café Yana gig. Alan Wilson was invited to accompany him on harmonica. It was his first experience backing a legendary bluesman, but he sounded as if he'd been doing it for two or three lifetimes already.

"He was brilliant," said Hoskins. "The Blind Owl is a hero to me. He really was; he was a brilliant man. And he played his instrument well — he played beautiful harmonica."

Around this time, Wilson was trying out some experimental harmonica techniques. Hoskins reported, "He used to take Kleenex and stuff it up his nose, because he played the harmonica and he wanted all the breath to come out of his mouth and into the harmonica."

As Wilson no doubt quickly realized, this would not really expedite blues harmonica playing, for it would prevent the nasal breathing that is not actually wasted air, but rather is necessary to maintain proper consciousness and a steady flow of aspiration. He apparently learned this quickly, and was never seen blocking his nostrils in this manner again.

While in Cambridge, Hoskins and Hurt stayed at Wilson's apartment for a couple of nights. "His apartment was pretty trashy," admitted Hoskins. "So was he, really. But he was a cool guy. It was sort of like the absent-minded professor. He lived in his head, and his head just drove him. He didn't have time to think about personal hygiene and stuff like that, because there was so much going on in his head. He was a smart man. He was a nerd, but he was a very special nerd. I mean, he could hang out with me any time. And boy, *that* is a privilege! He was a cool guy, especially when talking about blues or talking about music. Then I was kind of thinking, 'Gee, maybe *I'm* privileged to hang out with *this* guy!' Al was one of my most favorite people."

John Hurt was everything the folk revivalists and blues fans hoped he would be. His kindly demeanor matched his personable music, endearing him to audiences everywhere he went. The next blues "rediscovery" would be quite different. When the voices on the old records came to life in physical form, not all of them were exactly as Wilson and his friends had imagined.

In late 1963, a guitarist in California heard about the way Tom Hoskins had discovered John Hurt. He decided that if Hoskins could unearth an old blues singer, so could he.

This young man was John Fahey, a student at the University of California. As a recording artist, Fahey had released some of his work under the name "Blind Joe Death", which became a sort of blues alter-ego for him. With acquaintance Ed Denson, he had formed the Takoma record label for the promotion of his acoustic guitar music.

The Deep South was not new to Fahey; he had already been there canvassing for blues 78s. Now, however, he wanted to find a real live bluesman and record him for Takoma. The best prospect, and one of the most fascinating older bluesmen, was Booker White.

White had recorded in 1940 as "Bukka" White, the record company's corruption of his given name, pronounced in a Southern drawl. (To this day, uninitiated blues fans often mistakenly pronounce his name as "Byu-ka" rather than the intended, drawled "Bookah".) One of his songs was "Aberdeen, Mississippi Blues", and declared Aberdeen to be White's home.

In 1963, Fahey hoped the song still rang true. He sent a postcard to White in Aberdeen, addressed "General Delivery". Though White had moved to Memphis, he was still well known in Aberdeen, and his mail was forwarded by relatives. He recognized Fahey's postcard as a means to turn around a declining musical career, and made a collect phone call to California.

Within weeks, Booker White had become the latest blues rediscovery. Word spread around Cambridge that he would be visiting in April for a week-long coffeehouse engagement.

Members of the local blues cult were caught up in excitement and speculation, wondering what White would be like in person. Some of his pieces, such as "Bukka's Jitterbug Swing", were about partying and drinking. Others, such as "Fixin' to Die Blues", "Strange Place Blues", and "Sleepy Man Blues", were among the most intense blues anyone had ever heard. Their lyrics dealt with topics such as illness, death, and mental depression.

With this, White had a lot to live up to. His young fans, whose existence he had never imagined, were expecting him to be a sort of singing, guitar-slinging guru. The eagerness increased when arrangements were made for White to stay at Alan Wilson's apartment during the visit.

"It was the typical deal of finding a local person who was a fan that would put up the artist," explains David Evans. "Then you wouldn't have any hotel expense. The people at the coffeehouse booked these musicians in for several days, several nights, and they'd find some folkie that had a spare bed. Do things on the cheap. It was sort of like your duty to the music, you know, to put up these traveling artists. And of course Al was only too glad to do that."

As a musician, White was still strong. Wilson got to experience his blues both at the shows and during informal demonstrations at his own apartment. It was a thrill for him to learn some of his favorite bottleneck guitar licks from the very man who had recorded them.

Evans recalls, "He would learn stuff and then get in touch with me. He'd come over, report on his progress, and show me stuff. 'This is how Booker does that.' The bottleneck licks in particular, 'Aberdeen Blues' and 'Jitterbug Swing'. I think those were the main ones that Al had more or less mastered, or gotten to the point where he could do them, reproduce them, and show them. He was quite excited about being able to do that, being able to do those pieces. Because we'd heard them from the old records and could not figure out how to do them just from listening to the records."

Wilson is usually remembered as a shy person who suffered, to some extent, from social awkwardness. However, he lost his reserve when dealing with people on a musical basis. He held legendary bluesmen like White in high esteem, but never hesitated to talk to them, learn from them, and play with them if appropriate. Most older artists recognized his genuine interest in the music, and readily taught him whatever he wanted to know. Most of his peers recall him as having an uncanny ability to connect with other musicians.

"He was very respectful of them," says David Evans, remembering Wilson's work with artists like Booker White, Son House, Skip James, Robert Pete Williams, and others. "But he would plunge right in with them, ask them questions and really ask them to show him things. He definitely wanted to learn. He was pretty forward with them, but not aggressive, and very respectful. I mean, he didn't take the attitude that now he'd learned it, you know, 'Look at me!' It wasn't that sort of show-off thing at all. I think they were impressed by his seriousness, and of course by his ability to pick up on what they were doing, which nobody else around them seemed to be able to do."

Diligently, Alan Wilson and his friends immersed themselves in Booker White's blues wisdom. Unfortunately, in the end there was a sense of disappointment about his rediscovery. He taught his fans a lot about real Mississippi blues, but he wasn't as wise and profound as he had hoped. Nor did his singing match the standard of the recordings they had so idolized.

White's voice had changed over the years. Evans explains, "We were all disappointed in Booker's singing. His voice had gotten rough and hoarse. On those great recordings from 1940 and earlier, his singing was just so pure and strong. He and Son House were the two great, powerful blues singers from back then, two of the great voices. Son would still have the voice, as it turned out. Booker's voice had become kind of a rasp."

White's personality was not what they had hoped for, either. He was happy to show them guitar techniques, but he had no philosophy or wisdom to impart. Not much of a sage, he didn't care to explore the depth and profundity of his old lyrics that had so intrigued Wilson. Rather, he seemed more interested in partying than in pondering the secrets of life, sex, and death.

"Booker's personality wasn't the sort of deep introspective guy that we thought he would be, based on his lyrics and themes of those 1940 recordings," Evans said. "Instead, he was this party animal, this rough, tough guy who looked like he liked to get in fights and play for dancing. So we really didn't know what to make of Booker entirely, and there was this lingering sense of disappointment that he wasn't what we thought he would be."

Musically, White had evolved beyond his 1940 style, which had been frozen in time "In fact, he was still very good," says Evans. "His music still evolved some past 1940. What we were experiencing in 1964 was the product of an evolution that more or less cut off maybe in the early fifties. But we didn't understand that; it didn't make sense to us at the time. ... He did well enough, but I think his rough personality made folk audiences uneasy. And the blues audiences just didn't know what to make of him. I also thought that tinny National guitar really hurt him too. I would have liked to hear an instrument with a better tone."

Throughout White's visit, David Evans and Alan Wilson interviewed him both formally and informally. They also played him a variety of records by other classic blues masters. When they expressed interest in Son House, White claimed that a friend of his, blueswoman Lillian Glover, had recently encountered House in Memphis.

This generated a lot of excitement. Previously, blues fans had believed that House, a contemporary of seminal bluesmen Charley Patton, and mentor to both Robert Johnson and Muddy Waters, was dead. House had recorded in 1930 for Paramount, then again in 1941 and 1942 for folklorist John Lomax. These recordings had been reissued on LP, and were considered among the most impressive in blues history by fans like Wilson.

It now appeared that Son House might actually be alive, and thus accessible. Blues fans were ready to take on another rediscovery. That June, Wilson's roommate Phil Spiro went to Memphis along with Dick Waterman. The trip was scheduled around Spiro's vacation from his day job at a technology manufacturing company.

Waterman and Spiro were accompanied by Nick Perls, a New York record collector who provided the car and a tape recorder for the expedition. Perls, a man of some financial means through his family connections, also had a plethora of audio equipment. He would later become known as the founder of Yazoo Records, which specialized in reissues of early blues, folk, and other roots music.

Through the Booker White interviews he and David Evans had conducted, Alan Wilson was partly responsible for the revelation that House was still alive. However, Wilson had a gig at a folk club during the planned expedition. He chose to make that his priority, and stayed behind, foreshadowing a lifelong inclination toward emphasizing his own musical development over the mere study of music. Evans, for his part, had a job at a summer camp in Maine during his break from school, and passed on the journey as well.

Dick Waterman, Phil Spiro, and Nick Perls left New York on June 10, 1964. They had no luck finding House in Memphis, but were able to locate Robert Wilkins, a former blues singer who had known him. Though he no longer sang blues, having dedicated to the church and to gospel music in 1936, Wilkins was friendly to their quest and willing to serve as guide.

This team traveled around the north Delta, at one point happening across Fiddlin' Joe Martin, who had performed with House in the late 1930s and recorded with him for Alan Lomax in 1941. As part of their folkloristic expedition, they made a recording of him on Perls' portable audio equipment, though he now played drums instead of fiddle due to a hand injury.

Through Martin, Perls, Spiro and Waterman found a source for a phone number of one of House's relatives in Detroit. The relative informed them that House was now living in Rochester, New York, and even provided an address. From Memphis, the blues researchers sent House a telegram asking him to call them collect, but their hopes were dashed when they never heard back from House.

Fortunately, another contact in Rochester knew House and was willing to drive to his apartment with their request and telephone information. This time, House responded, and called them on June 21, 1964. Dick Waterman would later recall that House claimed he was in good health and ready to play again. He invited them to come pay a visit.

On that same day, just a couple of hundred miles away, a much more famous — and sinister — historic event was occurring. Three young civil rights workers, Michael Schwerner, Andrew Goodman, and James Chaney were murdered by Klu Klux Klan members and their associates in Philadelphia, Mississippi. Their bodies would not be found until August 1964, and the killings became a notorious part of American civil rights history.

The trio of Northern white blues researchers had been fortunate not to encounter any significant race-related danger during their Deep South. Accompanied by the black Robert Wilkins, investigating an obscure form of black music and actively seeking other black artists, they could have easily fallen into trouble. Luckily, the worst experiences recalled by the three consisted mostly of tense conversations, hostile looks from local whites, and, on one occasion, being spat at.

On June 23, 1964, the team of Waterman, Spiro, and Perls met Son House at his home in New York. Ironically, he had been practically in their backyard all along.

Coincidentally, Skip James was rediscovered the same day in Mississippi by John Fahey, Henry Vestine, and Bill Barth. The team of Waterman, Spiro, and Perls had attempted to locate James in Missouri as they traveled back north toward New York, but to no avail.

When they finally met Son House, a guitar had to be provided for him to play, as he hadn't owned one in years. He claimed it had been only four years since he had played, and in fact he had in recent months played music casually with neighbor and musician Joe Beard. However, it had likely been as long as seventeen or eighteen years since House had practiced in earnest.

House was somewhat baffled by his new fans and their interest in a music he thought was long dead. He was unaware that his prewar recordings had been reissued, and asked if they were sure they really wanted to hear "this old music". With encouragement, however, he was convinced that there might be an audience for his performances, if he could get back up to speed on guitar.

While he could still sing with all the power of his old records, House's musicianship suffered from a hand tremor. This might have been affected by his extreme alcoholism, and in later years, Waterman (who would become his manager) learned to carefully regulate the older man's intake of liquor. With just the right amount, House's hand tremor became manageable enough for guitar playing. Too much drink, and he would become incoherent.

Despite poor health and rusty skills, House was booked at the last minute to play at the Newport Folk Festival, which was slated for July 23 through 26, 1964. Back in Cambridge, Alan Wilson was already looking forward to it as a high point of the season.

4 NEWPORT

Just before the Newport Folk Festival, Alan Wilson acquired an instrument that he had been longing for. It was a used National resonator guitar, previously owned by his roommate Phil Spiro. Wilson liked its unique sound, very different from other Nationals on the market, and was happy to pry it from Spiro's grasp.

In a letter to David Evans, Wilson explained how a convoluted exchange brought him the instrument he loved: "I bought a brand new National in Providence, Rhode Island. It was actually a better instrument than Phil's and cost more — one hundred and twenty five dollars. However, it is treble-heavy and sharp, whereas Phil's is bass-heavy and mushy, which I like. So we traded even, though I kept the new case, custom-fitted and a beauty, and a forty-five dollar value. Thus Phil's guitar is the new one and mine is Phil's old one. I am very happy over all this and I love that guitar. If I lose it, I will probably quit music, for I have found that most Nationals are sharp and treble heavy, and that mine is perhaps a unique instrument. At the moment it's the only guitar in the world I can play."

Evans was out of state, keeping in touch with the Cambridge scene via letters from Wilson. Unfortunately, he missed out on the Son House and Skip James rediscoveries as well as the Newport Folk Festival due to his responsibilities. "I was temporarily out of commission, working as a counselor for a summer camp in Maine," he explains. "And, of course, before leaving, I knew that the Son House expedition was being launched, and had gotten word of the rediscoveries of these people. And here I was, stuck up in Maine!"

Wilson rarely wrote letters, but in these exciting times, he made the effort to keep his blues partner informed. On July 26, he wrote, "Son was found in Rochester about three weeks ago and recorded some GREAT tapes — unfortunately using an untunable borrowed guitar, an indescribable horror next to which my hulk is a $350 Gibson or Martin. It's the best singing since the classic era. Unfortunately, these tapes were all flukes, for Son arrived in Cambridge with an old age tremor, making guitar playing impossible unless he was drunk. When drunk he was a gas musically but otherwise incoherent, totally unable to handle a crowd. We put him on medication, which helped some, but his repertoire is now small and that is another hassle."

At times, House seemed unsure of whether he was onstage or in a pulpit. As Wilson related, "At a short gig at the Unicorn, he when sober was pathetic. When he was drunk, he: a) played the best blues I have heard up to the time, an occasion; b) gave the crowd ten minute sermons which were not only nonsensical but nearly unintelligible, and c) took as long as five minutes to tune his guitar." Later, these bizarre sermons became a regular part of House's show, interspersed with the blues his audiences had come to hear.

The old man's health soon gave way under the stress of his rediscovery, and he ended up in the hospital instead of at the Newport Folk Festival that weekend. Wilson reported to Evans, "Son was scheduled to appear at Newport on Saturday and Sunday afternoons. Unfortunately, on Thursday night, he was in the emergency room of a Newport hospital with truss, appendix, or hernia. I'm still not exactly sure. As of today, Sunday, he remains there."

Wilson could sense an underlying unhappiness in House's alcoholism. He said, "Even before this catastrophe, Son was tired, homesick, and puzzled. I guess he must be completely out of it by now. I haven't been allowed in to visit. Son is still mentally alert and musically vital, but with age has acquired a certain pathos and the type of weakness which leads to alcoholism. Death is an obsession, at least when he drinks. The ineffable sadness of Son coupled with the constant rigors of medicinal and daily drinking quotes, both intricately measured to ensure best performance, have drained the managerial brain trust to a point of mental exhaustion and spiritual collapse."

The "managerial brain trust" consisted primarily of Dick Waterman. He later became House's official manager, and would spend years attempting to help regulate the old bluesman's drinking so that he could continue functioning on a daily basis. House's alcoholism was so severe that later, in 1970, he would pass out in the snow after a night of drinking. He ended up with frostbite which impaired his fingers and created another hurdle for his musicianship.

Though House didn't make it to the Newport Folk Festival, several other legendary bluesmen were in attendance. Wilson had the opportunity to interact and play music with a number of them, including Skip James. In his letter to Evans, he made frequent references to James as "the great god Skippy".

In Wilson's musical pantheon, Skip James was one of the most exalted figures. His unusual guitar tunings and distinctive high-pitched singing were very unusual in the rural blues tradition. Wilson had been studying his 1930 recordings with great fascination, and even started singing in a high pitch like James. This would result in the pure high tenor for which Wilson became so well known, and which gave Canned Heat's two hit singles their instantly recognizable quality.

The voices of Wilson and James had some inherent differences, however. Wilson's speaking voice was of normal male pitch, whereas the speaking voice of James was naturally rather high. It is also noteworthy that James often sang in a true falsetto on his records, whereas all of Wilson's commercially issued songs were sung in a high tenor. (He did experiment with a true falsetto which can be heard on "bootleg" recordings of early live shows, but this was not utilized on his records.)

Though Wilson developed his own unique vocal style, Skip James was, without a doubt, the most significant influence. "He is the greatest, by far, of today's blues singers," Wilson wrote of James just after his 1964 rediscovery.

There were high hopes all around for Skip James. Wilson wrote, "Ed Denson, manager of Booker and Skippy, says, 'It mustn't happen again,' (referring to Booker's 'comeback' flop). I said to [Tom] Hoskins that all of us should work to ensure that the world will become aware of this man's genius, and he agreed. I hope it works out; at any rate, Skippy's comeback has started with a bang when he completely shocked, amazed, and delighted the festival in what all agree was the festival's great moment (I wasn't there, being back in Cambridge for the gig) at the Saturday blues workshop."

Unfortunately, the grand vision for a Skip James comeback didn't turn out as Wilson hoped. James was sick with cancer, and illness made it difficult for him to recapture the standards of his earlier work. "All of us were kind of disappointed in Skip," says David Evans. "His playing and singing became mannered."

Later, Wilson too would lament the listlessness of the rediscovered Skip James. At this time, however, it was thrilling just to see him in person; here was the great god Skippy! A Saturday gig at the Club 47 caused Wilson to miss out on James' onstage performance, but he was happy to see a more intimate performance. "I heard him at length at the performers' house, playing before small and quiet gatherings," Wilson wrote to Evans.

Wilson's letter makes it clear that, from an artistic standpoint, he was quite enamored of Skip James. He wrote, "Skip's voice is just as high as it was, ninety percent as good, and even sweeter in tone. He may have been insane in 1930 (though I now seriously doubt it) but he is now beautifully and profoundly sane, almost the definition of gassy (that is, deep and profound) sanity. As he plays, he is absolutely relaxed, every guitar nuance and vocal phrase the result of the calm inner workings of this unsurpassed musical mind. There is no facial emoting or bodily swinging as in all the others. Only when he comes up with an exceptionally beautiful moment does his manner change, for his face bursts into light with the most serene and rapturous smile I have ever seen. He did three versions of 'I'd Rather Be the Devil', two of which reduced us all to mumbled incoherencies."

Another thrill for Wilson was being asked to accompany James on harmonica. He noted that James expressed a definite artistic viewpoint, making it clear that harmonica accompaniment was not appropriate on every song. Apparently, Wilson felt that some other bluesmen allowed accompanists to play out of politeness rather than for musical reasons. He seemed refreshed by James's musical honesty.

As Wilson described the encounter to David Evans, "He was almost as happy — in his placid way, for he never becomes excited — with me as I was with him. Though I never could have guessed it, I fit better with Skip on some pieces than with any other singer. Others didn't work at all, such as the fast, irregular ones like 'If You Haven't Any Hay', which he now does on guitar. Those which did, however, were so fine that Skip asked me to record them with him. Even in this he showed his uncompromising and perfect taste for, considerations of friendship and hospitality being thrust aside, he selected only those three of four pieces for consideration of recording. Only Skip requested that the harmonica be silent on those numbers on which it was less than perfectly compatible, unlike the others with whom I have played in the last year."

Wilson felt reluctant about the idea of actually recording with James. He wrote to Evans, "As for recording I doubt if it will happen. Anyway the idea scares me. Nothing must mar this man's comeback. I will, however, travel as far as Chicago to hear him play and, if possible, play with him."

Unfortunately, Skip James was not always polite to Wilson or others around him. This was documented in Wilson's written report of Newport to Evans, and later recalled by music historian Stephen Calt in his controversial James biography *I'd Rather Be the Devil*.

When Wilson started playing Skip James licks on his "new" National guitar at Newport, James himself was there. Apparently, Wilson's skill aroused some jealousy, and James lashed out at him.

The content of his remarks did not actually address music, but more personal matters. According to Calt's later account, James suggested that Wilson needed to take a bath and lose some weight if he wanted to perform blues.

If Wilson felt hurt by this treatment from his musical idol, he didn't show it. Later, he wrote to Evans in a matter-of-fact tone: "Skip disliked me from the start. Due to my personal filthy appearance and curious ways. In fact, after I had talked music and played with him and it became logical for him to speak to me at all, he immediately pointed out, in a respectful manner, several of my personal deficiencies which in context I took as being a frank appraisal of those things which would bar meaningful friendship."

Others have confirmed that Wilson was, at times, a bit lacking in the personal hygiene department. However, this verbal attack seems a rather extreme response. In his book, Stephen Calt painted a picture of a grim and somewhat demented Skip James; other blues scholars have verified that he was indeed unpredictable and sometimes outright nasty. Some reports indicate that his rude behavior even extended to urinating and defecating in cars, homes, and other inappropriate places.

John Fahey recalled Skip James as a "jerk" who viewed himself as a musical genius, and behaved condescendingly toward others. Originally, Fahey had sought out James merely to learn more about his unusual guitar tunings. In later years, he claimed that he had never meant to kick off a "rediscovery" career for the older musician.

Wilson did not seem to feel terribly hurt over his own exchange with Skip James. In later years, he would deal with James again, and was not shy about doing so. In April 1966, James stayed with Wilson and David Evans in California while on tour. Wilson interviewed him at length about his music, and while James was indeed temperamental as documented on recordings of those interviews, he was notorious for behaving that way with nearly everyone.

Alan Wilson's encounter with Robert Pete Williams was also memorable. Like John Lee Hooker, Williams was difficult to accompany, but Wilson appreciated the subtlety and distinctiveness of his music.

Writing to Evans, Wilson explained the appeal of Williams: "He doesn't play music for dancing or partying. While the rest of the greats (save the great god Skippy) played excitingly extroverted music for the dancing and partying (and with depth, too) Pete sat in his room all night with but two or three onlookers (His music remains totally unpopular) playing pure 'head' music. Next to Skippy it was the best of all, topping even Son House by a slim margin. Long, gripping performances, with incredible guitar virtuosity. Even Phil [Spiro], who doesn't dig Pete, had his head turned inside out by one of Pete's 'mind maps'."

On backing Williams, Wilson commented, "On Thursday night I played guitar with Pete in his room absolutely alone for nearly an hour, and I can assure you that this is one of the world's most thankless tasks. Maxey and Welch proved it on the Folk-Lyric album, and I found myself also in a nearly hopeless position. However, a few times we jelled, and both Pete and I knew it, and were digging it. It was quite a time."

Bottleneck performer Mississippi Fred McDowell was also at Newport. Wilson was a great fan of his music, but at a late night blues jam, McDowell's wife Annie Mae stole the show. Wilson admitted, "McDowell is, of course, a soulful and introspective performer, but his music is mainly for all-night song, dance, drink, and fuck fests. I suspected this from the records, and I don't think he'd ever play alone in his room. Fred in his all night parties played just as you have heard, rocking back and forth, diverting lyrics first to one group and then another, and his solo bottleneck passages often shoot off electric sparks. His wife Annie dances, claps, sings in a more or less random but — or maybe therefore — exciting manner. Any wandering instrumentalist or singer is wholeheartedly accepted into this mob scene. The scene becomes more sensual, until once out of embarrassment even Fred had to restrain Annie from her ecstatic behavior — which was affecting me in a way in which sixty year old women seldom affect me."

Mississippi John Hurt, on the other hand, tended to direct Wilson's mind to more spiritual matters. Of Hurt's Newport performance, he wrote, "Definitely outclassed but still good and, as [Geoff] Muldaur (he wasn't at the blues house but I ran into him once) said, he is in his last incarnation and about to merge with the all. John alternated between the two parties, raising his gentle voice under rowdy conditions which fazed him not one bit. After a chorus he would be submerged by the stronger voices around him, and he would patiently pluck the guitar and wait. At the Jug Busters 15 minute marathon he would wait endlessly till the stronger voices got their signals crossed. In the resulting silence he would raise his voice toward some chick and gently proclaim, 'Tell me baby, why do you treat me so mean?' A very amusing scene."

During the summer, Wilson had several gigs at the famed Club 47, which was a central point in the Cambridge folk scene. This encouraged him to expand his repertoire and polish his vocal style. He reported his progress to David Evans: "I have written several originals, with stock words but distinctive guitar and melodic line. My voice is improving, mainly through getting used to a microphone and utilizing it to negate my voice's weak aspect — no power — and enhance its strong point — purity in the upper register."

All the hard work was beginning to pay off with "fealty and progress in this world of folkies", as Wilson put it. To Evans, he described his own shows the weekend of Newport: "Saturday was my third night at the 47 club, the other two being in June. All three have been with Lisa Kindred and Jerry Corbett, save for last night when Corbett didn't show and Don MacSorley was the replacement. I play harp behind them and split sets as soloist, (6 sets, I get the 3rd and 6th). The first night I was allowed only 4 number sets by a nervous Byron [Linardos, club manager], but the 2nd nite I was allowed two regulation 7-song sets, and was well-received (not too much chit-chat) despite deplorable (even for me) stage presence and a case of nerves. They liked Lisa and Jerry better, though, and I sweated awhile before I found I was booked in again for last night."

David Evans says, "This was probably some of Al's first work for pay on the stage. Al wasn't exactly a shining light of that scene. This was summertime; it would have been a slow season then because most of the students were gone. Probably for very low pay."

It was a humble gig, and not really a blues audience. Wilson, however, was pleased, and justifiably proud of his rapidly improving bottleneck technique. He wrote: "Last night I played very, very well (I don't boast like this often), and the crowd was swinging along with A FEW LINES, ABERDEEN, and then 'big beat' tunes. In the last set I tried a frightening gamble: two slow, Skip Jamesish originals... and there was *not a peep* for all but the last chorus of the second (and then just a peep or two!) Needless to say, all 14 were delta blues style. No ragtime!" Wilson's "big beat" term here likely referred to songs associated with Muddy Waters, who sometimes used it as a catchphrase when describing his style of blues.

The "frightening gamble" paid off, and Wilson was invited back to the Club 47. He told Evans, "This means, I think, that I am going to continue at the club once or twice a month. This, in addition to projected work at a coffeehouse being run by O.D. (my guitar student Pat's buddy) will make for musical expression, experiment, and improvement."

O.D. could not be tracked down for interview, but Evans recalls his coffeehouse: "That's where Al and I played. It was in Boston, on Charles Street. It was a little place upstairs. I think Babe Stovall played there later also, maybe in the spring. It never had much of a crowd, but we had a regular weekly gig. It was actually advertised slightly, with fliers. Maybe it lasted one or two months."

Wilson was creating his own niche in the blues he had embraced. It had become part of his identity, and sometime in early 1964, he and his friends expressed their connection to the music by forming a club or secret society. The group was documented by John Fahey and in Wilson's writings to David Evans.

Evans and Wilson were apparently the main forces behind this blues fraternity, each individual member being called a Snake Man. This might have had some connection to the John Lee Hooker song, "Crawling King Snake", and the phrase may also have had a sexual or phallic connotation.

David Evans was unable to recall the exact origins of the "Snake Man" group. he says, "It was probably something Al or somebody would have coined, some term for people who could play the music, or people we thought could. Like a sort of club or fraternity or something like that. Blues appreciation was all very cultish."

In his July 1964 letter to Evans, Wilson made suggestions on the ranking of the various Snake Men. He wrote, "As Phil [Spiro] is not practicing or improving and still can't sing, I suggest that [Bob] Wilfong be made third Snake Man and that Laurie Forti and Phil and my student Pat be placed on an auxiliary stand-by basis." Bob Wilfong was a guitarist, and Laurie Forti a keen record collector. Nothing else could be discovered or recalled about Wilson's student Pat.

When guitarist John Fahey came to Boston in 1965, he was invited to be a Snake Man, but declined. He said, "They tried to get me interested in it. They referred to a secret society. As far as I know it was just Wilson and Evans, and they tried to get me interested in it. I got scared."

In California, however, the ranks would expand. There, Bob Hite and Henry Vestine joined Wilson and Evans in some kind of blues fraternity which might have been a descendent of the Snake Man group.

Blues scholar Marina Bokelman, who would meet Evans in California and became his girlfriend, remembers becoming the first female member of the group. At that time, circa 1966 or 1967, their activities involved the wearing of a symbolic leather strap around one wrist. Bokelman did not, however, recall referring to herself as a Snake Man or Woman. It's possible that by that time, the group simply did not use the "Snake" reference any more.

In the aftermath of the Newport Folk Festival, the revival of Son House and his musicianship continued. Dick Waterman says, "When we found Son, he was a major-league alcoholic. He had no motivation to play; if he had a guitar, he would pawn it. He could still sing, though. He could always sing, and he could play slow blues things."

The fiery bottleneck work heard on his 1930 recordings, however, had slipped away from Son House with age and alcohol. He could barely remember the guitar parts to his own songs. This sudden interest in his music from young white fans had been a shock, and he didn't seem quite sure how to react.

Fortunately, House's old recordings were still around. Even better, there was someone who had obsessively deciphered each note on every one of these recordings. Al Wilson had learned every Son House song he could get in his ears, little guessing that he would end up teaching the songs to a befuddled House later on.

Shortly after the Newport Folk Festival, House got out of the hospital. He was encouraged to sit down with Wilson every day for practice, and together the two reviewed old licks, guitar parts, and lyrics. Soon the older man was making his own "rediscovery" of the talent that had languished unused for so many years.

Dick Waterman recalls that Wilson's assistance was essential to Son's career. He says, "Al Wilson taught Son House how to play Son House. I can tell you, flatly, that without Al invigorating and revitalizing Son, there would have been no Son House rediscovery. All of Son's successful concert appearances, recordings, and him being remembered as having a great second career — all that was because of Al rejuvenating his music."

Waterman's recollection has been characterized as hyperbole by some, including scholars like David Evans. To be sure, Wilson's assistance was more an example of *reminding* Son of his old music than of actually teaching him. However, the reminders were desperately needed. House's delight in the process was evident as he watched Wilson play guitar, occasionally exclaiming, "My recollection's coming back to me now!"

It didn't take House long to relearn his repertoire; the practice sessions lasted for a couple of weeks. "It was like when you break a bone, and you go in to rehabilitation," explains Waterman. "Al spent a couple of hours every day with Son, intensely teaching him. Al infused that old music into him, filling him up with the framework of his old playing."

On April 12 through 14, 1965, Son House was scheduled to record an album for the Columbia record label. Fellow artists on the Columbia roster included Bob Dylan and the Byrds, and House was given a one thousand dollar advance on his work. For the time, that was a respectable figure.

Such attention from a mainstream record company was unheard of for an elderly bluesman. Most blues was being recorded for niche labels such as Vanguard or small companies like Takoma. Columbia came on board because of a push from producer John Hammond, who had wanted to record the legendary Robert Johnson. Since Johnson was long dead, Hammond figured that recording his mentor House would be the next best thing.

Dick Waterman had officially accepted the role of House's manager, and invited Alan Wilson to provide guitar and harmonica accompaniment on the album. Hammond was dubious of this at first, not knowing Wilson and not seeing many credentials for him at this early date. However, he was finally persuaded to allow Wilson to play on the second day of the session.

Wilson backed House up on a total of four items, two of which, "Empire State Express" and "Leevee Camp Moan", were released on the album. The remaining two, "Yonder Comes My Mother" and an alternate take of "Leevee Camp Moan", remained unissued until the Son House Columbia session was released in its entirety as a 1992 double CD set. It is generally viewed as an essential blues album, and stands as one of the finest efforts to come out of the "rediscovery" era.

It was becoming clear that Alan Wilson and his good friend David Evans were headed down different paths. Both were dedicated to blues, but Wilson was a musician first and foremost. Evans was finding his place more as a scholar and researcher of the music. Both were stellar guitarists and knew the old blues songs well, but in the end, Wilson will always be known as a musician, and Evans as an academic.

Evans comments on the shift that took place: "Al was more into playing with the musicians at that time, and accompanying them. I kind of left them alone out of respect. Of course, I became a researcher, documentarian, and music recorder. I guess I felt that it was kind of wrong to impose myself on the musicians, say, as an accompanist, or to record myself with them. And to some extent, even to play with them. It introduced an intrusive element into the music. And that's also how I was trained as a folklore graduate student — not to contaminate the music. Which in a sense you do, no matter how good you are, how much you've gotten into it."

Wilson, for his part, respected the academic standards of folk purity, but did not live his life based on those principles. He wanted to *play* music. "Al was basically a musician," says Evans. "He was interested in the history of it, but wasn't one to document it by going out, making field recordings, and discovering new talent and new artists. He found his territory in playing with them. He just enjoyed doing it. And he didn't try to overwhelm them or overplay, which a lot of people do. He wasn't trying to show off; he was really trying to play something appropriate and complementary to whoever he was with."

Around this time, Wilson and Dick Waterman brought Son House to the Ontario Place, a coffeehouse in Washington, D.C. It was operated by Bill Givens, who also ran the Origin Jazz Library record label and was well educated on blues. He interacted with Wilson on various occasions, and has good memories of him.

"Everyone loved and respected Al," said Givens. "I knew him briefly when I was running the Ontario Place. He and Dick Waterman and Son House came down to Washington and we put Son up, put him on at the coffeehouse, and I got to know Al a little. Al and I were friends in that we were part of the old blues mob and that, but we weren't close in any way. ... People respected Al. He was regarded as having the best general knowledge of music as a *reader*. He was a real great guy, and had a reputation of being the world's foremost unlettered musicologist."

Givens, like nearly everyone else, was amazed by Son House's intensity. "He really was something," said Givens. "Of all the people who were rediscovered, he, I think, was closer to the bluesman he'd been, say in 1930, than the others. In my coffeehouse, our two house musicians were Skip James and John Hurt, and they were both quite good, but Son really go down as a much, much younger man would have. Skip and John both showed that they were in their sixties and getting on. Not to knock their performances of the sixties, but they weren't quite as good as they had been. Son, if anything, was better."

The musical re-education of Son House had convinced Dick Waterman of Alan Wilson's blues credentials. He says, "Al wasn't up there showing off. He was interested in, 'What can I contribute to the music?' He was just drawn to Negro music, and he couldn't do anything about it. He had to get into music. ... Al was the ultimate white Negro! People said that about Elvis, but Elvis was not unique. He was a poor Southern white boy singing the blues, singing Arthur Crudup songs and Junior Parker songs. But as a blues singer, Al was really the ultimate white Negro."

Though it seems unlikely that Wilson ever thought of himself in such terms, Waterman's assessment is interesting. As someone who was conscious of his many differences from those around him, and had been harassed for those differences while growing up, it seems likely that Wilson would have identified with the oppression suffered by African-Americans. Perhaps that was indeed part of the attraction of the blues.

To Wilson, blues had become a source of happiness and acceptance. For a shy young man, it provided a way to connect with others. According to Waterman, approval from the likes of Son House was very important for Wilson.

"If you could wish something for somebody," muses Waterman, "like to fall in love or have a nice house, a mansion on the hill or whatever, all I could wish for Al would be for some old bluesman to say, 'That boy can flat-out play!' That was Al's mansion on the hill. ... Sleepy John Estes would say, 'Where's that boy? Bring me that boy; I want him to play with me!' That was happiness for Al."

Wilson tended to withdraw into his music. Once in a while, he had romantic partners, but his musical relationships got priority over personal affairs. "Music was Al's happiness in life," recalls Waterman. "Music was 1A and 1B, and everything else was 2. The spectrum of ways that Al could find happiness was very limited. ... In Cambridge, we thought Al was asexual! If some woman wanted Al Wilson, she would have to have a *mission*, and pursue him. She would have to go after him. Because he wasn't the kind of guy who, after the show, would go down to the bar and say, 'Here I am! I'm the guy who played that slide guitar; look at me!'"

According to most friends, appearances weren't Wilson's strong point. Waterman explains his attitude in Cambridge: "He didn't care much about the way he dressed, or his hair, or anything like that. He must have bathed sometime; maybe he did, but I don't know! He didn't give much attention to hygiene. His glasses were often cracked, and he'd use paperclips to hold the frames together. He didn't like loud music, so he'd stuff cotton in his ears. But then he had these little cotton tails hanging out of his ears. Little cotton tails sort of sticking out of the left and right ears — like a bunny rabbit! And he always wore plaid lumberjack shirts, every day of the year."

When he played the blues, Wilson found, superficial appearances didn't matter as much. People might think he was strange, and a few felt that he needed to bathe more frequently, but such concerns faded in the face of music. Few listeners could deny Wilson's talent. He had grounded himself firmly now in an artistic foundation, and would soon be ready to start building his own creative works.

5 BLIND JOE DEATH

In 1965, guitarist John Fahey came to Boston. At that time, he was a student at U.C.L.A., taking a break from his studies to play a few coffeehouse gigs on the East Coast. The year before, he had rediscovered Skip James with the help of Henry Vestine and Bill Barth, Now, he would become a direct influence and pivotal figure in Alan Wilson's life.

Wilson, in turn, ended up influencing Fahey's artistic development. Years later, Fahey acknowledged his importance: "I loved Al a lot. If I hadn't learned that stuff through him, I couldn't be playing what I'm playing today. I learned a lot from him. While he was teaching me to write my thesis [in California], I learned about modes and stuff. A lot of blues and ragas and stuff, I never would have done had it not been for him. And I surely never could have done my thesis either!"

By the time he and Wilson met, Fahey had been active in the music world for some time, both as performer and scholar. A brilliant if rather obscure guitarist, he had recorded under his own name as well as the "Blind Joe Death" pseudonym. Later, he would claim that his sole reason for rediscovering Skip James was to ask a question about guitar tunings. Alan Wilson held his work in high esteem, to the point of filling an entire notebook with meticulous transcriptions of his songs.

Fahey had a gig at a Boston coffeehouse called the Odyssey. Wilson made a point to be there. After the show, he approached Fahey and introduced himself. "He asked me if I'd give him a guitar lesson," Fahey remembered. "'Sure,' I said, looking at this nerdy person. Because he was essentially a nerd, except for the music. Which doesn't mean I didn't like him or anything. I'm just saying how he was perceived, and how you had to relate to him and stuff."

Wilson was invited to come visit Fahey the next day for the requested lesson. "he came over to where I was staying, and he had a notebook," recalled Fahey. "He opened the notebook, and he had all of the songs down that I had recorded so far. In notation, or tablature. And all he wanted for a lesson was to fill in a couple of difficult passages he hadn't been able to transcribe. But he could play every one of my songs note for note! I wanted to kill him!"

Before this, Fahey had believed that nobody else could possibly play his material. He utilized nonstandard tunings which he thought would be difficult for others to decipher; however, Wilson had figured them out, and was obviously a musical equal. Fahey's first reaction was frustration. "Boy, was I mad!" he said. "There he goes, playing it note for note."

As the visit progressed, Fahey began to consider ways he might turn Wilson's skills to his own advantage. Wilson's ability to transcribe music, and analyze it using notation, was a strong point that Fahey himself lacked. "I thought something fruitful might come out of this relationship," he said. "So we hung out that week, and a few more weeks, and listened to records and compared notes. He liked songs with just one chord, and the fewer notes the better. His ideal song was a three-note song, like 'Mississippi Boweavil Blues' by Charley Patton. That was perfect. And he *hated* the ragtime progression. So what he was left with was Son House, Skip James, and a few others. He would have liked Geechie Wiley. I cannot remember much that we did except get together and compare notes on blues singers, guitar things, and so forth."

Around this time, Wilson was playing his beloved National guitar obtained from Phil Spiro. Fahey couldn't understand the guitar's appeal, and said, "He had this awful National guitar. It was not one of the loud kind; it wasn't bright. But he liked that. I don't know why. I didn't like it very much. I couldn't figure it out — why would anybody want it? Wilson liked to play on that guitar in open G minor, which is a very unusual tuning. I don't think he even had a wooden guitar. If he did, I never saw it."

Wilson tried to explain to Fahey why he loved his National. His ears were very sensitive to tonal variations as well as volume. "That's what he liked, because the tone was clearer to his ears," said Fahey. "There were fewer weird overtones. It was awfully quiet. One of the things Wilson talked about was the tone of the guitar. I think he talked about the tone more than he talked about anything else."

Wilson didn't care much for guitar plectrums, preferring instead to play using his fingernails. On his right hand, his fingernails were kept exceptionally long for this purpose. Bassist Richard Hite, who spent time with Wilson in California, once recalled that Wilson's thumbnail became so long that it appeared "grotesque".

At one point, according to Fahey, Wilson would experiment by wedging match sticks under his fingernails for guitar picking. This bizarre technique did not work well and was abandoned. As Fahey suggested, it sounded rather more "like a method of torture" than a useful means of picking guitar strings.

Evans was making regular appearances as Wilson and Fahey got to know each other. He had become intrigued by blues master Tommy Johnson. "Dave Evans used to come by," Fahey remembered. "He would sing these imitations of Tommy Johnson songs, like 'Canned Heat Blues'. And he was so serious about the way he did it; it was kind of funny."

In later years, Evans got even more serious about Johnson, writing his biography and analyzing his musical style as part of a master's degree thesis. This led to a renowned career as one of the preeminent musicologists of his time.

In 1965 Cambridge, however, Evans was just another student obsessed with an obscure bluesman. Wilson, for his part, seemed to be getting a little frustrated. He was drinking more, and while friends never recall him behaving poorly as a result of drunkenness, the alcohol provided one more challenge to his already poor hygiene.

Fahey recalled, "Wilson's little tiny bedroom was cluttered with beer bottles. He drank himself to sleep, I guess. [Phil] Spiro wondered how he got from the doorway to the bed, because there was, like, four feet of beer bottles. And so one night Spiro waited up to see how he did it. Wilson came in, came up to the room, and *dove* over the beer bottles to his bed!"

Fahey also had a memory of Wilson living somewhere else in the Cambridge area. Apparently not having learned much from his experience with the heroin junkies, he rented a space which he opened up to various and sundry inhabitants. "He lived in a flop house that he paid the rent for," said Fahey. "And anybody could come in there and sleep. That was after Phil Spiro, I think."

Wilson had a girlfriend for a while during this period. Fahey said, "When I first met him he had this kind of round girlfriend that actually kind of looked like him... but was somehow still attractive. You know, kind of short and fat, but still pretty good-looking." It's unknown how long this relationship lasted.

Eventually, Fahey saw opportunity in his relationship with Wilson. He asked Wilson to travel to California with him and tutor him on the technical aspects of music, such as notation and scales. This would help resolve the challenges Fahey had been experiencing in doing his thesis on Charley Patton at U.C.L.A.. He promised to pay Wilson what he could, and give him a place to live.

Wilson agreed immediately. He had been slowly coming to the conclusion that he must leave Massachusetts for greener musical pastures, and this seemed the perfect opportunity. As he couldn't drive, and might not have wanted to go to a strange place by himself, Fahey's offer was perfect for him.

Apparently having broken up with his girlfriend, Wilson had been expressing feelings of loneliness. Fahey assured him that he would be able to find a suitable woman in California. "That was something he complained about," said Fahey. "He said, 'I can never find any girls.' And I said, 'I used to have the same trouble when I lived on the East coast. I had much better luck out west.' And that's true. So that was one of the enticements, plus money, to get him to come out west. He wasn't very happy in Boston... for various reasons."

In August, Fahey was ready to head back to Los Angeles. First, however, he wanted to stop in Richmond, Indiana. "A record factory used to be there," he explained. "I wanted to take photographs of it, which I did."

During Fahey's Richmond sojourn, Wilson visited Son House in New York one last time. According to a later letter to his family, he also performed a gig or two, most likely at coffeehouses or the like. However, he was frustrated that the shows didn't result in much income for him.

Even worse, Wilson ended up losing his beloved National guitar, which was stolen right out of his arms. John Fahey recalled, "He told me in New York he was talking on the street and this guy asked him if he needed help carrying his guitar." The innocent Wilson handed his instrument over, and the thief ran away with it.

Wilson could never find another National that had the specific tonal qualities he loved so much. The loss of the unique guitar was heartbreaking. Weeks later, he wrote to a family member, "I loved that guitar like a near and dear relative, and it's all very painful."

According to Fahey, Wilson took a bus and met him in Indiana. As they headed west together, one other item was missing from Wilson's possessions. He had inadvertently left his eyeglasses behind, and on the road to California, his poor vision meant that he couldn't enjoy much of the scenery. "He couldn't see anything practically the whole way," remembered Fahey.

Inspired by Wilson's defective eyesight, Fahey began calling him "Blind Al", in the fashion of the "Blind" blues singers of olden times. Some examples included Blind Lemon Jefferson, Blind Willie McTell, Blind Willie Johnson, and so on. Such singers were typically more profoundly blind than Wilson, who without glasses was near-blind, but would eventually (circa 1969) obtain a driver license contingent upon usage of his corrective lenses.

"Blind Al" evolved into "Blind Owl", as Wilson's round face had an owlish appearance. A scholarly and wise nature is also traditionally associated with the owl, and Alan Wilson certainly had those qualities as well.

Fahey would also refer to Wilson as "Owl Krishna Wilson" or "Aouhl Krishnawilsuhn", the corruption of Wilson's middle name evoking their mutual interest in Hinduism. The "Blind Owl" nickname, however, was the one that took, becoming famous along with Canned Heat. Wilson seemed to like the appellation, and would amass a collection of stuffed owls over the years.

On their journey, Fahey found that Wilson's aversion to social interactions rivaled his own. On the way to California, they stopped in Albuquerque, New Mexico so that Fahey could visit his mother and stepfather. He felt no great enthusiasm for it. "At the time, I couldn't stand visiting; it was a pain in the ass to me," he explained. "Wilson thought that what he should do was sit in the corner in the half-lotus position and read a book, and stay out of the conversation. Because he didn't know them, and he'd never see them again. I mean, he was just trying to be nice! But they got mad. They didn't say anything, but the next time I saw them, they were mad because he wouldn't join in the phony sociability. If I had my way, I would have sat in the corner too."

6 BLIND OWL'S WESTWARD MIGRATION

After arriving in California on September 15, 1965, Alan Wilson and John Fahey got an apartment in Venice, a part of Los Angeles. "We lived in a black section," Fahey recalled. "It was slums in Venice, a black slum area."

As Wilson told his family in later correspondence, the apartment cost twenty-two dollars a month, a sum that the he and Fahey split. They had two large rooms, a kitchen, bathroom, closet space, and also a large patio with a barbecue pit. The West Coast was enjoyable, and Wilson wrote in the same letter, "I am delighted with the people I've met here, and also the beautiful weather."

Their apartment was but a few blocks from the ocean. Wilson enjoyed swimming in the summer and fall, and also appreciated the West Coast sports scene. He wrote, "It took me about three days to switch allegiance from the Red Sox to the Dodgers, who for my money are the most exciting team in baseball (and also the best!)."

At home, Wilson gave daily lessons on music theory, and helped Fahey with his musicological analyses for the Charley Patton thesis. Apparently he took naturally to the role of teacher, for his student would later grumble that he often "spoke as a professor", and that his scholarly manner became "annoying".

In the role of guitar technician, Wilson accompanied Fahey to a few shows. "He had perfect pitch, and perfect relative pitch," said

Fahey. "He was really useful to take on gigs, because he would tune my guitar and make it perfect." Wilson was extremely fussy about guitar tuning, which would occasionally cause him to be berated in later years, as he spent an inordinate amount of time tuning onstage with Canned Heat.

Based upon conversations during their drive from the East Coast, Wilson ended up writing liner notes for the Fahey album *The Transfiguration of Blind Joe Death*. His story is surreal and extremely bizarre, an example of the eccentric creativity both he and Fahey possessed. The notes appear under the pseudonym Charles Holloway.

"While we were on the way, he asked me a lot of biographical questions, and some serious questions," said Fahey. "And when we got out there, and we found an apartment to rent, he put a whole lot of this stuff together, into a story. It was the last thing I expected him to do. And, those are what made up the notes to *The Transfiguration of Blind Joe Death*."

Wilson didn't neglect his own artistic development, and continued expanding his knowledge of Asian music. Fahey had purchased an Indian veena before leaving Boston. When Wilson got his hands on it, he took to it immediately, learning to play basic ragas in only three days. Fahey decided that it was best to give him the instrument.

"I bought it in Boston that summer from the Indian Appreciation Society for about ninety-five bucks," said Fahey. "Yeah, I couldn't learn to play it. But he could! And he went to the U.C.L.A. library and got a library card and some books ... and learned a lot about modes and scales out of those books. He used to sit in the half-lotus position for hours. Yeah, he would go off into ... I guess you could say he could concentrate very well and ignore everything else."

Around this time, Wilson began expanding his mind through the use of psychedelics. Fahey recalled, "He started taking acid probably three or four months after we moved out there... he'd stay up all night and then in the morning he came around to school,

U.C.L.A." Others have recalled that Wilson appeared occasionally at the university and sat in on a few folklore classes with renowned professor D. K. Wilgus. It is also possible that he took some formal instruction on the veena from another professor, Gayathri Rajapur. (It is unknown whether or not Wilson was under the influence of LSD while receiving any such instruction.)

While they were living together, Fahey felt it necessary to make Wilson improve his cleanliness. "Wilson refused to take baths very often," he explained. "And he usually stunk. When he lived with me, I had to frequently fill up the tub with water and soap, and then threaten him, force him to take his clothes off and take a bath. And I'd buy him clothes and underwear and stuff. But he didn't smell too good. Very bad..."

Though hygienically challenged, Wilson was intellectually intriguing to Fahey. The two shared some spiritual interests, as Fahey recalled: "I found him stimulating. I listened to him talk, and we exchanged all kinds of theories about religion."

Of Wilson's spiritual perspective during the time they lived together, Fahey said, "Well, he had adopted the Hindu view, I think from ... I would guess it was the Sivananda Yoga Society, in Boston. That's where he'd picked up these Hindu ideas." Though he could not be considered a devout Hindu, Wilson was a keen practitioner of Hatha Yoga, a Yogic branch of physical exercises. Throughout his adult life, he could often be observed positioned in various *asanas* or Yoga poses.

Fahey also claimed that they visited a swami, or Hindu monk, together. He recalled, "I remember one thing that he said. The swami said to us, 'You are God.' And Wilson said, 'That's interesting.' Then he turned around and said, 'I'm God. But you're God too.'" The identity of the swami in this story could not be determined.

The two also attended a speech by a philosopher whose name Fahey could not precisely recall. He could only explain, "This guy is a very good writer, very peaceful writer. We had both read him and went to see him. When he gets onstage, he starts yelling and screaming and everything. And half the people that ask him a question, he makes fun of them. 'What a dumb question!' He talks, and it takes an hour."

The show had a surprise ending. "Wilson and I both saw it," Fahey reported. "He disappeared off the stage! That's what we both saw. Suddenly he's not there. And I've talked to other people who went to see him lecture; they said the same thing. Probably what he does, he's so spellbinding, you don't notice him walking off. Because I don't believe in magic."

California seemed to be good for Wilson, who became healthier, according to Fahey. In mid-October, he even found a girlfriend. Gone were the days of drinking so much that a mountain of beer bottles surrounded his bed. "When he lived with me he didn't drink much," said Fahey. "See, I think when he came out West he kind of blossomed."

Shortly after moving to Los Angeles, Wilson met a young bluegrass musician named David Polacheck. Polacheck played the five-string banjo, an instrument that looked promising to Wilson.

"I never really was a blues musician," explains Polacheck. "But I had an idea that I'd like to learn a little slide guitar, which was what he played. So we exchanged a few lessons. I showed him the five-string banjo, and he showed me slide guitar. He showed me a few guitar pieces, and transcribed the tablature."

Wilson ended up playing ragas on the five-string banjo. One of these would be recorded in 1966 for Fahey's Takoma label, but never saw issuance.

During their time together, Polacheck was impressed by Wilson's obsession with modal music. He remembers, "He was interested in any kind of music that was modal in character. Besides traditional country blues, Alan was just fascinated with classical Indian music. Both musics are structurally non-harmonic in character. Many recordings he would listen to intently, and he would go to the concerts that were being held. He was passionate about his interest in the music. He wasn't interested in anything that wasn't basically modal."

At one point, Polacheck played a Bill Monroe record for Wilson. Although the music wasn't modal, he thought it might be appreciated for the depth of feeling and the high quality of the singing and playing. Monroe is, after all, known as the "Father of Bluegrass" for good reason.

Polacheck recalls, "I thought it was really great, with a lot of emotion and everything that he would like. I said, 'Do you even like this?' He listened to it very carefully, sort of smiled, and said, 'I guess I'm incorrigible.' Anything harmony-based, with chord changes, he couldn't get interested in. No matter how good it was — if it wasn't modal in character, it just wasn't interesting to him."

After living with John Fahey for a couple of months, Wilson began moving out in November 1965. Bill Givens, who operated the Origin Jazz Library record label and knew him from the rediscovery of Son House, came to visit around that time.

Givens reported, "Al was living partly with a girl whose name I don't know, and partly with John Fahey. He helped Fahey enormously with his Ph.D. ... He would come over and do musical transcriptions that John needed for his Ph.D. And, in return for that, John fed him and gave him whatever pocket change he had, two or three dollars, to get him through the day."

They were poor and Wilson's diet was monotonous. "Al ate the same thing every day," said Givens. "He cooked some spaghetti that John had on hand. He poured it out, put some margarine on it and some Kraft cheese out of a shaker, and some garlic salt. And that's what he ate. Every day he came over, he came right for the cabinet, got the spaghetti out, without a word, made himself some spaghetti, then they got down to business."

During the final day of Bill Givens' visit, Wilson appeared at Fahey's home to pick up the last of his belongings. Through his notorious absentmindedness, he managed to cause a great deal of disruption.

"Wilson was waiting for a ride," said Fahey. "He didn't have a suitcase or anything! He was at my place, and this record collector, Bill Givens, came by. He had to get to the airport that night be eleven. So he was just hanging out and he had a suitcase, and he set it down by the door. When Wilson left, he took the suitcase! He thought it was his suitcase, I guess. And so time gets around to get Givens to the airport. And, no suitcase! We raced all over town and found Wilson's apartment, more or less by instinct. We walked in, and there was the suitcase. And Wilson says, completely oblivious to everything else, 'You know, I have a *problem*. Where did this suitcase come from?'"

Interestingly, Bill Givens told the story a different way, recalling that Wilson did have a suitcase identical to his own. He said, "Al had just moved out. He had moved in with a girl. ... And we both had plaid Grasshopper suitcases. Al was coming back to pick up his. I was sleeping in what had been Al's room over the three, four, five days I was down there. It was a terribly stormy November evening. I had a thirty day round trip excursion airline ticket, and if I didn't get off by midnight that particular night, which I think was a Saturday, I would lose the return half of the ticket, which was worth about a hundred and twenty five dollars to me, which was a lot of money back then. So John was gonna take me to the airport and I was gonna catch a flight, maybe nine o'clock."

While Givens was waiting at Fahey's place, Wilson appeared to pick up his items. Givens remembers, "Al comes in, we sit down and talk, and Al picks up a suitcase and I didn't notice it and John didn't notice it because Al had a Grasshopper which he'd packed previously, and off he went. John said, 'Well, better get you to the airport.' So I said, 'I got a couple of things to put in my suitcase,' took a look at the suitcase, opened it. It was Al's suitcase. And my suitcase, with all the traveling, business stuff for my record company ... Al had taken off with it! Not knowing that it was my suitcase."

With little time to spare, the two tracked down Wilson. "John said he thought he knew where Al would be," said Givens. "We tried three or four different addresses... and made contact with Al in an old apartment building. I was feeling I was getting the real local color! We switched suitcases. John in a car he'd probably paid fifty dollars for, was rattling all over the road, drove like a mad demon to the airport and I finally got on the plane with about three minutes to spare. And that's the story. But Al was sorta like that. Aside from music, he was kinda out to lunch."

The identity of Wilson's girlfriend has been difficult to confirm, though it's possible that her name was Carol. John Fahey said, "Out west he met this girl. I don't remember her name. Jewish girl, a young Jewish girl. Nice girl, I liked her a lot. And he went to live with her."

Unfortunately, their relationship was troubled. Wilson admitted to Fahey that he was having problems with intimacy. "We told each other everything," said Fahey. "I mean, we were really close friends. ... When you say friends, though, you usually mean that you're emotionally close to the other person. Right? And, Al was... he didn't mean to be and he didn't want to be, but inside there he was closed off. From himself. And from everybody else."

According to Fahey's personal interpretation, certain emotions seemed to be repressed or even missing in Wilson. "Only if you got to know him really well would you realize that there were certain things that he didn't feel," explained Fahey. "He didn't have certain emotions like affection, or love, or even strong hate. He might get mad sometimes, but not half as bad as I can get, or anybody else."

Though Fahey was no psychiatrist, there is a ring of truth to his assessment. Even his own mother, Shirley Konecy, felt that he tended to distance himself from others, much as he was loved by his family. Years later, she would write to the members of Canned Heat shortly after Alan's death: "We all loved him as much as he would allow us to," and commented that he had "... insulated himself from everything except his music and his love of nature and beauty."

John Fahey felt that this seemingly limited emotional range had some connection to Wilson's preferences in music. "He had a very small repertoire of emotions," Fahey mused. "It was limited. Also his music was limited to the same kind of emotions. Like, he liked only modal music. It had to only have one chord. Like Son

House, Skip James, and Robert Pete Williams, he liked a lot. But that was about it."

Fahey believed that Wilson was attempting, albeit unconsciously, to get in touch with himself through music. This helped to explain his zeal when it came to the artists he liked. "Another thing was he used to listen to this stuff intensely," said Fahey. "And then come over and give us a report, like he was a newspaperman. And about who he liked. And he took this very seriously. ... And he would speak as a professor frequently. He did that. And I think he was trying to find his emotions. Yeah, and he was looking for his emotions in music."

Wilson's live-in experience with the girlfriend didn't last long. They broke up within months, and he moved in with Barry Hansen, a music student he had gotten to know shortly after arriving in California. The two were able to relate well, and Hansen remembers Alan Wilson as a good friend.

"He stayed on my couch for at least two months," says Hansen. "He knew all kinds of musicological things about what made everything tick, all the way from blues to Indian music to any kind of classical music. He would want to hear anything new that I had, or he'd discover something and he'd say, 'What do you have by so-and-so?'"

Hansen's record collection aroused Wilson's interest in European classical music forms. "During the time he stayed with me, his favorite composer was Anton Webern," says Hansen. "Webern wrote very short pieces, so his entire life's work fit on four LP records. It was very concentrated music, very intense and organized. I had bought that set of records because I was a music major, and I studied it. I'd had it for several years at that time. And when Alan found I had that, *that's* what he wanted to listen to. Every night before he went to bed, he'd play that. Not the whole thing all the way through, but he'd pick a side or two off of it. He certainly played that more than any other record during the time he was staying with me."

As Hansen recalls, Wilson's musical interests were very wide-ranging. Throughout the next few years, the two would often visit and listen to music together, usually at Hansen's house because he had more records. As he recalls, "[Alan] would want to hear anything new that I had or he'd ask; he'd discovered something and he'd say, 'What do you have by so-and-so,' and it would not necessarily be blues. In fact it would probably be classical music or some music from some other part of the world that he'd want to hear."

Hansen had a piano, which Wilson attempted to play. He quickly found, however, that it was badly out of tune. The instrument produced dissonant and, to him, almost painful sounds. After hearing Hansen play it one day, he declared, "If you're gonna do that, you have *got* to tune that piano. I just can't stand to hear it the way it is."

"I was a poor student," says Hansen, "and I didn't want to pay a piano tuner. So we went out together and found the fork that you use, or the tool that you use to tune a piano. We went to a music supply store and found one; I think it was about five bucks."

When they got back home, Wilson took over. Hansen says, "Alan had never tuned a piano before, but it was just kind of an experiment. He started with the middle of the keyboard, and never quite got the lowest or the highest octave in tune. But he got the rest of it sounding okay."

David Evans had moved to California a few weeks after Alan Wilson, in order to attend the folklore program at U.C.L.A. Eventually Wilson moved out of Barry Hansen's place and in with Evans, who recalls, "I rented part of a duplex on one of the canals in Venice, and Al came in as a roommate. That would have been during the spring of 1966."

At times, there were other guests. "Skip James came to Los Angeles and had an extended stay at a coffeehouse," says Evans. "He stayed with us, and we interviewed him over the course of two or three days."

While staying with Evans, Wilson began experimenting with a combination of guitar and sitar parts to make his own instrument.

"I remember Al got a sitar bridge and put it on a guitar," Evans describes. "It was so that the string actually rested on the bridge. You see, a sitar bridge is flat; it has a long flat part there. On the guitar, the string runs over kind of a sharp bridge; it just sticks up, just a little thing with grooves and then the string sort of runs over it. But with the sitar bridge, the part that the string runs over is about an inch long and so it sort of rests on the bridge and gives it that buzzing twangy sound. Al was trying to get that sound on guitar."

Evans was more interested in researching music than in creating odd innovations. Wilson, long out of school but always a scholar, accompanied him on local "field trips" that led to the desert of Ridgecrest, California. There, in February or March 1966, they met the Reverend Rubin Lacy, a former blues singer.

For a year or so afterward, Evans and Wilson made periodic visits to Reverend Lacy, always dressing formally out of respect. "Al would actually wear a suit and tie, as we all did," recalls Evans. "He and John Fahey and I, if you can imagine that, going to visit Reverend Lacy on a Sunday! On the first visit, we rediscovered him, so to speak. Sometimes it was John and Barry Hansen and I, maybe all four of us, but usually John and Al and I. We'd make these visits to him up in Ridgecrest. It's a very scenic drive through the desert; it's called Red Rock Canyon. That was neat, too. Al liked that."

Although his greatest passion seemed to be for trees and wooded areas, Wilson did appreciate the desert as well. According to Fahey, this was because of the sparse desert landscape which to an artistic mind could suggest the sparseness of a modal music arrangement. "He liked the desert," said Fahey. "And he said, 'What I'd really like to see is tundra.' Tundra is, like, up at the North Pole!"

On the first visit to Ridgecrest, as Fahey has recalled, he, Evans, and Wilson stayed for a couple of days. They spent the night in a nearby motel room. As the sun approached the western horizon that evening, Wilson left his companions. Outside, he disappeared in the vast sand dunes for two or three hours. On returning to the motel room, he explained that he had been "gamboling" in the desert.

7 THE BEAR AND OTHER CALIFORNIA DENIZENS

Not long after arriving in California with Alan Wilson, John Fahey introduced him to Bob Hite. His relationship with Hite would grow quickly, and would prove to be one of the most significant — and complex — in Wilson's adult life.

All the local blues fans knew Hite, for he had one of the largest record collections anyone had ever seen. A man of large stature and lust for life, he collected prewar blues 78s with an enthusiasm that was matched by his physical appetites. Though generally a good-natured and generous man, Hite tended to extremes in his living, thus sometimes creating hazards for himself and those close to him.

Coming from a musical family, Hite received plenty of artistic encouragement from his parents. Prior to becoming a housewife, his mother had performed with an East Coast music group, Mal Hallett and his Orchestra. His father had played trumpet with bandleader Sammy Kaye before getting a job as a Greyhound bus driver to support his family. Bob Hite became intrigued with records as a youngster, first exploring his parents' collection, and soon investing in his own LPs, 45s, and 78s.

Blues and R&B were particularly fascinating to Hite. While he collected all kinds of music, his own career as performer would focus on blues and blues-based forms. In 1968, he said, "I like to watch the record go around on the record player. I like blues; if it's funky, if I like the way the guy's singing, if I like the way the guy's playing guitar, if he's in tune, I like it. I think I listen to the blues almost every possible waking hour of the day. I wake up in the morning, prepare myself for the day — by whatever means that I decide to prepare myself for that particular day — and turn on the record player. If I have to go somewhere, the record player is on until the last minute, when I've got my coat in my hand and I'm walking out the door."

Bob Hite and Alan Wilson bonded immediately through their mutual interest in deep blues. Aside from the music, however, the two could hardly have been more dissimilar. Hite was a burly, loud, outgoing character who loved to be the center of attention and the host of the party. He loved indulgence in food, sex, and whatever mind-altering substances he could get his hands on. In a way, his presence would provide a balance for the shy and introverted Wilson, who preferred to withdraw into the shadows.

Accustomed to having his own way and throwing his weight around, Bob Hite could be difficult to deal with at times. As teens, he and his best friend Claude McKee had amused themselves by holding up neighborhood newspaper delivery boys and bullying them out of any money they had collected. One story, from his younger brother, suggests that Hite acquired his very first record by shoplifting it from a local store. (In interview, however, Bob Hite himself claimed that he began working as a shoeshine boy at age five so that he could afford to purchase records.)

Another friend was a guitarist named Mike Perlowin, who had gotten into the scene through John Fahey. "John and I became tight," recalls Perlowin. "John was the one who introduced Alan to me, and that's how I met Alan."

Their collective interest in preserving the blues led Wilson, Hite, Fahey, and Perlowin to become involved with the early development of Canned Heat. In the beginning, however, the vision wasn't a band, but a record label.

Mike Perlowin says, "John and Alan and I decided we were going to start a record company and reissue some Library of Congress recordings. Bob Hite had the tapes." However, when they got together for meetings and discussions, they ended up playing music together. The Library of Congress recordings were set aside.

In November 1965, the four formed a jug band. This lineup featured an actual jug played by Hite. It was not much of a commercial enterprise, however, and it's uncertain whether the band actually ever played in public.

In later years, Hite would recall inviting Fahey, Wilson, and Perlowin over to his parents' house where he was living at the time. After an evening of listening to records, they were chastised by Hite's mother and ordered to turn the volume down. Eventually, they turned the record player off and switched to their own instruments, with Fahey and Perlowin on guitars, Wilson on harmonica, and Hite on jug. That night was the inception of Canned Heat, in Hite's bedroom.

Wilson soon began practicing on Perlowin's electric guitar, sensing potential in the technology of amplification. Neither had the money for a proper amplifier, however, so they were forced to improvise. "We plugged into an old tube tape recorder," Perlowin recalled. "That was our amplifier. It worked! It sounded like shit, but it worked."

Before long, their jug band was mutating into an electric blues band. John Fahey promptly dropped out in disgust. Perlowin recalls, "John immediately said, 'If you guys are gonna play electric, I don't want any part of it." Decades later, Fahey stated that he always respected Wilson as a musician, but didn't care for the sound of Canned Heat as a band.

Wilson, Hite, and Perlowin were left as a trio. They soon decided to add a bass player, Stuart Brotman, and a drummer, Keith Sawyer. A few days later, Perlowin and Sawyer dropped out. Sawyer was replaced by Ron Holmes, and Perlowin by Kenny Edwards, a local musician who would later play bass in Linda Rondstadt's Stone Poneys. With this lineup, they performed a couple of gigs at the local

Ash Grove club for five dollars apiece, as Hite would recall in later interview.

Stuart Brotman had been introduced to Alan Wilson at the University of California. "We knew each other from classes at UCLA in the music department," remembers Brotman. "I think he was studying South Indian singing and veena. He said that he was studying with Gayathri Rajapur." It is also possible that Wilson did not have Rajapur as a formal teacher, but was, rather, inspired by her work.

During this period, Alan Wilson lived for a time with Mike Perlowin and another friend, Mike Bass, who would end up on staff at the Ash Grove club. "We shared an apartment in Venice," says Perlowin. "Bass had the only bedroom, and Alan and I basically slept on the floor. We were just basically young hippies in Venice."

Along with an apartment, Perlowin and Wilson shared an unfortunate misadventure around this period. Wilson had been letting his hair grow longer, and while it wasn't past his shoulders, it was still long enough to present danger from the overzealous Los Angeles police department.

One day in the spring of 1966, Perlowin was driving down the road with Wilson in the passenger seat of his car. Wilson had a "joint" of marijuana in his pocket. Suddenly, Perlowin noticed a police car next to them, and felt a sense of doom. "I was behind the wheel," he remembers. "I looked over, and the guy in the car next to me flashed a badge. They saw two guys with long hair, and said, 'Let's see what we've got!'"

When he saw the police officer, Perlowin panicked and shouted, "Alan, swallow the joint!"

Wilson pulled the joint out of his pocket and stuffed it in his mouth, but this didn't avert the danger. "As soon as Alan reached for the joint, they knew they had a couple of live ones," says Perlowin. "Then their car was in front of us; I had to brake to stop. The next thing I know, there's four cops. One is on me and the other three are on him. Two of them are trying to pry his mouth open and one is sticking a gun in his face. 'Spit it out or I'll pull the trigger, I swear to God I'll pull the trigger!' ... And Alan swallowed the joint anyway. I think one of the cops punched him in the stomach but I'm not sure."

Both young men were arrested and taken to the police station. After a day or so, both were released on bail. When their day in court came up, all charges were dropped. "They took the car apart," says Perlowin. "They found three seeds and a pipe containing some residue. Under California law, that's not admissible evidence because it couldn't have been consumed. Had they found the joint, we could have been guilty of a felony and gone to jail for two years."

Bob Hite was still living with his parents, and Alan Wilson frequently appeared there to immerse himself in Hite's record collection. There, he encountered Bob's brother Richard, who was younger than Bob by eight years and Alan by nine.

In many respects, Richard was a toned-down version of his brother. Though not as aggressive as Bob, Richard also tended to be somewhat portly and self-indulgent. He was also a kind and generous man, and, in later years, would be well respected as a knowledgeable musicologist. He outlived Bob by two decades, long enough to lament that he was tired of being compared to his brother.

At his young age in the mid-sixties, Richard was already learning to play electric bass. John Fahey had given him his first guitar lessons, and Alan Wilson continued to teach him on occasion. Several years after Wilson's death, Richard would end up joining Canned Heat as bassist. While his relationship with the band and its legacy was often stormy, it wove a constant thread throughout his adult life, just as with his brother.

Even in the early days, Richard was involved with Canned Heat on the sidelines. He recalled, "At the beginning they were doing mostly covers. Because I remember my brother one time asking me to write the words down to 'Spoonful' by Howlin' Wolf. I used to get to do that kind of stuff too, write the lyrics down. I think probably the first country blues thing they started fooling around with was 'Big Road Blues', which actually at one point was a song called 'Straight Ahead #13' or something like that. It's when they first started taking the country blues and electrifying it."

When Wilson came to visit the Hite family, Richard observed his intense concentration and ritual while listening to his favorite sounds. "He would sit in the yoga position on the floor," said Richard. "He smoked Pall-Mall cigarettes, and they're non-filter. He would take the end of it and wet it, so he would have this wet, soggy non-filter cigarette. He'd just sit there and listen, and wet his Pall-Mall cigarettes ... he'd be there for hours on end."

Richard recalled that Wilson had distinctive musical fixations. "He used to always be interested in frequencies of tone in blues songs," said Richard. "For example, he would decide, 'Sic 'Em Pigs' or something like that, the D occurs forty-seven times. He was really into that, how many times the tone would occur in a song. And he would make these charts, and stuff like that. ... And he was also concerned [with] the positioning of songs on an album. The order, but having to do with musical keys. Because keys ... it's hard to explain. An open D on a guitar, that D sound is a happy sound. Whereas the E chord is a lower sound; it's not as happy-sounding. And so he would arrange songs so they would sort of, you know, work."

In contrast with the music-obsessed Wilson, Richard was often interested simply in having a good time. These youthful spirits were somehow attractive to Wilson, who Richard remembered as a friend as much as a music teacher. Wilson would even call off guitar lessons sometimes, so that he and Richard could play games outside.

"I was still in junior high school," Richard recalled. "When Alan would come over to listen to records or something like that, he would usually spend more time with me than with my brother, which used to piss my brother off quite a bit. Alan would be out there playing handball with me or something like that. My brother would come out and yell — "Rrraagghh, what's going on!?' — and he'd take the ball and hit it on the roof so we'd have to stop playing, and stuff like that."

Despite Bob's annoyance, Wilson continued taking an interest in the younger Hite brother. "He was real friendly to me," said Richard. "I mean, I would ... play a record or something like that and say, 'Here, write the music down for me, exactly write all the parts and everything,' and then he showed me, really taught me how to play guitar. He took an interest in that, him and John Fahey. But I wasn't really interested at the time. But he was sort of like a playmate in some ways, because when he would come over, he would spend time with me and play Scrabble."

Richard's girl friend at the time was Marty Wynoff. She also encountered Wilson, and noticed his distinctive fixation on certain areas of interest. "He was almost like a prodigy," she recalled. "He could do music real well, but other skills he was utterly lacking in. He didn't have the basic skills."

Occasionally, Wynoff joined in the Scrabble games, and remembers Wilson's talent for this pastime: "He whomped the shit out of us! He wouldn't play a word unless he could get fifty points. He could play all his letters, and he could do it, a lot. I mean, he was amazing."

Together, Richard Hite and Alan Wilson also amused themselves by making home recordings. "I've got some acetates somewhere of him and me playing together," said Richard. "The old acetates they would tape Canned Heat stuff on, I had little disc recorders, so I would take the blank side and record Alan and I and stuff like that. He was just like one of the kids, really."

Mrs. Hite, for her part, treated Wilson like one of the kids. "I can remember my mother telling him to take a bath before he came to her table," says Richard. "[She would] tell him, 'If you're gonna eat at my table, you're gonna be *clean*. ... Oh, he smelled; oh God! You'd really have to tell him to wash. I mean, it just wasn't important [to him]."

At times, Wilson's blindness combined with his absentminded nature made for problems. Richard remembered a mishap that took place after Canned Heat became famous: "They were playing for the President of Mexico's son or daughter's wedding. And they had just finished playing. Alan took off his guitar and was going to lay it down on the table, and — he was going to lay it down on the presidential wedding cake!"

Bob Hite managed to save the cake, and the day. Richard said, "My brother had seen him about to put the guitar down, and my brother *tackled* him!"

Wilson spent a great deal of time playing music with Bob Hite, who was primarily a singer, though he dabbled with trumpet and jug. His vocals were in the "blues shouter" vein, one of his great strengths being his knowledge of traditional blues verses and his versatility in adapting traditional lyrics.

Typically, Hite's songs were individualized by adding, eliminating, or adapting verses according to his own tastes. In concert, he might sing a song differently than on the record if he felt so inclined. This was a traditional manner of blues composition, similar to the way that many rural blues singers worked with their material. Hite's knowledge of the blues vocabulary was so thorough that it's easy to imagine him singing and improvising for hours on end, just as the legendary Big Joe Turner did on the streets of Kansas City. His extensive record collection provided him, and Wilson, with plenty of source material for adaptation.

Unlike some later blues revivalists (and, more frequently, non-musician commentators), neither Hite nor Wilson seemed to feel any moral, personal, sociological, or musical conflict connected with the fact that they were Caucasian men playing music created largely by African-Americans. In 1968, Hite would explain, "If you really can feel the blues, you can be capable of coming up with blues lyrics. I'll disagree with a lot of people that say you have to be black to do that. Hell, I lost a lot of women! And I missed a lot of payments on my furniture. And the furniture man has come to my house and taken my furniture away ... and I ain't black."

Hite would also compare having long hair with being black, in terms of the social stigma he had encountered. On Canned Heat's United States tours, he recalled occasions when the band members had difficulty getting service in restaurants and other establishments, all because of their hair.

Some correspondence among Wilson's family members contains suggestions that he did not enjoy having his hair long, but felt compelled to do so to help maintain the band's image. This, however, has not been confirmed through any of Wilson's own comments, so we cannot be sure of his actual feelings on the hair styles of the day.

In 1966, another key member of Canned Heat joined the lineup. Guitarist Kenny Edwards was replaced by Henry Vestine, who was born in Takoma Park, Maryland and moved to California as a teenager with his family. He was an old acquaintance of John Fahey, and had participated in the rediscovery of Skip James. By 1966 Vestine's career included a variety of studio work, as well as a stint with an early Mothers of Invention lineup. Band leader Frank Zappa ended up fired him for his excessive drug use, foreshadowing issues that would plague Vestine throughout his life.

Like Bob Hite, Vestine was a fanatical record collector, and very knowledgeable about rural blues styles. His own guitar style was in the modern vein pioneered by B. B. King; other influences included Freddie King, and Albert Collins.

Vestine's interest in the blues had evolved from purchases of rock and roll records. "It was kind of rock and roll into blues," he explained. "They were sold by the same record stores. I would go into colored record stores to find rock and roll records, and there I encountered blues records. I would say there are two styles I like equally well: the Mississippi Delta stuff, and the B. B. King style. I just like the way it sounds. I like the rhythms of it a lot. I like the singing, the verses, and the words in the songs."

Shortly after Vestine joined the band, Frank Cook replaced Ron Holmes on drums. He was experienced as a professional musician, though his background was based more in jazz than blues. In the past, he had performed with musicians including Chet Baker, Shirley Ellis, and Dobie Gray.

At this point, Canned Heat wasn't much of a profitable venture. Alan Wilson had already written to his family and requested that his bricklaying tools be shipped to him, so he could work at that trade if necessary. His other main source of income was John Fahey, who still hired him occasionally to provide musical transcriptions and occasional instrumental accompaniment for records.

During the end of 1965 and the beginning of 1966, Wilson and Bob Hite had gone though several different names for their band. "I think the first name of the band was Little Something and the Nothings," said Richard Hite. "That was the first acetate they ever did. They borrowed my equipment that I had. I was just learning to play bass, so they would take my amplifier and stuff when they had to play gigs and stuff like that. Take advantage of little brother!"

Eventually, Hite, Wilson, and Vestine settled on the name Canned Heat, an idea from the 1929 Tommy Johnson record "Canned Heat Blues". The name appealed to Wilson for various reasons, not all related to music history. He explained, "I liked it because it has to do with potential energy — like the fear or the expectancy of exploding. So that's why I went for it."

Of course, Wilson certainly appreciated the traditional blues connotation of the name Canned Heat, and noted another local band which had a similar idea. "I always liked the name the Stone Poneys had, although I don't like the band too much," he said. "Because that refers to Charley Patton's song."

Wilson liked the "Stone Poneys" name so much that at one point, when that band had temporarily broken up, he and Hite considered taking the name for their own band. However, the group had already gotten used to the name "Canned Heat", so that was what it remained.

Wilson's roommate Mike Bass had suggested the name Canned Heat. He and Wilson were visiting with guitarist Steve Mann, whose musical associations included Janis Joplin and Frank Zappa. Mann joked, "Why don't you dress up like cops and call yourself The Heat?" Bass responded by recommending *Canned* Heat for a band name.

"We were talking about the heat, meaning the police," said Wilson. "Someone said, 'Why don't you call the band The Heat?' And so Michael exploded from his chair, as he is wont to do, and suggested *Canned* Heat. So that was it; everybody thought that sounded pretty good."

In the early days of the band, the official name was the Canned Heat Blues Band. Sometime in 1967, however, it was changed simply to Canned Heat. This maneuver was thought by many, including Wilson, to render the band more palatable to the general public.

While attending U.C.L.A., Wilson's friend David Evans met Marina Bokelman, a fellow student also intrigued with blues music. In late 1965, she became his girlfriend, and they moved in together the following spring.

"I met Dave on the first day of grad school," Bokelman remembers. "That would have been September of 1965. We got acquainted and found out that we both loved blues. He had talked about Al; I knew that this was an important friend to him. I met Al through Dave, and then the three of us were friends. Dave and I seriously got together in December of 1965, when we fell in love, I guess you might say. We started living together the following spring."

Their house was located off the Pacific Coast Highway, shortly past the turnoff for Topanga Canyon. Bokelman describes it as a humble sort of residence: "It was a shack, there on the coast. We had a shower which had frogs in it. The shower was full of frogs. Hence a special enjoyment when we listened to 'Bullfrog Blues'! They weren't big frogs; they were small frogs. You'd often go into the shower and there would be three or four of them on the walls and on the floor, and stuff like that. You got used to it."

Their house became a gathering place for the local blues circle. Robert Pete Williams once stayed there for several days when he played in Los Angeles. During that time, Wilson interviewed him at length, and produced a two-part feature article on him for Barry Hansen's *Little Sandy Review* periodical.

Wilson spent much time playing, analyzing, and listening to music with David Evans and Marina Bokelman. He would often spend the night on their couch, and Bokelman came to know him well.

Wilson's habits included an odd sleeping position. "He always slept on his back with his knees up in the air," says Bokelman. "I never observed him to sleep in any other position, which was fascinating. I've never seen anyone else sleep like that. I wouldn't think it would be easy to do! It was endearing, because it was totally weird and unique. I'd never seen another human being sleep like that — it was just Al."

Bokelman accepted Wilson's many eccentricities, and hoped that her home could be a refuge for him. "I think he had a difficult time in the social world," she says. "I would describe Al as a terribly wounded person — wounded to the point of being maimed. It was just something I knew."

As she recalls, Wilson was prone to depressive episodes. "When he was bummed, you could almost see the black cloud around him," she says. "It was a visible depression, in his body language. ... He would become more taciturn, not want to speak, and be kind of listless. It's like the light would go out. You couldn't get him into, 'Let's talk about Garfield Akers — which one of these four extant cuts is the best?'"

Wanting to help a friend in need, Bokelman did what she could for Wilson. "I liked for him to come over," she says. "For one thing, it did satisfy the mothering instinct. I would say to Dave, 'Let's have Al come over and stay for a couple of days.' Basically so that I could feed him. Or someone would say, 'Al hasn't been eating,' or, 'Al doesn't have much money,' or is subsisting on some substandard alleged nutritional item. And so I would say, 'Let's have Al come over.' And then it was just fun. All these discussions and arguments would take place, endless kinds of theoretical discussions about music. We might spend several days transcribing lyrics, and maybe hours playing back a verse or a line, to get what the guy was really saying."

Bokelman noticed that Wilson tended to be clumsy. She ascribed this not just to his poor vision, but also to his introversion. "He was very nearsighted and he was so extremely absentminded," she explains. "Very much absorbed in an internal world. It was partly from being introverted — I mean, he was an introvert — but partly just because so much was going on inside of his human consciousness. He was just thinking about music at the time and hearing music in his head, and so literally he would stumble walking across a smooth floor. I think just because the internal activity was so great. And that's what gave him his perception: the intensity of that inner focus."

At times, Wilson continued to pull his hair, a nervous habit he'd had for some years. "I remember that habit of him twisting and pulling his hair," says Bokelman. "The balding area was along the part of his hair. It wasn't bald in the sense that it was slick; he hadn't actually pulled *all* the hair out of the spot. But it was very thinned out along the part area."

Bokelman felt that Wilson's nervous habits and clumsiness were related to his depression. "When there's so much going on in your mind or if your emotions are very painful, the world begins to recede a bit," she comments. "He was inattentive and somewhat careless with physical reality at times. There was a physical component, but there was another component working there too. Because I've been around Sonny Terry, and he didn't bang into things. And he was even more blind than Al, because he couldn't see anything at all. But Sonny was present in the world, and knew how to survive in the world. He was *there*, in his body and functioning."

Wilson's friends took his eccentricities in good humor. Bokelman recalls a comment comparing him to Blind Lemon Jefferson, a famous blind bluesman who performed on the streets of Texas. As David Evans discovered through field research, many guitarists claimed to have worked with Jefferson as a "lead boy", assisting him and guiding him around safely. Most were exaggerating and a few had never even known Jefferson, but the claim sounded impressive.

"Dave and I had a personal joke," says Bokelman. "There were a lot of musicians who recorded and made 78s and then recorded later on. But it was like everyone claimed to have been Blind Lemon's lead boy. Well, Dave and I would affectionately say to each other that we could say that we were Al Wilson's lead boy. ... Dave would joke to me and say, 'I was Al Wilson's lead boy.' We looked at Al with kind of a protective feeling, the way you would look at a child."

Beyond her role as one of Al Wilson's caretakers, Marina Bokelman made her own mark in the blues revival. "I think it's the degree of which the tradition lives inside of your consciousness, and is expressed through you," she says. "I always say it's the sounds you hear inside your head, and the full range of availability. I think that's what makes you a tradition bearer. You can't help yourself — this is what you have to do. The tradition compels you in a way. Then I think you're a part of the living stream."

Continuing to keep the blues alive in her own way, Marina Bokelman is one of the notable blues scholars of her time. While health issues have posed a challenge to her guitar playing in recent years, she is one of the most authentic and traditional female blues players from the 1960s era. She has not sought a career as a performing musician, being satisfied instead to play and sing her music mostly among friends; however, this, if anything, only serves to enrich her deep blues purity.

Spending time with Alan Wilson was, for Bokelman, a rare treat. "The way his mind worked, it was totally, absolutely brilliant," she remembers. He listened to music very hard, and had an extremely discerning ear, and an extremely analytical grasp. He wasn't a seat of the pants musician. I mean, he did play by ear, but he had a tremendous technical grasp. No one else has come after him who has the same ear for the music."

To her, Wilson seemed extremely confident in his abilities. "He was confident to the point that another person might consider it arrogant," she says. "But he wasn't arrogant in the sense that he would deliberately set out to crush someone, or showboat. It was the natural arrogance of someone who is very young and very talented. They know that what they know is right. And they know that the way they're doing it is the right way and the best way. He was certainly a perfectionist. He could be harsh or ruthless in his judgments, about if something wasn't very good. ... He was extremely opinionated. We all were. But he had technical perfection to back it up, because he was very good. It was beyond technique — he was a genius. And a certain arrogance belongs to genius, because you know you're in a different category. For good reason."

The blues has historically been male-dominated. However, Marina Bokelman wasn't one to be left out. Her blues skills and knowledge could not be denied, and soon she was accepted into a fraternity that might have been descended from the secret blues society formed by David Evans and Alan Wilson in their Cambridge days.

In the spring of 1966, Bokelman noticed that Wilson, Evans, Henry Vestine, and Bob Hite were wearing identical leather thongs around their right wrists. "It was a leather thong wrapped twice around the wrist, so that it crossed over, and then tied with a double knot," she says. "Eventually it would rot off, and you'd put another one on. The guys were wearing them, and then I noticed. ... The leather thong, that was some kind of, not club, but symbol of a connection. I imagine a Three Musketeers thing, 'We're all together.'"

After observing this, Bokelman applied for membership. "Al had one, and Bob had one," she says. "Dave got one, and then I wanted one, because I considered myself to be part of the band too. There was a record store further down Westwood Boulevard, below Westwood Village, and Bob was working in the record store. I remember going there and basically saying that I wanted to be included, and have a thong. So I did, and we all wore them. There wasn't any special meaning, except that we were all connected. ... So it was like an initiation to have one, but in a sense it was a meaningless initiation, because no knowledge was passed, no secret handshake. It was just, the thing got tied on, and then I was one of the guys."

When the photo for Canned Heat's first album was developed a year later, Wilson took Bokelman aside to talk about the leather thong on his wrist. "You can see it on the first album," she explains.

"Afterwards, Al commented that it was very important that it be shown. He pointed it out; he said, 'I sat like this so the thong would show up in the photograph.'"

The circle of friends had their own blues jokes that nobody else could understand. "There were just jokes, things you could say," recalls Bokelman. "We had certain catchphrases. Like, some writer had written in a book about the blues that so-and-so's blues were always intensely personal. So that became sort of a humorous thing. We would characterize something as 'intensely personal', and then there would be this kind of smile that would go around, because everyone knew what *that* was about. Taking ideas and pushing them into the ridiculous."

One joke arose out of John Fahey's blundering attempts to transcribe Charley Patton's lyrics. Patton's bizarre pronunciation rendered his singing nearly impossible to understand, and even some of his contemporaries such as Son House found his singing unintelligible. Fahey was already finding his thesis a challenge, and Patton's seemingly tongue-tied delivery compounded his problems.

At some point, Fahey decided that the Patton song "Gonna Move to Alabama" contained the words "Great God yo deed I are." In 1968, Wilson commented, "What did that turn out to be? 'Gonna move to Alabama, great God yo deed I are.' That's what Fahey thought it was. ... I know it's not true; it's just ridiculous."

The words became a common exclamation in their little blues circle. Bokelman remembers the phrase "Great Lord yo deed I are" as an alternate interpretation. She says, "You could look at each other, somebody could say something, and the other person could go, 'Great Lord yo deed I are!' I say that to myself sometimes now, because there's no one to say it to. Because there's no one now that gets the joke. There were certain things like that; they were little pet things."

While they were all immersed in the blues, Alan Wilson remained interested in other kinds of music. Once, he brought a Frank Zappa album to Marina Bokelman's house. She had known

Zappa years ago as a high school friend, and Wilson knew that she would want to hear his first release, *Freak Out!*

"He liked Frank Zappa and the Mothers of Invention," recalls Bokelman. "The Mothers album came out and I hadn't seen it yet. I think it was Al that loaned me the album and said, 'Here, you'll be interested in this, because you knew the guy.' I subsequently got my own album."

Wilson found much to appreciate in Zappa's work. Much of the music was progressive and avant-garde, which intrigued him. Bokelman says, "It was because of all the factors of originality, technical perfection, subtlety, and flat-out weirdness. And just for pushing the musical envelope, he respected someone like Zappa."

While spending time with Bokelman and Evans, Wilson often used a "hulk" guitar for playing around the house. Evans would later make the concept famous in a musicological article for the now-defunct *Blues Revue* magazine. He now recalls, "A hulk was a cheap wooden guitar, not necessarily large in size, like a Kay or Stella. It had a hollow, thudding sound without much blending of the individual strings when sounded together. It was especially good for slide."

This was appealing to Wilson, as Evans explains: "Al figured that the old bluesmen probably played mostly cheap guitars, and they managed to sound great on their old records. I think the idea of the strings *not* blending in lush harmonies especially appealed to him. This was certainly counter to the 'folkie' aesthetic and is still one of the reasons why many acoustic revivalists can't come close to recapturing the old sound. In my opinion each string has to speak for itself, and Al intuitively realized this. I know he always kept a hulk for playing around home."

Wilson was also noted for his usage of an unwound third string. Evans picked up this practice, saying, "Al used an unwound third string and advocated this, based on his observation of traditional bluesmen. I use one to this day. It's easier to bend, and has a much different timbre from a wound string. Most folkies use a wound third, which is how they come when you buy a set."

Marina Bokelman remembers some of the other aesthetics they held dear as blues purists. "When you listen to the 78 [record]," she explains, "there is the quality that blues purists prize, ones like myself who don't like the scratches to be taken out, who like OJL better than Yazoo." Here, she refers to the Origin Jazz Library and Yazoo record labels, which were competitors in the tiny niche market for early blues reissues.

The blues purist got used to a few pops and scratches, and after a while, they presented no hindrance to the aural experience. "You listen between the scratches," says Bokelman. "So part of the aural quality is from the 78 recording, but part of it is because the guys were not playing very elevated instruments. So if you played a twelve-dollar guitar, you would sound more like an old 78."

Sometimes, the musical experiments with Evans and Bokelman involved altering the mind through the use of a popular herbal substance. Wilson liked marijuana, but felt that his musicianship was better when his mind hadn't been affected by it. Bokelman, however, felt that they played better when stoned, due to the relaxation.

Her experience is not uncommon, and many artists find that occasional drug or alcohol use can act as a creative tool. A substance-induced "high" is, however, no substitute for the artist's diligent efforts. Relied on excessively, any consciousness-altering agent — including television, sugar, or adulation — can become a hindrance. It seems that Wilson tried to remain aware of this, despite being a regular "pot toker" throughout his adult life.

"He did have a theory that he was extremely vehement in defending," recalls Bokelman. "It was that we only *thought* we played better stoned. And that it was an illusion; we only thought we were better because we *were* stoned." The controversy over this matter raged on for some time, and Wilson eventually insisted that a proper experiment be conducted to settle the matter.

Wilson, Evans, and Bokelman recorded themselves playing while unaffected by marijuana, then while stoned. Later, they listened to the tapes while straight, then got stoned and listened to them again. "This was the idea of a scientific experiment," says Bokelman. "The idea was to prove that we were not as good when we were stoned — although we ourselves thought we were." The experiment, while interesting and no doubt enjoyable, changed nobody's opinion.

When altering his consciousness, Wilson liked to absorb himself in nature as well as music. In the backyard of Bokelman's house, he could commune with the local plant life. "It was in kind of a semi-rural area," David Evans remembers. "There was kind of a little cove or settlement, a little valley in the mountains. You'd go right to the back of the house and you were kind of up in the hills, in the wild there. Al liked to go up there; he liked to go out in the wild."

Once, Evans had a rare psychedelic experience in the backyard. He admits, "I tried acid two or three times. Alan did a lot more than that!" When they took it together on one occasion, Wilson wanted to be outdoors. "We went up on the hill," says Evans. "We were looking at leaves, rocks and things, and it was flashing with weird colors and all that. He was really into that sort of thing, into contemplating nature when he was high on something — especially acid because of the colors and distortion of it all. He really appreciated the beauty of it."

8 THE CANNED HEAT BLUES BAND

In 1966, Alan Wilson began solidifying his musical vision for Canned Heat. A very important part of this was lead guitarist Henry Vestine, whose style had managed to intrigue Wilson. This was a feat that no other modern electric guitarist short of Elmore James had managed to accomplish.

In 1968, by which time his style had matured and he had switched from a Telecaster to a Stratocaster, Vestine commented on his influences: "Certainly my main influence, I would say, was B. B. King. I used to listen a lot to Freddie King. I like Albert Collins a lot. I like Albert King a lot, but I don't play anything like him. The way he plays guitar is a completely different technique than the way I use, so I'm kind of avoiding playing the lines he plays or making them sound like him. The thing that I most consciously copy note for note — but I don't do this much any more — is B. B. King licks. Like on slow blues, that stuff really sounds great. But I don't do that so much any more."

Wilson explained his concept for Vestine's place in the band, and his perspective on modern lead guitar styles: "What I wanted to do was take that real neat lead guitar that Henry played, and put it over a more interesting background than often appeared on the postwar records like Albert King. The funny thing is, I feel differently about it now. I now think that backing on Albert King records is pretty neat, in its own way. But at the time the band started, I didn't like any of that stuff. I hardly knew who B. B. King was! Then here was Henry, and all I knew was that I really liked what he was playing. I thought it was *great*. But I didn't know too much about the background of that kind of music, and I didn't like what I'd heard. So I tried to put it over the Mississippi stuff that I play. I don't know how to describe Henry, but I detected the spirit, although never the letter, of certain country attitudes. I'm talking about his style on the Telecaster, of percussive vocal quality, and only being interested in four or five heavy notes, instead of all twelve. He's not really concerned about the other seven notes so much."

In the summer of 1966, Canned Heat got to see the inside of a recording studio for the first time. This was facilitated by local rhythm and blues mogul Johnny Otis. Bassist Stuart Brotman recalls, "That was the session that we did one night in Johnny Otis's studio, which was called El Dorado studio, I think. He ran the board. Everybody was very relaxed and professional; felt like we were doing something important. We were making a demo, to see if we could solicit any interest from anyone."

Unfortunately, nothing came of the session. Verve, Elektra, and United Artists all rejected the resulting demos. The recordings were shelved, to be released years later as the album *Vintage Heat*.

Wilson was broke, and depression was beginning to set in, making everything seem hopeless. In August, he detailed the band's woes in a letter to David Evans, who was in the Deep South doing field research. "With me, you lose," he wrote. "We're probably finished. As a working band we're finished now. I'm scared — my future is a nothing, I've no money (to say the least!) and there seems to be no way for me to turn."

Trying to explore other career options, Wilson made some solo recordings for John Fahey, perhaps hoping that he could release an album on the Takoma label. These included ragas played on the veena, jaw-harp, and chromatic harmonica.

Fahey was not impressed. He later explained, "The ragas were so long and slow. Al never really learned to play very fast. He learned to play accurately and correctly, according to the books he had, but they were slow. None of the tapes were worth issuing. So I didn't pay him anything."

On Fahey's 1966 album *The Great San Bernardino Birthday Party*, Wilson played his veena on the song "Sail Away Ladies". He was credited as "Mysterious" Al Wilson. The album's liner notes, written by Fahey, describe his attendance at girlfriend Linda Getchell's birthday party, accompanied by Wilson, David Evans, and Barry Hansen.

In mid-August 1966, Canned Heat broke up for a short period. Wilson would later describe their failure to break into the music business as "ignominious", apparently finding the entire turn of events to be humiliating. In later interview, Bob Hite would recall spending this period on his family's couch, watching daytime soap operas and being scolded by his mother to get a job.

During the autumn of 1966, Alan Wilson and Henry Vestine formed a short-lived band. Called the Electric Beavers, this group included a horn section and various rhythm sections. It never performed in public, but was said to have cut some demo tracks which have never surfaced. The identity of other band members could not be determined. Two of the recorded items would later evolve into Canned Heat tracks, Wilson's "An Owl Song" and the instrumental "Marie Laveau", released on the *Boogie With Canned Heat* album.

A number of sources have reported that around this time, Alan Wilson and Taj Mahal rehearsed as a potential backup band for singer Janis Joplin. Such sources include the books *Janis Joplin: Take Another Little Piece of My Heart* by Edward Willett, and *Love, Janis* by Laura Joplin. The latter claims that Stefan Grossman was also part of these sessions, which were done at the behest of producer Paul Rothchild.

However, according to the account of Stefan Grossman, Wilson was not involved with these sessions. Rather, the rehearsal band consisted of Grossman, Mahal, and guitarist Steve Mann. Taj Mahal was not available for comment, and the other parties said to be involved are all deceased.

In November 1966, Alan Wilson, Bob Hite and Henry Vestine decided to give Canned Heat another try. They re-formed with the same rhythm section of Frank Cook and Stuart Brotman, and through one of Cook's connections, got a gig performing at a U.C.L.A. party. (According to a later interview with Bob Hite, however, Brotman had a prior engagement with an Armenian group that evening, so bassist Mike Rosso, a friend of Vestine, sat in on bass with Canned Heat.)

In the audience that night was Skip Taylor, an agent with the renowned William Morris booking agency. Taylor always had his eyes and ears open for new talent, and when he saw Canned Heat, he knew he had found something with potential.

The next day, Taylor and his partner John Hartmann propositioned Canned Heat, offering to manage them. The band members agreed, so in a bold move, Taylor and Hartmann left William Morris to form their own management company. Under their experienced guidance, Canned Heat began getting local bookings.

Skip Taylor was diligent in his promotional efforts, with the goal of securing a recording contract. Some of his techniques were early forms of guerilla marketing. He says, "Hartmann and I both started coming up with these promotional ideas, one of which was to come up with these bumper stickers and buttons. They said, 'Canned Heat is the blues'. We'd pass them out to people and leave them lying around at parties."

The two then escalated their efforts to include record companies. Skip recalls, "Then we took these bumper stickers, and it was everything from 'Canned Heat is the blues' to 'Canned Heat is happening'; we had a couple other little sayings. We started putting them on bumpers of cars in record company parking lots. Like, we went to Capitol records and we just plastered them on every car there. Went to Liberty and did it there, we did it at Columbia, we did it at Warner Brothers. And so pretty soon, the record companies started talking within themselves about, 'Canned Heat — is that one of our acts?' And all of these record companies thought that they already had them. And none of them had them! So we started kind of a little mini bidding war. Where at least in their minds and our minds, that there was something happening, that all these companies wanted them. Meanwhile, none of them had even seen them!"

Ultimately, however, it was a performance at the Los Angeles Ash Grove club that got Canned Heat signed to Liberty Records. Singer Jackie DeShannon, who was married to the head of Liberty's A&R department, attended one of their shows and brought her husband's attention to the band. He was impressed enough to offer them a record deal, which was readily accepted. Recording sessions were scheduled for May 1967.

During the early months of 1967, Canned Heat played more and more frequently. In January, bassist Stuart Brotman had to leave the band due to other musical commitments, and was replaced by Mark Andes.

As Alan Wilson and the others were learning, this job wouldn't be all fun and great music. "There were certain venues the band members hated playing," remembers Marina Bokelman, who attended many of these early shows. "There was one at the beach on an old pier. It was a metal building or something like that. The acoustics were such that when they performed there, Bob said that he had tears streaming down his cheeks from pain the whole time he was singing. Because of the way the noise fed back and hurt their ears."

Canned Heat's first tour outside of the Los Angeles area was in February 1967. They ventured up to Northern California and played a variety of shows, one opening at San Francisco's Fillmore Auditorium for the Grateful Dead. Another was at a cocktail lounge in the working-class suburbs of Fremont.

Alan Wilson's friend Barry Hansen had recently begun working for the band, and remembers the trip well. In some accounts of the band's history, Hansen has been referred to as their first road manager, but he clarifies this to describe himself more humbly as a roadie. "Road*ie* would be a better way of putting it," he says. "I did not participate in the management of the band, booking gigs or anything like that. My job was hauling the instruments around and setting them up. That's basically what a roadie does."

For transportation of their equipment during this 1967 tour, the band owned a Volkswagen bus whose sides were emblazoned with the words "Canned Heat Boogie Bus". At the end of the tour, Barry Hansen drove the Boogie Bus down the coast on Highway 1 back to Los Angeles. He was accompanied by Wilson, who wanted to see the country.

As Hansen recalls, it was an excursion filled with incredible views. He says, "With the band's equipment in the back, we drove down that road, and just marveled at the vistas of the seaside. Mountains that go right down to the sea is basically what the scenery is. This road is kind of carved precariously into the sides of the mountains, hanging above the ocean. It's just a spectacular drive. And Alan was just marveling about the mountains and the trees and the ocean. That was, I guess, my first inkling of how attuned to nature that he was."

The drive's only difficult moment came when they encountered another motorist who was apparently intoxicated, and wavered erratically down the highway. "We wound up being behind somebody for a while who was either very drunk or very stoned," says Hansen. "He was going about ten miles an hour and wavering all over the road. Alan got quite upset that anybody would endanger peoples' lives by driving like that."

Upon returning to Los Angeles, Barry Hansen would leave the band's employ, disgusted by the fact that his duties had come to include scoring drugs for the band members and washing their dirty laundry. Bassist Mark Andes left in March 1967; he would eventually find success in the band Spirit.

Andes was quickly replaced by Larry Taylor, who hailed from New York City, and already had a distinguished career. At the age of 18, he toured with Jerry Lee Lewis, and later became a session musician for the Monkees (he can be heard on "Last Train to Clarksville" and "(Theme From) The Monkees").

Taylor was influenced by various forms of roots music, including country and blues. In a 1968 interview with Marina Bokelman, he explained, "I've always been around blues, listened to blues, even from when I first started playing. ... I've been around a lot of country music. I was raised around a lot of it, you know, in Tennessee, when I was young. Then I played with Jerry Lee Lewis — he's like, kind of a rockabilly. And there's a lot of a blues influence in his stuff. You know, kind of his mixture. ... I played country music with him too. He played country music, then he'd turn right around and do a blues, a B. B. King tune."

Larry Taylor's work with Canned Heat would mark the band's sound during their days of greatest commercial success. Today, he's renowned as a master of his instrument, one of the world's greatest bassists in rock or blues. In recent decades, he's performed with the likes of Tom Waits, Charlie Musselwhite, and other luminaries. In the 2004 blues documentary *Lightning in a Bottle*, and at the 2012 tribute concert for the late guitarist Hubert Sumlin, he could be seen performing on the upright bass. He also plays lead guitar occasionally, to good effect.

As Canned Heat began gaining momentum, it nurtured the band members' artistic dreams. For Alan Wilson, it also represented hope on a more personal level.

Frank Cook, the band's drummer, befriended Wilson and was gaining some insight into his plans for the band. According to Cook, Wilson hoped that success with Canned Heat would also spell success with women. Cook says, "His thought that was if he was able to be in a hip rock and roll band, that would be the only way that he would be able to be involved in a love relationship. He thought that he would be loved by women because of the art he did. That's not unusual, except there was a real desperation. He felt that he was too dorky, too shy around women. He was incredibly naïve in that area."

Willing to help, Cook thought he knew someone who could at least provide Wilson with casual companionship. "He wanted to get laid," says Cook. "So I told him, 'Okay. Let me set this up.' I remember the night very well. I told my wife at the time I was gonna go out on a mission, to get Al laid. She said, 'I think you ought to.'"

Cook picked up Wilson in his car, and drove him to a large apartment building where the lucky girl lived. She had already met Wilson once, and Cook figured that she could be persuaded to have sex with him — it was, after all, 1967, when free love was the fashion! Leaving Wilson in the parked car, Cook went into the building, up the stairs to the second floor, and into the girl's apartment for preliminaries.

"We got loaded together," said Cook, "and he was waiting in the car. I asked her if she could sleep with my friend, and she said, you know, 'Okay!' And so then I came downstairs. She was in an apartment house, and I came out the front door and said, 'Okay, look. Marilyn's ready.' I think he'd already met her. 'Marilyn's ready. All you need to do is go up there; it's apartment number four upstairs. Push the door open, walk in, go up to the second floor, fourth apartment.'"

Wilson could hardly believe that it was going to be this easy. "She's really — "

"Absolutely!" Cook assured him. "All set! Don't worry about it. Taken care of. All you need to do is walk in there and you're gonna get laid."

"Really?" Wilson implored.

"Yeah yeah yeah! Go on!" Cook encouraged Wilson out of the car and drove off into the night as Wilson headed for the apartment building.

"So I leave him there," Cook recalls, "and I see him the next day. I say, 'Well, Alan, how'd it go, huh?' And he said, 'Instead of pushing in on the door, I pulled back on it, and it locked.'"

Frank Cook's setup had seemed flawless. Only the Blind Owl could mess that one up, and it seemed to somehow symbolize his general problems with the opposite sex. "If you think about it, there was nothing standing in his way of doing it," says Cook. "It wasn't that he was that ugly that he couldn't; obviously he could. But he pulled the door the wrong way. I mean, that was all set up; that was a deed done. All he needed to do was walk in and walk upstairs. And he pulled the door and locked himself out."

At some point in 1967, Alan Wilson did find a girlfriend that he would date for a couple of months. The exact identity of the woman is unknown, and Wilson's friends remember her only as "Pokie".

David Evans says, "She was kind of short, a little on the dumpy side, with kind of short, curly, light brown hair. She was very quiet, kind of shy, and seemed like she was glad to have a boyfriend that was interested in her. ... It seemed to be as much a platonic friendship as anything. I think they found each other nice, or maybe tolerable. Nice to have attention from someone of the opposite sex. Maybe it was just kind of a holding hands kind of thing."

Bokelman remembers Pokie, and recalls that Wilson seemed befuddled about how to carry on a romantic relationship. "Al had a sort of tender cluelessness around the opposite sex," she says. "I think she was equally clueless to Al, and that it was sort of like Hansel and Gretel! Neither of them had a clue of how to relate or bond or anything like that. So those things never last long."

Though he wanted a relationship, Wilson didn't seem to understand how to connect with an intimate partner. "I would have said that he was a very wounded person," observed Bokelman. "And that he didn't have a clue, really, when it came to intimacy of any kind. I think he didn't know how it worked, just didn't know how two people got together and were close. I don't think he had a clue what women were really like, or too much of a clue as to that part of himself. That was unexplored territory."

David Evans remembers that eventually, Pokie just wasn't around any more. "I don't recall that it lasted long, and I think it just sort of drifted apart," he says. "I remember asking Al, 'Whatever happened to whatever-her-name-was?' And he said, 'We don't see each other any more.' It wasn't like they had a big falling-out. I think they just kind of drifted together and drifted apart."

Marina Bokelman comments, "We all have to have certain places inside of ourselves developed before we can do any kind of pair bonding. And I don't think those places were developed in him. You know, I think he came in [to life] with his music and stuff, but in other areas of being human, I think he was just a babe in the woods. And that was part of what was painful. It can be painful to be a human and just kind of not have the hang of it."

Fortunately, the band was keeping busy around this time, and one hopes that the music brought pleasant experiences to Wilson when his personal relationships proved less than fulfilling.

One of the best places to see a Canned Heat show was the Ash Grove club in Los Angeles. "If I was going to pick a Canned Heat or blues band venue, I would say the Ash Grove was really the perfect place," says Marina Bokelman. "It had good acoustics for what it was, and it was the perfect size. I myself had sung at the Ash Grove, and David and I often put up bluesmen who performed there. Robert Pete Williams always stayed with us. We were part of the chauffeuring system, to make sure that Son House got there, and that kind of thing."

The Ash Grove, located at 8162 Melrose Avenue in Los Angeles, had been founded in 1958 by Ed Pearl. Named after a Welsh folk song, the establishment was a nexus of roots music activity. On occasion, it also provided a friendly venue for left-wing social activists, though the primary focus was music. People from all backgrounds and social categories could be found in the Ash Grove audience, ranging from hipsters and hard-core folkies to high-class ladies in fur coats.

Ed Pearl recalls, "Traditional music was always number one on what the Ash Grove did. ... Basically everyone came there, and all political differences and racial differences and so on were left at home. And people got along. We never had a racial fight or anything."

Alan Wilson had been involved at the Ash Grove since moving to California. Occasionally he sat in on music sessions, and when he was able, offered his home as quarters for traveling artists.

Sometimes this was at the place he shared with David Evans, and occasionally interviews would take place, as with Skip James who stayed with them in the spring of 1966.

"He [Alan] was around the Ash Grove before Canned Heat existed," Pearl remembers. "And he came and volunteered to house one person after another. He was living on the Venice canals, as I recall, and he did that. I would drive him back and forth, and we became friends through that. ... I knew he played the harmonica, he liked to sing and so on, but I didn't really know how the quality of his singing and his great artistry was, until he did it with the group, because he never played before me until Canned Heat was formed."

In late 1966 and early 1967, Canned Heat performed frequently at the Ash Grove. Occasionally, they would play up to six nights in a row. Ed Pearl says, "Canned Heat was actually the Ash Grove house band for several months, when they were just starting. ... They would play on Monday nights, and they could take all the money. We would take whatever we could sell in food. As opposed to having a hootenanny, or playing a show that nobody came to. So that was filling up a Monday night, basically. And one or two of the guys would sit in with other people. That happened a lot."

One staff member at the time was Mary Katherine Aldin. At the Ash Grove, she fulfilled a wide variety of tasks including employee scheduling, press releases, band contracts, bar and kitchen inventory management, and ticket sales. In later decades, she would become known in blues circles as a journalist and historian. However, she points out that at that time, neither she nor the members of Canned Heat thought of themselves as blues scholars. "At that time," she explains, "I was *not* any kind of scholar — I was a blues *fan*, and so was Al."

Aldin says of the Ash Grove, "Whenever there was a blues artist playing there, all of them, especially Al, would be in there every night sitting right at the front or as close as they could get, paying close attention, learning by watching the masters at work. This would be artists like Son House, Skip James, Mississippi Fred

McDowell, Lightnin' Hopkins, Mance Lipscomb, etc., and later the electric bands like Buddy Guy and Junior Wells."

The Ash Grove had a unique audience, consisting of fans who truly appreciated traditional bluesmen and acoustic folk artists. Aldin remembers, "Ash Grove audiences were very knowledgeable and *very* particular. If you made noise during an acoustic performance you would be shushed by everyone around you! Of course Canned Heat was a different story — unlike the solo acoustic traditional artists we usually booked, they were loud, electric and *young*."

With assistance from Ed Pearl, Canned Heat was able to work the Ash Grove's reputation to their advantage. Their shows connected with blues fans who were knowledgeable about the roots of their music, as well as rock and psychedelic music fans. By pairing Canned Heat with older bluesmen on the same bill, the Ash Grove provided hard-core boogie along with a solid musical education for new listeners.

"They [Canned Heat] brought in a totally different crowd," says Mary Katherine Aldin. "Ed Pearl often used these occasions to book an older, more traditional act on the same bill as Canned Heat, in order to expand the young audience's knowledge of the music. And I think that was smart, and worked most of the time."

The younger Canned Heat fans wanted to boogie, not just sit and listen. "Canned Heat's audience was not scholars and folklore students, they were young kids, wanting to drink and party and have a fun time," recalls Aldin. "I used to call them the 'boogie till you barf' crowd, meaning that as a comparison to the usually more adult and more staid audiences for the traditional musicians. Of course Canned Heat was really all wrong for the confines of the Ash Grove — they were a festival band, a dance band, and it must have been hard for their fans to have to just sit still and listen. There was no dancing at the Ash Grove."

Henry Vestine's guitar playing was so powerful that audiences accustomed to folk music were literally blown away. "When Henry first played at the Ash Grove, that was really an amazing experience for me," says Ed Pearl. "I was leaning up against the wall, and Henry started off playing. And the sound of it bounced off the wall. I was leaning against the wall; it pushed me off the wall. I'd never had that experience before! I'll never forget, my entire body was filled with the guitar. That was the first time I ever heard something so loud. Henry was an incredible guitarist. I mean, absolutely wonderful."

At one point, a local motorcycle gang paid a visit, foreshadowing Canned Heat's reputation in later decades as a biker band. "The Hells Angels came into the Ash Grove," remembers Pearl. "They loved the Ash Grove, and the head Hell's Angel came to ask if he could talk to me. I said, 'Sure.' He said, 'I love this music, but when I get excited, I break chairs.' He said, 'But I'll pay for it!'"

Pearl balked. The chairs at the Ash Grove were of a particular design that was no longer manufactured, so buying a new one would not be an option. However, he wanted to meet the unique needs of this rowdy music fan. "I'll get you a chair!" he promised the Hell's Angel, and produced a cheap folding chair suitable for destruction. "He didn't break it," recalled Pearl. "And they loved Canned Heat, by the way."

Documented on tapes from this time period, Canned Heat's repertoire at the Ash Grove included the following items sung by Bob Hite:

- "Big Road Blues
- "Bullfrog Blues"
- "Can't Hold Out"
- "Catfish Blues"
- "Dimples"
- "Dust My Broom"
- "Evil"
- "Five Long Years"
- "Goin' Down Slow"
- "Got My Mojo Workin'"
- "Hair Parted Down the Middle"

- "If You've Ever Been Mistreated"
- "I Wish You Would"
- "Louise"
- "Man Got Your Woman"
- "Pet Cream Man"
- "Rain Keep A-Fallin'"
- "Rollin' and Tumblin'"
- "Sloppy Drunk"
- "Terraplane Blues"
- "Three Hundred Pounds of Heavenly Joy"
- "Wang Dang Doodle"

Alan Wilson sang the following items in his high tenor vocal style:

- "Dust My Blues"
- "Help Me"
- "61 Highway"
- "Madman Blues"
- "Must I Shake 'Em On Down"
- "Someday Darling"

Wilson performed the following songs in a falsetto style:

- "Blues With a Feeling"
- "Cherry Ball"
- "You're So Fine"

Drummer Frank Cook would occasionally sing "There Is Something On Your Mind". Bob Hite and Alan Wilson sometimes performed "Dealing With the Devil", with Hite on lead vocals and Wilson providing backup, somewhat in the style that was later documented on the song "Boogie Music" in 1968.

Now and then, Mary Katherine Aldin had the opportunity to spend time with Alan Wilson outside of the Ash Grove. As fellow blues fans, they occasionally went to shows together, and got together to discuss music. "I spent a bit of time with him," Aldin says, "and occasionally went to his place. He was living at that time in a garage, using a space heater on the floor for warmth. I remember being really surprised that he was living in such conditions but he seemed content there."

Comparing notes on contemporary blues performances was a favorite pastime. Aldin says, "We talked as fellow fans, but not about recordings — more about the live music that was around us. As mentioned previously, he was always in the club to hear the older blues artists, and we often talked about them and how they did/didn't measure up to their earlier recordings."

When Fred McDowell performed at the club, Wilson and Aldin spent some time socializing with him. The evening led up to an interesting after-hours dinner. "One night after the Ash Grove closed, a few folks — me, Al, I think Barry Hansen, Steve Mann, one or two others — were going out to get some food," she says. "One of us, probably me, was charged with driving Fred McDowell to his motel after the club closed. We invited him to go to dinner with us and to our surprise he agreed."

The group selected a Chinese establishment, but the menu proved confusing to McDowell, who seemed baffled about what to order. Aldin recalls, "We went to a Chinese place, and we got in and got settled and started looking at the menu, and Fred's face just shut down. It immediately became clear to me, and also to Al, that he either couldn't read, or else had no idea what the Chinese dishes were."

Wilson navigated this potentially awkward moment with ease, covering for the older bluesman. He began conferring with Aldin about the menu, going over each item within earshot of McDowell. "Well, this one has rice and beef with a kind of gravy over it," he suggested, "would you like that one?"

Catching on, Aldin replied in kind. "Oh, I don't know, I kind of like the look of this one that has chicken with vegetables."

Once he heard them describe the food, McDowell's relief was obvious. "Al swung into action very smoothly," says Aldin, "engaging me in conversation so that Fred could hear us discussing the various dishes and what they were. ... Fred immediately jumped in and said, 'I'll have that chicken one,' or whatever, with a big look of relief on his face."

Though some have recalled Wilson as having few social graces, this incident makes it clear that he was acutely aware of the feelings of others. In a discreet way, he helped Fred McDowell preserve his dignity. The experience ended up being pleasurable for everyone, as Aldin remembers: "Once the food came we passed all the dishes around anyway, so Fred got to taste many different kinds of food — he told me later that it was the first time he had ever been to a Chinese restaurant and he really enjoyed it."

When Alan Wilson and Canned Heat took the stage at the Ash Grove, they played to increasing numbers of regular fans. For many listeners, these shows served as an introduction to blues, and for a few, the music would change their lives.

One frequent audience member was Roger Handy, a young harmonica player who idolized Alan Wilson. He says, "Alan was just a total god to me. I always went to hear Canned Heat, and I'd park myself right in front of Alan's Super Reverb amplifier so I could hear him play harmonica and hear him play slide guitar to best advantage. He was just something else. Alan was just consistently really good, really awesome, all the time. You always knew what you were going to hear. It was just so good. So good."

Handy had met Wilson through Mike Perlowin, who had participated in the founding of Canned Heat over a year ago. "I was in a recording band at the time," says Handy. "We thought we'd be a big pop sensation. Mike was a guitar teacher, and he was also in the band at that time. He took me over to Alan Wilson's house one night, and we sat around and talked and so forth, and I heard Alan play for the first time. Mike picked up the guitar and played, and Alan played along. They played 'Rollin' and Tumblin'". I was amazed. I mean, Alan could — he could sound like God."

Whenever he could, Handy went to see Canned Heat. He remembers, "The announcement every time they would play was that they were L.A.'s favorite blues band. That was one of their designations. So as a result of going there, I would hear groups like J.B. Hutto and the Hawks, Howlin' Wolf, Muddy Waters, people like that. I quickly recognized the importance of the music, and how amazing it was that this group — Alan and Bob and all these other guys — how important they were because they were continuing on with this tradition."

At some point during this time, Roger Handy requested a harmonica lesson from Alan Wilson. This was granted, and Handy was given directions to Wilson's apartment.

"Alan was living at an apartment, on the ground floor," says Handy. "It was on a street which was called Gretna Greenway, just about half a block down, or south, from Montana Avenue. It was in the rear of a house or apartment. ... As far as I know, it was Alan's place exclusively. It was kind of a little bachelor pad, or a studio apartment, with a single bed. It was kind of a big one-room sort of situation. It had a refrigerator and all that stuff in there."

In Wilson's apartment, Handy saw musical instruments everywhere. "There was a regular door that went into another room," he recalls. "It was just crowded with musical instruments of all sorts. All sorts of exotic looking stuff. Like, there were sets of vibes and xylophones, and marimbas and congas or whatever. There were all kinds of percussion instruments and stuff. It was just this jumble of stuff. And I remember thinking, wow, this cat's serious."

It was early in the day. Wilson was still waking up, hadn't put his glasses on, and seemed a little disoriented. "When I went, it was in the morning," says Handy. "I sort of rousted him out of bed, I think, and when he got up he had a white V-necked T-shirt on. I had the distinct impression that he had just gotten up out of bed shortly before I arrived, or maybe right when I knocked on the door. He looked a little fuzzy around the edges. He had his glasses off, and when I was looking at him, he had that look ... kind of like he was looking, but you know he wasn't seeing real well! Kind of like, 'Whoa, what, where, who — who are you?'"

However, Wilson didn't seem to mind being rousted out, and he was ready for some breakfast. "He wanted to know, did I want a bowl of cereal," Handy remembers. "And he poured himself a bowl of cereal — it was Cheerios. He poured some milk on it and was walking around eating cereal. He didn't sit down and start scarfing it up; he sort of carried it around with him, sat down and took a bite out of it or something. Then he played a couple of 78s that he had in a shelf right there up next to the food. There was a space, so he had part of his record collection set up right there next to the soup and what-not."

Next, Wilson played an LP by an artist Handy had not heard before. Handy was astounded, for the harmonica player on that record sounded much like Wilson. "Who's that?" he asked.

Wilson replied, "God."

The deity was Little Walter Jacobs. The first person to successfully utilize amplification for the instrument, Jacobs is known as the father of modern harmonica. He had been a sideman to the great Muddy Waters, as well as a successful solo artist. Naturally, he was one of Wilson's main influences, and his work is essential listening for anyone interested in blues harmonica.

When the record was done playing, Wilson wrote some numbers on a piece of paper and gave it to Handy. "When you leave here," he instructed, "go to a record store and buy these two albums." He had written the catalog numbers for *The Best of Little Walter* and *The Best of Muddy Waters*. Both items were on Chess Records.

Handy remembers why Wilson didn't just tell him the names of the records: "Whenever I would be around those guys, they would always refer to various albums and singles with the label name and number. So he wrote down the numbers, which he knew off the top of his head. In record collector-speak, everybody knew what you were talking about. You'd be a real rube if you were to actually say the title and the artist. So I thought that was really funny. But it was very impressive, the way he had that all committed to memory. I went out and got both those albums, and all of a sudden I knew, 'Oh yeah! This is what's going on here.'"

At one point around this time, Alan Wilson thought he had a chance to see his harmonica hero perform in person. When he heard of a Little Walter gig in the area, he called Mary Katherine Aldin from the Ash Grove to see if she wanted to accompany him. Other blues fans heard about the show, and the excitement escalated.

Aldin says, "Al called me and said, 'Little Walter is playing at a club in Venice! Let's go!' Now, this was a rarity — a great Chicago blues harp player whom Al idolized was playing right near where he lived! So of course I said yes, never having seen Little Walter live myself. So a bunch of us all went over there, and there was a big sign: 'Live, tonight, Little Walter and His Chromatic Harp'."

Wilson and his friends were in for a bit of a letdown, however, "We got in there, and lo and behold it wasn't Walter at all," says Aldin. "It was George 'Harmonica' Smith, an L.A.-based musician who also played both standard and chromatic harp. George often performed at the Ash Grove and was a good friend of mine. ... I looked at George up there on the stage and looked at the audience — who were loving what they were hearing — and looked at Al and said, 'Huh?' At the break we went up to George and said, '*What* is going on here?' George looked a little bit ashamed of himself but basically said, 'A gig is a gig and I need the work.'"

Wilson, for his part, took it all in stride. Though he had been hoping for Little Walter, he seemed happy to see George "Harmonica" Smith instead, and got a laugh out of the misleading billing. "Al wasn't at all upset at having been led astray," recalls Aldin. "He thought it was hilarious."

Since mastering the harmonica, Alan Wilson had periodically given lessons to beginners, occasionally making a few dollars here and there through such work. His later schedule with Canned Heat would mean less time available for mentoring others. However, players throughout the decades since his death have been inspired by Wilson's playing. In this way, the education continues.

One of Wilson's primary lessons was about finding one's own style as a musician. With Roger Handy, he emphasized that individuality is key to artistic excellence, especially in blues. Handy says, "You listen to Little Walter, you listen to Sonny Boy Williamson, you listen to Slim Harpo. Now those are three dudes. When you hear those cats, they're all playing great stuff, but they're all different. ... All of them are really great; they've got their own sound."

Wilson was developing his own sound on the harmonica as well. Though heavily influenced by the masters who had come before, he went on to make his own innovations, and he is now remembered as one of the finest players of his era. "I even realized that at the time," says Handy. "He synthesized all that stuff, and learned from all those sources, and then came out with this totally individual sound! In his playing, I hear a lot of Big Walter, a lot of Sonny Boy, a lot of Junior Wells. I can hear all these little bits and pieces of stuff that he used as a point of departure, and then refined it and put his own spin on it. It was just totally amazing!"

Generous with his skills, Wilson taught Handy the essential elements of blues style. His playing was already notable for its full and rich tone. "He taught me basically that the sound is coming totally from inside your mouth," explains Handy. "There's a point of contact with the air, how you channel the air in your mouth and where you channel it from. He was really on top of whatever it took physically to play the harmonica, in terms of breath control and all that."

According to Handy, there was a physical element distinctive to Wilson's playing. He reports, "There was one thing I noticed about him which I didn't see when I watched other harmonica players play, and I've never noticed it to the same degree even after I've looked for it in other harp players. That is that way, when he blows notes either in or out, his cheeks would either suck in really deep for the blows, and out really a lot, like a chipmunk or something, when he was blowing out. And it's the way. If you blow just like he showed me how to, you're going to do that. It's like when you watch that trumpet player, Dizzy Gillespie, though that's a really wild example of it! And, of course, there's no draw on the trumpet. But when you would watch Alan playing, you could always tell. It was fun just to watch the cheeks go in and out, just like a bellows or something. That was a kind of peculiar hallmark of his playing."

Wilson played so hard that he wore out harmonicas often. Barry Hansen says, "He would wear out harmonicas very quickly. When he could afford it, he would buy new ones frequently, because he always thought that a harmonica was best when it was new. He sucked and blew on them so hard that the reeds would get kind of flabby. So after he used a harmonica maybe for a couple of weeks of gigs, he didn't have any use for it."

Hansen also witnessed Wilson retuning his diatonic harmonicas. An example of his retuned harmonica can be heard on "On the Road Again". In this instance, the retuning involved raising the pitch of the sixth draw reed. "Five Owls", from *Living the Blues*, also features a retuned harmonica.

Not all of Wilson's harmonica experiments were successful; one recalls his Cambridge attempt to achieve superior airflow by stuffing his nostrils with tissue. That hadn't worked out, but Wilson was still curious enough to try anything that promised to improve his music. For a while, he tried soaking his harmonicas in water, which he had heard was somehow beneficial.

"I remember onstage, he'd have a cup or something," says Barry Hansen of this phase. "It was kind of an oversized coffee cup. He'd fill it with water and put all the harmonicas he was going to use in that." Later on, however, Wilson would tell Roger Handy not to soak his harmonicas, so he apparently concluded that this technique was but a useless ritual.

Alan Wilson's musical innovations were frequently accompanied by explorations of another kind. Since moving to California, he had become more and more interested in expanding his consciousness with herbal or chemical assistance. This usually meant marijuana, and sometimes LSD, but Wilson was curious enough to try other mind-altering substances as well.

Roger Handy recalls one of the more bizarre experiments with drugs. "On the first night that Mike Perlowin took me over there, when we first went into Alan's pad, it was at night," he says. "Alan had evidently been sitting around working out lyrics or practicing or something. He had what I thought at first were, like, little remnants of reefer. Kind of little half-smoked cigarettes and stuff, like little roaches lying around."

When he inspected the "roaches" more carefully, and asked a few questions, Handy found that Wilson and his friends were attempting to dry banana peels for eventual ingestion. He says, "Upon observing the scene there a little bit closer while we were talking and stuff, I noticed what these were, and they even lit some up while I was there. They were smoking banana peels! At the time, you see, there was a song by Donovan called 'Mellow Yellow'. And there was kind of a popular folklore, that if you smoked banana peels you'll get high."

This was something Wilson just had to try. Analytical scholar that he was, he put the banana peels through several different processes to determine whether there was anything to the popular legend. "He had all these kind of banana peels lying around in various stages of decomposition," remembers Handy. "I guess he was letting some of them dry out naturally, and some of them he'd put in the oven. So he'd evidently been trying to get buzzed off this stuff. I think the general consensus was, among him and Mike Perlowin, that it just wasn't gonna work. It *didn't* work, you know. But they were giving it a shot anyway!"

Wilson knew marijuana would get him high, and loved to smoke it. Marina Bokelman said, "He liked dope; he appreciated good dope. He didn't suffer personality change [from marijuana]. He became more Al. He would really get into the music, a favorite thing to do while stoned. That would be really good for listening to music. He had maybe more animation with the cannabis, rather than people who just become totally quiet and space out. He didn't do that. It was more of a stimulation to the intellect or the musical facility."

Although tobacco cigarettes didn't get him high, Wilson smoked them also. "If you want to say addiction, I would say smoking, certainly," says Bokelman. "He probably smoked a couple of packs a day; he smoked a lot."

Non-filter Pall-Mall brand cigarettes were Wilson's preference. Roger Handy recalls the situation when his harmonica hero wanted to bum a smoke: "He asked me for a cigarette, because I had cigarettes. I pulled one out and I lit it up, and he said, 'Could I have a cigarette?', or whatever. And I handed him one of my cigarettes, and I smoked filters. He grabbed the cigarette; he just promptly twisted the filter off, discarded it, and lit the cigarette and smoked it, just like that."

Wilson had a very specific reason for taking one drug. As Canned Heat became successful and started touring extensively, he began suffering from insomnia, and took "reds" or "downers" to help him sleep. The term "reds" was street slang for barbiturates, in this case of the secobarbital variety, that are illicitly distributed. Richard Hite has recalled that they were often known as "bandits".

To Barry Hansen, Wilson once explained why he had begun using reds. "He had a hard time sleeping, so he got into taking those reds," says Hansen. "I knew that. That's how he first started taking them."

Sometimes careless with his drug consumption, Wilson occasionally ingested substances without knowing for sure what they were. Once, he found some random pills in his pocket. Presuming that they were safe, he gave them to the teenage Richard Hite.

"I remember one of the first times I ever got high," Hite recalled. "Alan gave me a bunch of pills he had in his pocket. And he was just like, 'Oh, they're there, and I didn't realize they were there. Oh, here's these; try these.' And it was very strange. It was just like matter-of-fact, you know. They're there, so... That was when I was probably like sixteen." Wilson would have been about twenty-five.

9 CANNED HEAT'S FIRST ALBUM

Canned Heat went into the studio to record their first album in April and May 1967. That June, their first single, "Rollin' and Tumblin'", was released.

On June 17, Canned Heat appeared at the Monterey Pop Festival. Their performance of "Rollin' and Tumblin'" can be seen on the resulting film, with all the band members neatly clad in matching blue shirts. (Drummer Frank Cook has recalled his wife sewing those shirts for them shortly before the festival.) More of the music was released decades later as a compact disc set, on which "Bullfrog Blues" can also be heard.

The Monterey lineup made it one of the first great festivals of the era. It included soul singer Otis Redding, pop singers such as the Mamas and the Papas, the flamboyant guitarist Jimi Hendrix, and psychedelic groups like Jefferson Airplane and Country Joe and the Fish. Other "blues revival" bands, contemporaries of Canned Heat, included the Paul Butterfield Blues Band and the Electric Flag.

This was Canned Heat's first big show outside of the Los Angeles area, and with their first record just under their belts, they were excited. It proved to be a turning point in the band's career. Their performance was well received, and their picture was even featured on the cover of *Down Beat* magazine afterward as part of the festival coverage.

Barry Hansen recalls a strange outburst from Alan Wilson at Monterey. "I remember I saw Alan backstage," he says. "And just as I was talking to him, Mama Cass walked past. And Alan kind of turned to me — this was uncharacteristic of him, in a way — but he said, 'Can you imagine her and Bob Hite having sex?' He just kind of chuckled at the thought."

There were strange antics from other band members as well. Richard Hite remembers, "My brother and Henry were chasing Brian Jones around, of the Rolling Stones. Just staring at him and not saying anything. They'd go up to him and just — look at him."

The band's first album was released in July 1967. Simply entitled *Canned Heat*, it contained the songs from their first single and others from various blues sources. "Help Me" was the only song containing Wilson vocals; all others were sung by Bob Hite.

Most selections had roots in the early rural blues tradition. This included "Rollin' and Tumblin'", "Bullfrog Blues", "Catfish Blues", "Big Road Blues", and "The Road Song". Sources for these traditionally oriented pieces included Tommy Johnson, William Harris, and Howlin' Wolf (who, though known as a Chicago bluesman, had heavy influences from rural artists like Tommy Johnson and Charley Patton).

"Rich Woman", notable for Wilson's harmonica playing, is derived in part from Billy Boy Arnold's "I Wish You Would". Arnold had been heavily influenced by Bo Diddley, whose modal songs held a special place in Alan Wilson's musical pantheon. "Goin' Down Slow" is also significant for his harmonica playing. Wilson's amplified harmonica-oriented pieces were usually of relatively modern vintage, as early Delta blues items often were not structured for harmonica accompaniment.

The only Wilson-sung item on this record is a version of Sonny Boy Williamson's "Help Me". It had originally been recorded by Rice Miller. He was actually the second bluesman to use the "Sonny Boy Williamson" name, though he always declared himself "the original Sonny Boy". The other "Sonny Boy", also known as John Lee Williamson, had no connection to this song.

117

Musically, Wilson's version makes no significant departure from the traditional blues sound heard on the rest of the album, except for his unusual singing (and even that can be traced to the blues of Skip James). Lyrically, it demonstrates the way that Wilson often turned traditional blues lyrics into something personal. His lyrics are close to the original in most places; however, there are certain peculiar Alanesque distinctions.

First, Wilson does not include Williamson's verse about cleaning and doing other housework. Apparently this was not appealing to him, and not coincidentally, he had rarely been known to do much housecleaning in his regular life.

Wilson also includes one verse not sung by Williamson. It is a variation on a traditional verse, and the way it diverges from typical blues language is unique to Wilson. It is based on a certain traditional blues verse, incorporated into various and sundry songs throughout the tradition. The traditional version has been sung by the likes of Tommy Johnson as well as more modern practitioners, and typically goes something like: "The sun's gonna shine in my back door someday; the big wind's gonna come along and blow all my troubles away." Bob Hite sings it on this album, on "Big Road Blues".

Wilson sings an equivalent of this verse, but refers to the *moon* instead of the wind, singing that the moon will take all his troubles away. This change is unique in the blues idiom; neither this author nor several other blues experts could find any recorded precedent for this particular lunar reference.

The cover of the *Canned Heat* album represented the band's interest in rural, archaic pre-war blues. A particular set of cultural and period references are depicted on the cover, though none would have been readily identifiable to the average record buyer.

The band had, of course, been named after the Tommy Johnson song "Canned Heat Blues". Therein, Johnson sang about his addiction to a drink made from the cooking fuel Sterno. Described on its label as "canned heat", Sterno was used as an illicit alcohol substitute during Prohibition times. It was said to produce a sort of drunken high, though the physical side effects were unpleasant at best and deadly at worst.

Scholar and friend David Evans had been researching the life and music of Tommy Johnson. Most of this work took him into the Deep South, along with Marina Bokelman who lent her own abilities to his research. She remembers how they returned with information on Johnson's favorite drink.

"Dave and I had come back from Mississippi and Louisiana," she says, "where we were talking to everyone who ever knew Tommy Johnson, and all of his surviving relatives. From at least one source, if not two, we got an extremely detailed description of straining Sterno through a white handkerchief and adding sugar and lemon juice, things like that."

On the first album cover, the average record buyer would see only a group of longhaired musicians sitting around a table, which is covered with an odd assortment of objects. But to Tommy Johnson, it would have been clear what they were doing. To him, the paraphernalia — Sterno cans, handkerchiefs, sugar, and lemon slices — would have been as obvious as a razor, mirror, and a rolled-up dollar bill to a cokehead. The band was making the drink that was their namesake.

The bandmembers not only made the Canned Heat drink, they consumed it. According to Richard Hite, it was an initiation rite, and he too was forced to participate years later when he joined the band. He claims, however, that nobody in the group drank enough to feel any "high" or other effect from the beverage, as it was quite revolting.

"On the first album, they are actually drinking Sterno," Richard explained. "That was a prerequisite of being in the band. That's what they are doing on the first album cover, and the picture is reversed." The reason for the photo's reversal on the United States release is unknown. It might have been simple error, though Richard once speculated that it might have been purposeful on Liberty's part, out of concern for the obvious appearance of the trademarked Sterno label.

Marina Bokelman recalls that it was her idea to take pictures of the Sterno ritual for the album cover. "I think it was me that really insisted that they do this," she says. "I remember Dave and I did it together; we were the ones that brought back the exact information. So it's all there on the cover; it's the exact setup that Tommy Johnson used."

The band, three-fifths of whom were blues cultists at heart, knew that their symbolism was obscure. That was part of the attraction. "We didn't care whether the public would understand it or not," says Bokelman. "It's not really too understandable when you look at the table and see what the objects are. You can see the Sterno can, although because the negative was used backwards, everything on the album cover is backwards. So a discerning viewer can see that it is a Sterno can and make the inference. But I doubt that they would understand the pieces of lemon, the sugar bowl, the handkerchief, and that kind of thing."

The back of the album cover featured liner notes composed by Pete Welding, who was a good friend of Wilson. Welding wrote for *Down Beat* and other music magazines as well as operating his own record label, Testament. His notes provide an eloquent explanation of the blues tradition, which enabled Canned Heat to adapt old lyrics and instrumental forms to their unique style for the modern day. By reading these notes, record buyers would receive something of an education on blues in general.

Wilson commented on the liner notes, saying, "Pete said that in some of our songs we translate prewar influences or guitar parts into modern idiom, modern in terms of instruments employed. Now that's a real key factor. It might seem superficial at first, the instruments, but it ain't, because the prewar Mississippi style had kind of run out of gas before the amplification came along. I guess it's something to do with doing new things. They'd just about run out of the sounds they could produce on acoustic instruments. They'd come up with just about all of them. So the amplified instruments gave — same five notes, or a few more in some cases, same type of music but with new sounds. And then the rhythm section. Muddy Waters adding the big beat, as he says. That changed it around a little. So, I would agree with what Pete said there. That is true. That we're just taking, in some of these songs we're taking old musical backgrounds, and then sort of creating [a] different bunch of sounds and then throwing in Henry to boot, playing that lead stuff. So I'd say he was correct."

In fall 1967, Canned Heat began their first national tour. In later interview, Bob Hite would recall that they sometimes spent their nights in the homes of fans or fellow musicians, so small was the band's budget at this time. They were often marketed alongside rock-and-rollers, with whom they might share an audience, but little musical affinity.

Barry Hansen recalls, "Sometimes he [Alan] would come back from a tour and tell me about the other bands that played. He wasn't real fond of most of them, of the rock and roll bands that were out at that time. But he'd get to know musicians, and he'd say, 'So-and-so was a real nice person.' The first group that comes to mind that he said that about was the Iron Butterfly."

The band ran into problems when they played in Denver. Bob Hite had lived there for a while as a teenager, and called up some old school friends when he returned with Canned Heat. That night, the band was staying at the Rancho Manor Hotel, and one of Bob's pals came by to party.

Unbeknownst to Bob, there was an ulterior motive. In the years since they had last seen each other, his friend had joined the local police force as an undercover narcotics officer. As part of a larger sting operation targeting certain businesses and individuals, some drugs were planted in Bob's room. Ironically, this was not really necessary as most of the band members had brought their own illegal substances.

Before long, several uniformed cops showed up. They headed straight for the planted drugs, which had been jammed beneath a chair cushion, and arrested everyone in sight. Fortunately for Alan Wilson, he was not in the motel, having wandered outside to collect leaves. His lack of sociability worked to his advantage this time, and he was not arrested.

As for the rest of the band, they didn't have any money for bail or lawyers. Skip Taylor was forced to cut a deal with Liberty Records, selling their future publishing rights for $10,000 so that a legal defense could be mounted. For now, this seemed like a good enough deal, getting the band out of jail and back to work.

In the end, no time would be served over the Denver bust. In later years, however, the surviving members of Canned Heat would lament the loss of the royalties they had been more or less forced to exchange for their freedom. The incident would be memorialized in the song "My Crime", sung by Bob Hite and recorded for the band's second album in 1968.

10 THE BLUES ON ACID

Canned Heat hadn't been back long from their first national tour when drummer Frank Cook quit. He claims that this was, in part, due to a disagreement with the band's management about finances.

"There was a hassle about money," Cook says. "I didn't feel that they should get fifteen percent on top. They should share in the expenses and we should split the band seven ways. They were doing a job, and they didn't do any more than anybody else did. We got into a fistfight."

There were, however, other reasons. The music had a lot to do with it, as Cook's playing didn't quite fit in with what the other band members wanted. A shift in Henry Vestine's style meant that their blues were becoming more about volume and power. As Cook admitted, "I wasn't a power drummer." The band needed someone on drums who could keep up with their evolving sound.

The primary influences on Vestine's playing had been blues guitarists like B. B. King, Freddie King, and Albert Collins. Now, however, he was listening to contemporaries such as Eric Clapton and Jimi Hendrix. Their work inspired him to crank up the volume on his amplifier in order to get sustain and distortion effects. This approach was not traditional in blues, but Vestine was eager to explore new paths.

"We try to update it and do it a way we feel is good to do now," the lead guitarist explained in 1968. "The first one [Canned Heat album] was a good blues LP, but it's twenty years later than that style of music, and I'm not as much of a purist any more."

Vestine was still playing notes that had "vocal quality", as Wilson had characterized it. However, he was beginning to use these notes in different ways by adding "psychedelic" tonal effects. This took Canned Heat's blues in to new realms, sometimes not so gentle. At times, it sounded as if he had spiked a flask of blues whiskey with LSD and was now tripping on acid to a Tommy Johnson soundtrack.

"I play a lot of the same notes now," explained Vestine, "but I do different things with them. Like, I have an amp that will sustain notes, make the tone change, and all of those things."

Vestine's older style had been associated with the Telecaster guitar. "Henry is two creatures," explained Wilson. "The old Henry corresponds to the B. B. King thing, out of Albert Collins. It seems weird to use the name of an instrument to define a style, but the sound of a Telecaster or a Les Paul is sufficiently distinct that it's almost the difference between a six or a twelve string, which would be noted in a standard discography. All these types of guitars have pretty distinctively different approaches. Henry's old style is a Telecaster style."

In Wilson's mind, Vestine's new style was associated with British bands such as Cream. "His new style is influenced by the English thing," said Wilson. "Not fuzz tone, but sustained notes, broad sound, and less percussive variance in the line. There are not as many ups and downs in the percussion. No snapping strings or ups and downs in the rhythm, just more sustained, continuous tone."

In 1968, Wilson would dramatically proclaim of Vestine, "His old style is now an extinct phenomenon. Like the dodo or the passenger pigeon, it no longer exists on the earth. He says that he's already done it; he wants to do something else. That's where his head's at. And he can do the new thing okay too, although he ain't got all the bugs out of it yet. Now his approach is the sustained note thing, which is trying to pick up on another aspect of what a singer can do."

The vocal approach, which was what Wilson had loved about Vestine's style in the first place, was still present. "He avoids a large number of the frets which do not have vocal connotations," said Wilson. "He sticks to those basic notes, and relies a lot on bending back and forth between them, using neutral notes, all that stuff."

Frank Cook was replaced by drummer Adolfo de la Parra. He was from Mexico, where he had played in a variety of rhythm and blues bands. Recently he had immigrated to California hoping to break into the United States music scene. As it turned out, he fit right in with Canned Heat, impressing Bob Hite when he showed up at the tryout session carrying a Junior Wells record.

The band members were even more enthusiastic when they heard de la Parra's playing, and hired him immediately. He would turn out to be intensely dedicated to the band, sticking with them through thick and thin over several decades. After enduring the deaths of both Alan Wilson and Bob Hite, he would emerge as the leader of a reconstituted Canned Heat, and carries on the band's boogie tradition to this day.

With Adolfo de la Parra providing the power they needed on drums, Canned Heat went back into the studio. Their second album, *Boogie With Canned Heat*, was released in February 1968. It was a milestone in the development of the band's identity, defining the boogie sound for which the band is now so well known in music history.

As they recorded the album, Wilson found the modern multi-tracking capabilities of the studio to be much to his liking. Now, he could play any number of instruments on a given song, accompanying himself to his liking and ensuring that every note was just as he wanted it. This enabled him to create new and exciting instrumental arrangements.

Though he is often stereotyped as a "blues purist" or traditionalist, Wilson was actually quite progressive. This can be heard in his recorded work beginning with *Boogie With Canned Heat*. Henry Vestine noted this in 1968, pointing out that Larry

Taylor, Adolfo de la Parra, and Bob Hite tended to be more conservative in their musical efforts than Wilson and himself.

"In a way," said Vestine, "they're [Taylor and de la Parra] the most traditionally oriented in what they want to play, of anybody in the band except maybe Bob. Alan and I are kind of in the forefront of this experimental angle. They're kind of discouraged with that sometimes; they like nice set arrangements. But Al isn't that strict in only playing old-style stuff. He's a very experimental player."

Vestine was happy with this approach. He said, "I'm very partial to the style of the second record, because it's more our own music. I'm really interested in playing something that is my own music, as much as I can. ... I like real free jazz things, and I like to think that way in my playing rather than being restrained by having to play this lick or that lick."

When the band was in the studio recording their second album, Vestine's new style had caused a technical problem. In order to achieve the desired distortion effects, he had to play extremely loudly. This kind of volume mean that he couldn't hear anything else — including the rhythm he was playing over.

"Most of the guitar solos are overdubbed," explained Vestine. "To get the sound that I wanted to record with my amp, most of the time the amp was louder than what I could hear of the track through the earphones. So I kind of lucked out, really, and it turned out the way I thought it would, with the twelve bars or whatever. But I really couldn't hear what I was playing over at all, a lot of the time."

Despite the volume, or perhaps because of it, Vestine's lead guitar work on this album was very good. One standout track is "Amphetamine Annie", based musically on Albert King's "The Hunter". Here, Vestine's heavily amplified style creates a new and powerful blues sound.

The lyrics of "Amphetamine Annie", written and sung by Bob Hite, describe the ravages of addiction to "speed". One can barely hear Wilson's guitar; he plays a minimal rhythm part and seems to have had little input on this song. However, it is a classic Canned Heat track and one of the best recorded examples of Henry

Vestine's lead guitar playing. One can imagine that Wilson must have been highly pleased by this excellent work.

Wilson sang two songs on the album, one of which contained completely original lyrics and a horn arrangement. The other selections were sung by Bob Hite, who typically preferred to use lyrics compiled from traditional sources, or, in cases such as "Amphetamine Annie", those on which he had collaborated with the other band members or Skip Taylor.

The first Wilson-sung item is "On the Road Again". It contained traditional blues lyrics, mostly borrowed from various songs recorded by bluesman Floyd Jones. However, even borrowed and adapted lyrics could be indicative of Wilson's own thoughts and feelings.

According to Wilson, all the lyrics he chose to sing had meaning to him, even traditional lyrics not written by him. Without that personal connection to any given lyric, he had no desire to sing it. "The only psychological truth is what is applicable at the time, to the singer," he said. "So, if the words fit psychologically, then he can feel comfortable singing them."

Wilson found that the singing process was deeply individual. He commented, "Singing is pretty weird. It's really personal. Everybody's voice is different. You take ten guys that play the harp; it's more like they all play the same instrument. You take the same ten guys, say they all sing. It's almost like there's ten different instruments. Everybody's voice is like a unique instrument in the world. More so than other instruments. It's pretty weird."

Textually, the thoughts and feelings expressed in Wilson's "On the Road Again" fall into the same category as most of his lyrical subjects. Throughout his career, Wilson would sing primarily on themes of abandonment, mistreatment, and his own dissatisfaction with life. "On the Road Again" is the first of many songs with a similar topic, but is unique for its direct reference to Wilson's childhood separation from his mother.

The studio arrangement of this song is rather untraditional, though the song itself follows a standard blues pattern. It was a foray into the new realm of overdubbing, also known as multi-tracking. Wilson plays five of the seven instrumental tracks, accompanied only by the rhythm section which plays bass and drums at his behest. He explained, "On that one, that's the one song where I emerge as dictator. Told everybody exactly what to do, and would not tolerate any changes, at all."

To listeners throughout the decades, the most immediately striking element of the song — and the sound that immediately distinguishes it from other blues records — is the drone created using an Indian tambura. Sometimes referred to as a "tanpura", this is used to accompany instruments such as the sitar or sarod in classical Indian music. Here, it is overdubbed for a total of three tracks.

According to Wilson, the available tambura was of poor quality and lacked the normal buzzing aural quality heard with a proper tambura. The multiple tracks, however, enabled him to create an appealing "tinkling" sound. Just as the humble "hulk" guitar had become a distinctive element in primitive blues, Wilson's cheap tambura had actually helped to create a unique sound in "On the Road Again". It had taken his genius to turn a shoddy instrument into a sound that would have an instantly recognizable place in music history.

The results of his first on-record experiments with multi-tracking pleased Alan Wilson. However, it made the band's studio sound different from the sound of live Canned Heat performances. In concert, for instance, Wilson never played the tambura on "On the Road Again", sticking instead to the harmonica. Vestine played guitar during their live performances of the song, but did not appear on the recording. To the members of Canned Heat, however, such growing disparities in the band's sound were well worth it.

"In the future we'll be doing more of this kind of thing," Wilson said enthusiastically in 1968. "With the harmonica, I can have two or three bodies. 'On the Road Again' in person doesn't have quite the sound of the record, because I can only play one of the instruments at the same time. ... I love records for that. All the disadvantages of records are made up for in one way: it's just so much fun to be able to put down bottleneck and harp both in the same record. And to hear it back — it's really weird. You can play four or five things at the same time if you want to; that's really a lot of fun. Ooohh, I dig it!"

Multi-tracking was one way to compensate for the atmosphere of the studio, which some musicians find impersonal and sterile, particularly if they are accustomed to playing in front of a live audience or in less formal settings. As the band recorded their second album, it had become clear that studio recordings could not capture the raw energy of their live shows. They could, however, create something that was exciting in a different way, albeit irreproducible in the concert hall.

Wilson commented, "We have two scenes: we have recording, and live. Like any other group, or most groups, the result of the first album was somewhat surprising. You're posed with the sterility issue of the studio, the possibility of sterile sound, things like that. So we decided to try and compensate for this by doing things on the records that we couldn't do live, organizational type things."

Henry Vestine also got involved in the multi-tracking process. On "World In a Jug", which was based partly on an old recording by Garfield Akers, Vestine appeared five times at once at a certain point. This kind of thing flew in the face of conventional blues purism, whose values tended to insist that one should re-create the performance styles of old bluesmen as closely as possible, eschewing modern trappings of technology and electronica.

"There's a lot of stuff that's done for the effect of the sound," said Vestine about the album. "Like on 'World In a Jug', the building part right before the solo, I play a line where I appear five times overdubbed, just for the way it would sound. That's not so traditional, really. It's not to do it like a Garfield Akers song, but to update it and do it a way that we feel is good to do it now."

For some time already, Wilson had been intrigued with the concept of accompanying himself on multiple instruments. Years before Canned Heat existed, he had attended a Bob Dylan concert with Dick Waterman, and expressed interest in Dylan's harmonica rack as a way to obtain greater instrumental flexibility. He didn't actually care much for Bob Dylan's style, but the basic idea of playing guitar and harmonica simultaneously excited him.

Dick Waterman recalls, "I liked Dylan because of the lyrics; I liked the words. Al commented, 'Hey, he's pretty good.' That shocked me, and I said, 'But you hate this kind of music!' But what Al was interested in was Dylan's harmonica playing, and the rack, which meant that he could suck and blow and do all this other musical stuff at the same time. He liked the instrumental aspect."

Wilson was never known to experiment with a harmonica rack in public. A bit of experimentation probably would have led to the conclusion that racks are not for the serious harmonica player, as in blues playing it is helpful to have one's hands around the harmonica in order to help produce various tonal effects. Onstage, Wilson played either guitar or harmonica, giving his full attention to one instrument or the other.

"An Owl Song" was the second Wilson-sung item on *Boogie With Canned Heat*. Looking back on his career, this can be seen as a prominent turning point in his creativity. It was the first known song that he composed entirely himself. Lyrically, it was his first recorded departure from the traditional verses and phrases that made up his earlier songs, "Help Me" and "On the Road Again".

This was part of a conscious effort on Wilson's part. He now wanted to write songs using his own way of speaking, instead of relying on the familiar blues dialect. This process was documented in an interview with Wilson, conducted by Pete Welding and published in *Rolling Stone* as "Just Those Five Notes" almost two months after Wilson's death.

In Wilson's paradigm, expressed in this interview with Welding, the most elementary phase of blues composition would consist of singing traditional blues lyrics as they appeared on a previous recording. A second step, in the direction of greater originality, would feature lyrics from other traditional sources, used in an original fashion or mixed in a different combination than heard on previous sources for a given song. As an example of this second step, he cited "Rollin' and Tumblin'" and "The Road Song" from the first Canned Heat album, as well as his own "On the Road Again" from *Boogie With Canned Heat*.

As a third step in the direction of original songwriting, Wilson suggested the use of traditional phrases put together in new relationships. This could create traditional-sounding lyrics whose verses included traditional words, but were not the same as any heard on previous recordings. "Turpentine Moan" and "World In A Jug" from *Boogie With Canned Heat* were, according to Wilson, good examples of this approach.

FInally, a fourth step of originality would introduce the singer's own syntax, phrases, and ideas into the songwriting. This would signify a shift away from traditional blues lyrics, and toward the singer's own vocabulary, language, and pronunciation. Of his own items, Wilson referenced "An Owl Song" as a good example of this fourth step in songwriting. Of items sung by Bob Hite, Wilson cited "My Crime" as a song in the same category.

While it was more original than any of his previous songs, "An Owl Song" did include one notable traditional element. That was his use of the word "fairo", meaning girlfriend or sweetheart, in the second verse. Wilson had also used this term in "On the Road Again". Its ultimate origins are uncertain, and while it is common in archaic blues, it was not in widespread use at the time of Wilson's recordings. It is something of an anachronism in "An Owl Song", but by no means diminishes the effectiveness of the song, which is otherwise modern-sounding and even features a horn section.

According to one relative of Wilson, who requested not to be publicly identified, Wilson composed the song about an actual romantic interest that he was not able to pursue in real life. For some time (possibly since 1966), he had been seeing a female psychiatrist for his depression and related issues. Apparently he had developed a crush on the psychiatrist, and admitted to a family member that he had written a song about it. This theme would indeed fit the lyrics of "An Owl Song", with its references to a "money-taking woman" who patiently listens to Wilson talk about his problems.

Alan Wilson's increasingly personal approach to songwriting contrasted with the attitude of Bob Hite. "Most of the words I like to listen to, I don't want to sing," said Wilson. "The main thing is like, Bob feels comfortable singing a wide range of words, not directly applicable to his life, such as, 'I was born in Alabama and raised in Tennessee.' I think he thinks of them as *songs*; he likes to sing songs."

Because he now wanted each of his songs to have personal meaning, this meant that Wilson's repertoire was relatively small. "It's really weird," he admitted. "At any given time there's only about five songs that I know. Cause the main problem I've had is most of the [traditional] words sound good, but not coming out of me. So I'm getting more into writing my own words to get around that; it's an obvious solution."

Wilson's performances of blues songs were unusual partly because of his vocal distinctiveness. Many blues singers blatantly imitate their sources, but others develop a more unique voice. It is true that Wilson began by emulating the style of Skip James, but by the time he recorded, his singing had developed to the point where he cannot merely be classified as a James imitator.

David Evans comments, "I think Al did, at first, try to imitate the voices of his sources that he admired, as most of us do. Some people kind of take over the voice of people. There are all sorts of Howlin' Wolfs out there, Little Muddies and Little Elmores, even in the black tradition. And then there are musicians who try to put on a particular kind of voice or even a particular voice. Al, I think, did some of that; I don't remember it that well. But he came to the conclusion that he wasn't very good at it, and that you should sing with your natural voice. I mean, with a projection of your speaking voice, even if you had an accent in your speaking voice that was very far removed from that of black singers. They were mostly Southern, black, and had some range of accents within that culture. Basically they were singing with their natural voices, and in most cases not singing in a false voice, at least that's what Al felt. And so he felt that's what you should do, and you'd be most relaxed and sing at your best that way."

Wilson said, "For myself, I'm interested in avoiding Negro inflection of speech as much as I can. I think if a person sings Negro dialect, he's used to it because that's the only thing he's heard in records. But even if he's not aware of it, I think sometimes it creates problems. Like, some guys sing and they get hung up behind it. I think some of the reason is because they're singing syllables that they don't speak. And they don't think of it that way. This is applicable to rock and roll singers who do blues, or maybe John Hammond or The Doors' way of singing the blues. Those are extreme examples of grotesque ways of singing the words, in a way completely unlike speaking."

The concept of the "natural" voice and its place in blues, however, is complex. A distinction can be made between using vocal effects for purely aural purposes, versus imitating the dialect or pronunciation of someone from another culture.

David Evans explains, "In actual fact, a lot of the black blues singers do put on other voices or multiple voices. Charley Patton would be a good example. Or gospel singers too, like Blind Willie Johnson with his two different voices. But, of course, they are still within a range of voices within their culture. They don't try to usually sing like Bing Crosby. So, the opposite of that would be maybe a middle-class white kid trying to sing like Charley Patton. Al rejected that approach, and did wind up singing with his kind of Boston accent, which you can hear there. But it sounds good; it sounds natural to me. ... It came out real different in blues. His diction was fairly precise. But he had a good voice, and he sang with a lot of feeling. I think that's what came across in the records."

In terms of his distinctive high pitch, Wilson was, in a sense, not actually singing in his "natural" voice. While his on-record singing is not falsetto, it is much higher in pitch than his speaking voice, which was of average male pitch. (An example of this can be heard in the spoken recitation at the end of the 1968 song "Boogie Music".) His speaking voice was not naturally within the pitch range that he used while singing. Wilson's concept of the natural voice was, then, more related to pronunciation and dialect than pitch or timbre.

Mike Turner, a college student at U.C.L.A., was Wilson's housemate and friend during part of 1968. He recalls Wilson confessing a heavy Skip James influence. "Wilson was into Skip James, big time," recalls Turner. "He was really, really into Skip James, and patterned himself completely after him in his singing. He liked singers who weren't belters and shouters. He liked Skip James because of his pitch, which he thought was perfectly tuned and also unique. I don't remember him ever talking about any other blues guy personally so much. That's where his singing comes from. I remember him talking about singing in particular. How he'd found a niche that was *him*. Because if you think about it, almost all blues singers are belters and shouters. He wasn't too fond of that, and he was happy that there were guys like James who could sing the blues *softly*."

Along with reworking the blues to express their own creativity, Alan Wilson and the other members of Canned Heat made a point to support older blues artists, both in public and in private. Now that their own band was climbing the music industry ladder, they were in a better position to help the other musicians they admired.

One of these was pianist Sunnyland Slim, born Albert Luandrew in 1906. He had spent time backing Muddy Waters, Howlin' Wolf, Little Walter, and other Chicago luminaries, as well as forging a solo career. More recently, he had been making a living driving a cab in Chicago. Bob Hite and Alan Wilson met him in May 1968, during a chance cab ride after an Electric Theater Canned Heat show.

Hite and Wilson befriended Slim, persuading him to return to the recording studio. The result was the album *Slim's Got His Thing Goin' On*, released on a division of Liberty Records. Several tracks featured Canned Heat as Slim's backup group, with Hite in the role of co-producer. On *Boogie With Canned Heat*, Slim would play piano on the song "Turpentine Moan".

In 1969, this kind of work continued when the band encountered Telecaster guitar stylist Albert Collins in Houston. They urged him to move to California, where they introduced him to representatives of the United Artists record company. As a result, Collins began recording again. Throughout the rest of his career, which later included work for the renowned Alligator blues label, he would express appreciation to Canned Heat for giving his career a boost.

Even among hard-core blues purists, Canned Heat's dedication to the music could not be questioned. Hite, Wilson, and Vestine, in particular, seldom missed an opportunity to direct listeners to their sources, and often leveraged their own success to the benefit of older artists. This, along with their own respectable body of work, will be part of their musical legacy for decades to come.

11 A HEADFUL OF IDEAS

By the time *Boogie With Canned Heat* hit the streets, Alan Wilson's role as the band's musical director was firmly set. He was responsible for coordinating the arrangements, communicating between the rhythm section, Henry Vestine, and Bob Hite to ensure that each part fit neatly into place. Onstage, Hite appeared to be the leader of Canned Heat, and he certainly also did his part in coming up with song ideas from old records. However, anyone who spent much time around the band could see that Wilson was the inspiration behind their sound.

Wilson, however, didn't see his accomplishments as anything to boast about, and described his concept for the band very humbly. "It's no complicated thing," he explained. "I just came into it with a head full on the guitar, with a head full of ideas from old Paramount records. And Henry came into it with a head full of ideas from the modern way of playing the guitar. And just bang, there it was. That's all it was. ... I turned out to be mostly the arranger for the band. The other guys are very spontaneously inclined guys, who really play great — blowers, improvisers, that kind of thing."

Teamwork between the various band members, all of whom were technically superb players, enabled Wilson to work his magic as musical arranger. "Usually I just come in with a guitar part that I think will sound good," said Wilson, "and then each guy works out his own part independently. Larry almost always creates the bass lines; I don't create the bass line. All I do is like come in with a little seed. And then everybody sprouts out of it in their own way. I just spot out what I think is possible, maybe come up with a couple of suggestions. Sometimes I'll suggest a couple of things in the bass line. But generally, I just bring in the song. And this gives quite a bit of freedom in what everybody does; they just do their own thing *good*. So, I don't tell them what to do. They usually can figure out what to do better than I can do, 'cause they play their own instruments."

Larry Taylor commented on the relationship between Alan Wilson and Henry Vestine, in terms of their guitar playing: "Henry, he's in the modern vein, you know. Where Al's completely into the old and the country. And they really work together good. I don't know two guitar players I've ever heard that do work together like those guys. Just a natural thing, you know; it just *fits*."

Sometimes, however, the members of Canned Heat couldn't quite get on the same musical wavelength at the same time. In one instance of this, they wanted to record the song the band was named after, but were having trouble adapting Tommy Johnson's original guitar part to ensemble performance and the rhythm section.

In 1968, Marina Bokelman asked Alan Wilson why they didn't perform the song. Wilson seemed frustrated and blamed himself for their difficulties with "Canned Heat Blues". He said, "Because I can't play it... well, it's not so much that I can't play it as I can't do anything with it either. I just can't get anything happening with it. That's all. I can't do it."

Wilson could actually play the song, but the results were never quite good enough for him. "It would be kind of neat to be able to play the song; we're named after the damn song," he lamented. "I just can't think of anything on it. I've thought of it, but this is all in the realm of theory because I just can't play the damn song. It's not so much that I can't play it like Tommy Johnson can play. I just can't play it any way that sounds good to me. So I just don't do it, 'cause why do it?"

In 1969, the band would finally record a modified version of "Canned Heat Blues", sung by Bob Hite, for the *Hallelujah* album. It was simply entitled "Canned Heat", and is musically and lyrically distinct from the Tommy Johnson song. However, it fulfilled the band's collective desire to record some version of the "Canned Heat" theme.

Many of Canned Heat's songs involved the use of elements from archaic blues items. In Alan Wilson's opinion, however, there was one particular song perfect for adaptation to live ensemble format, working as a feature for Henry Vestine's lead guitar playing. "It's 'Bullfrog Blues'," he said. "But we can't find another one. We haven't been able to hit the winning combination. The ideal characteristic is where Henry can get [play] all the way through, and have a strong rhythm guitar part. The ideal song is where we get a good rhythm part and then have it lay, the lay of the land in such a way that Henry can do anything he wants over it."

For live performance, bassist Larry Taylor preferred songs whose rhythm had, as he called it, a "driving" feel. "There's certain things that just, for this band, come easier," he said. "Like the tune 'Bullfrog'; we've been doing this for a long time. ... It's just the type of tune that just got the kind of drive, and just makes me want to play it all the time, because it's got that certain drive, you know. ... Some of the songs don't sound that full in person; that's why we're afraid to do them. That's why I'm afraid, and I know everybody else feels pretty close to the same way."

The perfect pre-war blues, when adapted for the band, had to allow room for the tonal ranges of all instruments. Not every song fit into this category, as electrified ensemble playing was not typical of early rural blues performers; their songs were crafted for solo performance on acoustic instruments. In Canned heat, Wilson's role as rhythm guitarist was to play the traditional guitar part, which needed to be spare enough that it wouldn't conflict with the other sounds."

"You got treble figures, bass figures," explained Wilson. "'Bullfrog' just happened to be a song where all of the action took place in one hunk in the middle, which left all the top open for Henry, and all the bottom open for Larry. Anything where the action on the rhythm guitar is in the middle. And leaving the other ends open. Putting together an ensemble, it's good to spread out the tones so that all the action ain't in one place."

Discussing the adaptation of traditional material, Larry Taylor said, "In country blues, in the kind of stuff we do like mixing up country blues songs, you gotta kinda just be pretty simple in what you play, because you can't clutter it up. Because it's a set kind of thing, you know. It's a driving thing for bass. Like your 'Bullfrog', those tunes like that. That's country. The bass, you listen to the bass; it's just a real driving, repetitious type of lick. It's not mixed up or a lot of things happening, not a lot of notes. It's like country music; it's simple."

Occasionally the rhythm section's more modern sensibilities conflicted with Wilson's archaic, modal values. When Vestine was added to the mix, things got even more complicated, as during the *Boogie With Canned Heat* sessions when the band wanted to record Tommy McClennan's "Whiskey Headed Woman". Their rehearsals made it clear that Vestine would not be able to play lead throughout the piece as Wilson had hoped.

"I tried to find something like 'Bullfrog' that Henry could play over," said Wilson. "I looked through my whole record collection to try and find one. And, the best I could come up with was 'Whiskey Headed Woman'. That didn't fill the bill. It didn't really work out the way we planned, because Henry was originally supposed to play all the way through. But then the rhythm section could only relate to the guitar part by making the break and playing along with the guitar on the break. And so this created an up and down type of terrain that Henry couldn't play lead over, so then it turned out that Henry just played solo in the middle of the song."

Of Canned Heat's "Whiskey Headed Woman #2", Larry Taylor said, "We like to play and have a full sound, you know; that's our whole thing. And some of the things just don't come off like that onstage. Like 'Whiskey Headed Woman'; we never do the song, because it's just that kind of song. It's not a full type of song. It breaks a lot; it stops and stuff, you know. But the kind of stuff we like to do mainly is the driving stuff."

"World In A Jug" came down much the same way. Wilson wanted to feature Vestine's playing as much as possible, but this ended up interfering with the rhythm section. "The same thing happened on 'World In A Jug'," said Wilson. "Henry originally played lead all the way through. But despite the fact I tried to come up with things so concise that there would be no interference if he played lead, it didn't work. And eventually we just put on two rhythm guitars on each one, and then he takes solos in the middle. So they sound okay, but not originally what we planned them to be."

Both songs appeared on *Boogie With Canned Heat,* the Tommy McClennan song being listed as "Whiskey Headed Woman #2". However, due to the issues with these songs, the band rarely played "Whiskey Headed Woman #2" or "World In A Jug" during live performances. Many of their challenges were related to the band members' varying rhythmic sensibilities and preferences.

Wilson elaborated on these issues, saying, "The rhythm section has been unable to play these fifteen or thirty-three measure type things, with a hitch in them. Things like 'Traveling Riverside Blues'. We haven't been able to do that. The rhythm, the bass and the drums, they can do it, but it's just mechanical. They can't get away, so we can't do it. In the category that Henry plays lead on, the background part has to be concise, and also has to be twelve measures. In terms of the things I play today, unfortunately today, except for one-chord items, the twelve measure prohibition applies. We only have two forms: twelve measures, and twenty-four — that's the same thing — and then one chord."

Canned Heat's bassist and drummer were extremely skilled instrumentalists, and highly adaptable in the studio. In live performances, however, they wanted to play using the rhythm and structures that came most naturally to them. Larry Taylor commented, "When we go out [onstage] and then when Bob calls it [a song] off to do it, if we know it grooves and we know we've gotten a good groove on it, we'll play it. And we dig playing it. But a lot of the songs we do, we know there's little things, and we're hesitant sometimes to play it, you know. Which is ... not really too good of a scene; we should play just everything we can. Because the only way you're gonna get it down is play it."

Of the rhythm section, Alan Wilson explained, "Their way of feeling rhythm is based on evenness. It's the same way that the average Westerner has to learn — the average *any*, that I know of — has to learn how to play in five and seven and nine like the Greeks do naturally. That's their basic rhythm, and there's a jerk, a hitch. I used that word earlier, hitch. It's a non-technical word, but it describes it. The average one of these songs that is not twelve measures long is thirteen and a half. With two measures of singing, two and a half of guitar, and the singer kind of breathes in on that last half of a measure. And it is a different way of breathing. Musically, and every other way. These singers like to do it, whereas for the rhythm section, having that hitch in it is merely a disruptive feature. They want to play straight ahead; their concept of straight ahead is that period of four measures."

Some of the concepts that interested Wilson, such as songs with uneven measure structures, might have been better suited for solo arrangement. "Perhaps a forward stage of evolution is getting into patterns based on just breathing," he said. "And not that rigid. So that's one thing — that's actually why I think soloists have it over the bands, because the patterns are more flexible, because people don't get hung up trying to follow each others' patterns. Guys like Hooker."

Here, Wilson was of course referring to John Lee Hooker, one of his favorite bluesmen. Noted for his idiosyncratic timing and propensity to change chords only when the mood struck him — if ever — Hooker was notoriously difficult to accompany. He didn't follow the standard rules of Western music, and this was one of the things Wilson found so attractive about Hooker as an artist.

Much of the time, the band's challenges resulted in learning experiences and the creation of new sounds. Wilson understood the musical issues, and knew how to cope with them. He didn't deal as well with personal issues that arose between the various band members. As the main arranger for the band, however, he tried to ensure that everyone's voice was heard and each member's musical outlook respected.

In 1968, Marina Bokelman was making a short film about Canned Heat as a school project for her folklore degree. As part of this, she interviewed Wilson about Canned Heat's creative process. To her, he described a typical band practice session, in which constant disruption seemed to be the norm.

"I'll just come and sit down, play the guitar part," said Wilson. "Then Larry will start mulling around, and he'll start filling in the bass. And then Larry and Fito will discuss the matter. There'll be a few fights; somebody'll suggest throwing the song out. Somebody'll walk out for a while and then they'll come back. And then the rhythm section, they'll get it together, then somebody *else* will decide they can't make it. and then they can, but they'll get changed around. At various times, everybody will suggest dropping the song."

According to Wilson, song selection was determined by majority rule. He said, "It more or less depends on whether a coalition of three emerges at any given time who don't like the song. That's the key thing, at any given time. Now if it comes down that everybody dislikes it at a *different* time, and at any given time it's four to one, then the song manages to stay in the books. Every once in a while we go through the old repertoire at rehearsals and get mad and throw out songs. We throw out a third of the book and then we find out we don't have any songs left, and we have to go back and play them again."

Bob Hite said, "Alan will generally come up with a lick, and talk to me about it. Then we'll have a rehearsal; he'll present the lick to the band, and say to Larry, 'All right, what do you think you can play on this particular thing?' Or, maybe he's got an idea for Larry already. We get the music down ... there's a lot of changes. 'That isn't any good! Throw that one out!' You know, that's what we go through. Usually it'll take a little while to get into shape and somebody hollering, 'Yes, it'll work, it'll work if we just keep pushing!' Then it comes out."

Band manager Skip Taylor witnessed some of the band's quarrels, and commented, "Well, there was always a little dissension in the band, as far as Larry and Alan, and Henry and Larry. Larry just didn't get along with a lot of people ... and he would get rubbed the wrong way real easily."

Most of the time, the band members were tolerant of each others' quirks. Their nerves became worn at times, however. Larry Taylor, for his part, was a hard-core musician, not a party animal; his dedication to artistic excellence has since become legendary. The frequent distractions involving drugs, often purveyed by Henry Vestine and Bob Hite, frustrated him. This would eventually lead to a major falling-out between Taylor and Vestine.

Wilson told Marina Bokelman, "Larry is just uptight. And it filters down. ... Since we disagree on so many things, there's a lot of shouting goes on some of the time. And there's various scenes at rehearsals. It's really weird. It's not that you just come in with a song and rehearse it. As soon as you start playing it, at least with us it becomes like a very close thing. And if it doesn't sound good, people get like a revulsion reaction."

Wilson described one recent drama that occurred when the band tried to rehearse a new item: "This song we just added, first of all, Bob hated it so much he walked out. The rest of us rehearsed on it, he came back, then he decided he liked it. But this time *Larry* decided the thing was terrible and wanted to throw it out; we went through a big scene with that. And then finally Larry got his head straightened around. Now we play the song, but if it had happened that Bob and Larry hated it together, it never would have been learned. So that's what comes down at rehearsals, sometimes."

Another difficulty, for Wilson, was related to the band's developing sound — or, rather, sounds. In 1968 he described their music as a "schizophrenic scene", saying, "What Henry wants to do, in inclination, is growing further away from what I want to do. We both like what each other plays, but there's a big cleavage coming up."

Vestine's preferred sound was now the loud, psychedelic approach. "One category of songs is played at top volume, with the British approach to sound," explained Wilson. "But then if I'm playing harmonica or bottleneck, then more and more so in the future it's going to emerge as a whole different category of song, in which the volume may be as much as three fifths and no more of the peak volume reached on British oriented items."

Vestine's volume was necessary to produce the sustain and distortion effects he wanted. Wilson preferred listening to that kind of guitar playing on records, which allowed him to control the volume. He himself was not a loud guitarist.

"The volume necessary to produce the tone he [Vestine] wants is a volume which does not agree with the volume that I play lead at," said Wilson. "So it means like when I'm playing lead, we have a whole different situation. It's viewed by many as being a lot more conservative, and it definitely is in some ways."

Wilson was afraid, and rightly so, of losing his hearing from exposure to loud music. "It wipes me out," he said in April 1968. "I understand [Eric] Clapton just had a major ear operation. He lost a lot of his hearing, and they discovered *blood pools*, pools of blood hemorrhaging in both inner ears. So, I'm not ready for that! [Michael] Bloomfield I believe is having trouble hearing, and I understand a lot of the harmonica players in Chicago are starting to lose it. I have no interest in that *at all*."

In September 1967, Canned Heat opened two shows for Eric Clapton's band Cream in New York. One night, Wilson stayed around to watch the Cream's portion of the concert, but had to leave when the volume became intolerable for him. During a few of Canned Heat's performances, he observed that some audience members were likewise leaving when Henry Vestine's volume became particularly clamorous.

There seemed to be only one solution. In Cambridge, Wilson had stuffed cotton in his ears to protect himself from loud folkies. With Canned Heat, he resorted to actual earplugs, which he began wearing in August 1967.

On this decision, Wilson commented, "It passed the point where I'd wake up in the morning and my ears would buzz. I didn't mind so much when they buzzed after the job, but when I'd wake up the next morning and they were still buzzing, I said, okay, that's it. And so, I can't make that scene."

Earplugs and amplifiers seemed to be the winning combination. Wilson pointed out, "It's not completely insane to play this way, because if you play at a lower volume you just can't get the sound. Sometimes we're so loud people have to leave, and that upsets me. it's weird; it's like a price. You have to pay. ... But it's very easy to protect yourself; all you have to do is wear earplugs. That's all you have to do. It's just that people don't do that. So what I think is that they should play loud and everybody should wear earplugs! And then you'd get the sound and you don't wipe out your ears."

12 ON THE ROAD AGAIN

Throughout 1968, Canned Heat's management waged a campaign to create a viable commercial image for the band. They had made two records, and had a good following on the west coast, but had been unable to catch the attention of the greater record-buying public.

Liberty Records had persuaded the band to record a song called "Evil Woman" by Larry Weiss, a songwriter not associated with Canned Heat. Released as a single in October 1967 (January 1968 according to some sources) and later included on *Boogie With Canned Heat*, it wasn't the hit song everyone had hoped for.

Nobody at Liberty seemed to know much about hard-core blues, and they were uncertain of how to make the band palatable to the general public. "Liberty was just a straight, almost teenybop type of rock and roll label," says Skip Taylor. "They didn't have anybody like Canned Heat at all!"

The band, for their part, knew next to nothing about commercial promotion. Everyone relied on the management, primarily Skip Taylor, to sell the band. He came up with various concepts, some bordering on the gimmicky, to better appeal to the masses. The band wasn't particularly glamorous, so he worked on ways to make their relative homeliness seem somehow hip.

"We said, 'Let's give them all nicknames!'" recalls Skip Taylor. "You know, and made the Bear look like, 'Yeah, you can weigh as much as you want. Grow your hair long and let your beard grow and you'll *be* the Bear!' So Bob started becoming proud to be this big, husky, bearded, longhaired bear! And we tried to say, 'Remember, you're the *friendly* bear! Not the mean bear! Be the friendly bear!'"

Shortly thereafter, Henry Vestine was given the name "Sunflower" because of the way he leaned over his guitar with his long blond hair, which vaguely resembled yellow sunflower petals. When Wilson mentioned that John Fahey had already named him "Blind Owl", that became his official nickname in the band. Larry Taylor was "The Mole", and drummer Adolfo de la Parra was simply "Fito". One promotional poster of the time shows the band members dressed up in costumes depicting their different names.

At times, in the early days of Canned Heat, Henry Vestine had been called "The Preacher" as documented on tapes of live recordings. Hite also referred to Wilson as "Little Al". However, neither of those nicknames would stick for long.

In April 1968, Canned Heat released a new single, "Boogie Music". This upbeat, feel-good song features vocals by both Bob Hite and Alan Wilson, making it unique in their catalog of commercially issued recordings. It is also unusual in its use of a horn section, which was not part of the traditional Canned Heat arrangement. The lyrics, extolling the benefits of boogie music, are original throughout the bulk of the song.

At the end of the song, Alan Wilson provides a spoken recitation, attesting to the life-changing qualities of boogie music. Though many fans believe that Wilson composed this, it is actually an adaptation from a portion of occultist Aleister Crowley's book *Magick in Theory and Practice*. (The inner cover of Canned Heat's LP *Living the Blues*, on which "Boogie Music" appears, contains a note "Poem with apologies to Aleister Crowley". This is a reference to the "Boogie Music" recitation.)

It is uncertain why the band members chose to use this adaptation of an Aleister Crowley quote. Insofar as is known, nobody associated with Canned Heat actively embraced Crowley's teachings or followed his occult path. However, Wilson was extremely well-read, and included a variety of spiritual and mystical books in his intellectual consumption. It's possible that he read Crowley's book and felt that such an adaptation would be clever and humorous, as a kind of "inside joke".

After the end of "Boogie Music", one can hear a snippet of Charley Patton's 1929 song "Tell Me Man", on which he is accompanied by fiddle player Henry Sims. This snippet has been excised from some versions of "Boogie Music", but is intact on the LP (where Sims and Patton are also credited). According to one account, Bob Hite and Alan Wilson were influenced by "Tell Me Man" when they composed "Boogie Music", although the exact nature of the influence is uncertain and difficult to ascertain by listening to the music.

In 1968, Canned Heat bassist Larry Taylor spoke with Marina Bokelman about this supposed influence. He said of the Patton song, "Well, that's where they said they got the song ["Boogie Music"] from. But man, I don't hear no relation. So, we actually just wrote it ourselves, you know. I think. ... Now Al, evidently, the lick he's playing, he thinks or he says it came from that. But I can't hear it. To him it might be, you know. Just in his own head. But ... yeah, it doesn't sound the same."

"Boogie Music" was released with Wilson's "On the Road Again" as the B-side. "On the Road Again" was not considered potential hit material by the band or their management. All their hopes were on "Boogie Music".

Not much happened until summer, when a radio station in Texas began playing the new single. The strange thing, however, was that the B-side was getting more airplay than the A-side. Other stations picked up on it, and soon "On the Road Again" was getting so much airplay that Liberty reissued the single with the sides reversed. "On the Road Again", suddenly turning out to be the first Canned Heat hit, became the A-side and received the promotion.

The band was amazed, as was Skip Taylor. "Lo and behold," he recalls, "some AM station in Texas started playing 'On the Road Again', out of the blue. I mean, nobody can take credit for it at all. It just happened. And then they started playing it in Austin, and it moved up to Houston, moved to Dallas, and all of a sudden it started showing up on some of the reports that go to *Billboard* and *Cashbox* magazine. It was a breakout record in Texas. Everybody was going, 'What? Who?' And it just kind of spread, more and more, and then Liberty Records promo guys got behind it."

There were actually two different mixes released of "On the Road Again", according to Bob Hite's brother Richard. He remembers, "Out of the blue, it broke; it was in Texas or something. Then it started going up the charts and completely surprised everybody. When the record first came out, the relative volumes of the harmonica and the vocal were very close. So they had to actually remaster the thing, to come out to have a version where the vocal was louder." According to Richard, Wilson usually preferred his singing to be kept relatively low in the mix so that the vocal was similar in volume level to the instrumental accompaniment. Throughout his recording career, he had to be persuaded by Skip Taylor and the other band members to raise the levels of his vocal tracks to a normal level.

"On the Road Again" was a manifestation of Wilson's involvement with classical Indian music, which he studied closely along with the blues. "On the Road Again", inspired by this sound, involves a drone provided by the Indian tambura. Recent utilization of Indian instruments by rock and pop performers may have contributed to the 1968 commercial success of "On the Road Again".

The Beatles should, of course, receive a great deal of credit for giving the average late-sixties record buyer a superficial awareness of Indian music. A few, such as Wilson, had learned of the genre from other sources. However, most rock and pop fans would never have heard of, say, Ravi Shankar, without the Beatles. There can be little doubt that their work helped to open the door for "On the Road Again" by making the sounds of Indian instruments familiar and acceptable, in adapted form if not in standard raga form.

The Beatles had begun using the sitar as far back as 1965, on "Norwegian Wood". At that time, they were approaching the instrument from a point of relative ignorance, as none of them had yet commenced a proper study of Indian musical styles. In 1966, however, George Harrison took sitar lessons from Ravi Shankar and got more of a technical grasp on the sound.

The Beatles' Indian-influenced recordings culminated with "Love You To" on the 1966 *Revolver* album, and "Within You Without You" on *Sergeant Pepper's Lonely Heart's Club Band* in 1967. Throughout his later solo career, Harrison would further explore the Indian genre along with associated mystical themes. In 1997, he acted as producer for *Chants of India*, a Ravi Shankar CD featuring devotional mantras.

Alan Wilson had been listening to classical music well before the Beatles began using it. He had heard their albums and liked much of their work, but he did not use Indian elements in his music simply because they had made it fashionable to do so. For him, as for them, it was part of a natural creative evolution. The resulting music became part of a larger cultural movement embracing natural philosophies and Hindu Yoga practices.

David Evans remembers, "I know Al liked the Beatles and rock and roll; we used to listen to them. But Al would have worked on his own, and quite independently, because that's just the way he was. He wasn't a follower of trends — to say the least!"

Contrasting Wilson's use of Indian influences with that of the Beatles, Evans points out that the starting point of blues made his musical fusion distinctive: "He managed to blend Indian music with the blues. The Beatles, I think, were just kind of using it as a flavoring. They weren't applying it to blues, in any case. The kind of blues Al was using it with was very modal music, which of course Indian music is too. The theory of Indian music and the scales that it uses are really different from the blues, but there are points of affinity, and some of the modes could sound very similar to a pentatonic blues scale."

Money was coming in now for Canned Heat, and for Wilson as co-author (along with Floyd Jones, who also received songwriting credits) of "On the Road Again". However, in Wilson's case, this new income went largely unspent.

Wilson's lifestyle remained much the same as it had been since his move to California. When the band was in Los Angeles, which was less and less now, he often stayed with Pete Welding, David Evans, or Barry Hansen. And now there was a new place for him to stay, as Bob Hite was buying a house.

Bob had moved out of his parents' house in 1966, and lived for a while in a rented cottage on the beach. Then he moved to another rental, which provided him with very awkward sleeping conditions. His younger brother Richard remembers, "It was really funny. The floor was like at an angle, and the bed had to be up against the wall or it would roll. I mean, it was a real big angle!"

Finally, thanks in large part to Wilson's hit song, Hite had enough money to get the kind of house he needed for his large record collection. In fall 1968, he bought a home in Topanga Canyon. A wife, Verlie, joined him along with her son from a previous marriage. (This individual, Ed Marrow, would later become a jazz drummer.)

The new Hite property included some land on an adjoining hillside, with trees and plants that attracted Wilson. Lately, he had been having trouble sleeping, but found it easier to rest if he was outdoors. With its woodsy, almost mountainous terrain, Hite's backyard was a perfect place for him to spend the night when in Los Angeles.

Wilson once mentioned this to Barry Hansen, who explains, "He had insomnia, sometimes had trouble sleeping. Sometimes, he found, he thought he could sleep better outdoors than inside." Other bedtime quirks have been noted by Canned Heat drummer Adolfo de la Parra, who recalled in later interview that when they shared motel rooms, Wilson preferred the floor over the bed as a place to sleep.

Thus Bob Hite's backyard became a sort of refuge, a nesting place for the Blind Owl. As if to compensate for Canned Heat's newfound fame, he began isolating himself from the rest of the world whenever possible. He could often be found on the hillside behind Hite's house, sleeping, meditating, reading, or just getting away from people.

In one taped 1968 conversation, Hite declared his intent to work on a song during a quiet time when nobody else was home. Wilson expressed the opinion that this was an unrealistic plan, commenting that Hite's house was never empty. This seemed to be true, as the Topanga Canyon house quickly became a Canned Heat gathering space. It was usually filled with extended family, friends, friends-of-friends, and hangers-on who continued to party whether Hite was present or absent.

When he wasn't in Bob Hite's backyard or crashed out on someone else's couch, Wilson could sometimes be found in a house whose rent he shared with two college students. The house was on Rose Street in Venice, a suburb of Los Angeles. During the spring, summer, and fall of 1968, Wilson spent part of his time there.

One of his housemates on Rose Street was a young man named Mike Turner, who remembers, "We lived like college students. Rose Street was this scene; it was a bunch of U.C.L.A. students, a lot of whom went on to be film directors and stuff like that. They all lived in the scene around there and they all knew each other. Alan was, like, on the outside of that. The thing that we all did was we all rented these old houses, before it became real popular, and we'd split up the rooms."

Wilson, for his part, was no broke college kid any more. When they started hearing his band's song played on the radio, Wilson's roommates found it a little incongruous, and wondered why a rock star on the rise would embrace such a humble lifestyle. Turner recalls, "Basically, here was a guy making a lot more money than we were, and still living in a room, like a college kid's lifestyle. He was only around once in a blue moon."

When Wilson appeared, his eccentricity and talent always made a big impression. "He had perfect pitch, and he would tune his guitar off the telephone," says Turner. "It was a B-flat or something.

He said it was a perfect something, and explained to me why it was the perfect pitch to tune his guitar. I never saw him do it, but people told me he could transcribe music as it was played. He could transcribe it note for note, musically. And he was into a lot of other music besides blues. He was a lot into free jazz, and had a lot of Indian music. He liked classical music too."

No music snob, Wilson openly embraced some of the popular sounds of the time. "Alan brought home the Beatles' 'White Album'," Turner remembers. "He got it the day it came out, and I sat down with him and we listened to the whole thing. He thought it was really great, very creative. He wasn't so much a blues purist. He was into pop, even though he didn't collect it so much."

Nobody knew quite what to make of Alan Wilson. "He was kind of like an alien," says Turner. "There was an alien quality about him, and he was hard to get to know. He was pretty quiet, but I got to know him fairly well. He was a real sweet guy, a kind guy. He was very cerebral. I got the picture that he was the guy who didn't do what all the other band guys did. You know, they'd stay in a motel room and chase groupies or whatever. He seemed like the guy who would know where a good park was in each city. He was an intellectual."

Wilson was making what seemed like a huge amount of money. He didn't seem to have much use for it, however, aside from purchases of records and botany books. Turner recalls, "It was 1968, and he told me he made thirty thousand dollars that year. We just thought that was insane. It seemed totally incongruous and strange to him, I think."

The debauchery of rock and roll was equally strange to Wilson, and he to it. Popular bands seem to inevitably attract groupies, young women who make it their mission to sleep with musicians. Wilson, however, didn't quite know how to deal with the groupies, even though some might have presented opportunities for romantic relationships.

The groupies, for their part, didn't know how to deal with Wilson. Apparently he was rebuffed by them on more than one occasion, though it's uncertain whether or not this actually caused him much dismay. Mike Turner says, "I heard they [groupies] were into the group as a band, *except* for Alan. I remember him talking about the scene and stuff, that he wasn't into it."

In August 1968, the band played in Hawaii. One story goes that during an off night, Wilson sat in for a solo set at a Maui club without revealing that he was part of the famous Canned Heat. There, he met a girl, became involved with her, and brought her back to live with him in California.

"He had some girl friend that he met in Hawaii," remembers Mike Turner. "She came back to live with him. ... I remember him being real happy when he brought that girl back. She was sort of a plain girl, kind of chubby."

Sadly, things didn't work out, and the relationship only lasted a few months. "She kind of disappeared," says Turner. "I don't know what happened. He had bad luck with girls, didn't have too much happening there."

Wilson would write a song about this love interest, which was never recorded commercially but surfaced later among bootleg collectors. In the lyrics, he describes enjoying the girl's company and taking her to watch the sunrise at Haleakala, a volcanic national park in Hawaii. Set to a John Lee Hooker style guitar part, Wilson's words also feature a twist on a traditional blues lyric, in which he declares his intent to go to Maui to get his "hambone boiled".

13 TALKING TO THE TREES

In September 1968, Canned Heat toured Europe for the first time. Their music had a significant following there, as European listeners have historically been more appreciative of blues than American music fans. To "purists" among the listeners, the extensive knowledge of traditional blues displayed by Alan Wilson, Bob Hite, and Henry Vestine authenticated their blues credentials, regardless of skin color or geographic roots.

"People in Europe just took to Canned Heat," remembers Skip Taylor. "Because it was more pure and it wasn't rock and roll. It was kind of defying the system. And all these music associates could sit down with Bob and Alan and just have a field day. They could ask them questions that nobody else on earth could answer. So they became like the darlings of the whole music trade set over in Europe. There were just so many music magazines and publications — you could just do interview after interview. So the band grew over there tremendously."

Despite the band's popularity, Wilson didn't seem to be extremely fond of touring. In part, this might have been due to the busy schedule and many inconveniences preventing him from spending time outdoors while on the road. In addition, he expressed his distaste for the prerequisite travel by plane.

"I got the feeling that it [flying] was maybe anathema to him," says Marina Bokelman, recalling the band's increased tour schedule of late 1968 and early 1969. "There must have been a discussion where he made some kind of vehement remark. Hasty methods of travel were not for him. ... I know that touring was very hard on him. I know that he didn't like it. I don't think that he was psychologically suited to it. It was too hasty, and there was too much pressure. He wasn't happy around touring; there was a discomfort and maybe some certain remarks."

Despite his love of the music, Wilson apparently dreaded touring so much that he frequently missed scheduled airplane flights. Richard Hite has recalled that in such instances, the rest of Canned Heat would go ahead without him, and he would take a later flight. Others have recalled Wilson being semi-forcibly escorted back from his nature excursions in order to make flights or gigs with the other band members.

Bringing his sleeping bag on tour, Alan Wilson often eschewed motel rooms and slept outdoors whenever he could. This was odd enough, but things became even stranger when he began packing his own food, including large quantities of brown rice and a camp stove. At one point, his suitcase fell open in an airport and large quantities of rice spilled everywhere, much to the other band members' embarrassment. Wilson, for his part, seemed oblivious to the trouble his eccentricities were creating.

Skip Taylor accompanied Canned Heat on tour, and remembers Wilson's increasingly quirky behavior: "We'd check into a Holiday Inn or a Hilton or whatever, and he had his little hot plate kind of thing, and a little stove, and he'd take his bagged food. That's his things, and off he'd go! 'Well,' he'd say, 'what time do I have to be back? What time are we leaving?' I mean, right when we'd check in, he'd go, 'What time are you leaving for the gig?' 'Is there a sound check?' or 'When do you want to see me in the lobby?'"

Then Wilson went off by himself in search of the nearest woods. He was often forced to settle for some kind of park, or perhaps a bit of vegetation at the corner of some parking space or empty lot. When he returned to the motel, he was often messy and disheveled from being so very close to nature. However, he was still not very interested in bathing, much less primping before going onstage.

Skip Taylor says, "He'd come back and he'd either have slept or just walked, as far as the woods. He'd come back with mud all over him, tree limbs and pollen. ... And he'd be ready to go to the gig; there was no change of clothes or anything! 'Okay, here I am! Let's go!' You got to just expect that of him and love him for the guy he was."

Occasionally, Taylor tried to help Wilson clean up his act. He recalls: "If I wanted him to look a little better onstage, it meant me going out and buying him clothes. He'd put on anything, and being Alan, he could put on a brand new shirt and pants and look like he'd slept in it overnight. He was never much of a fashion plate, but it certainly didn't matter to him."

Clearly, Wilson was as different from his fellow band members as he was in childhood from his school mates. "Alan was extremely introverted," says Skip Taylor. "He was very hard to talk to, but when he would say something, you better have your ears open. Because it was always going to be meaningful and it was always going to be upfront. But I can't say that I ever got really close to Alan, or that I know of anybody who did. He kept to himself, and was happy that way."

Sometimes, Wilson did tire of his solitude. However, he had spent so much time in the world of his own mind that it was difficult for him to relate to other people — particularly those of the opposite sex. It's possible that his need for personal connection became redirected in some way through his love of nature. Much like the nature mystic and writer Henry David Thoreau, he seemed to get more satisfaction out of trees and shrubs than women.

Skip Taylor speculates, "I would say he was more asexual, and he was more affected and endeared by trees and plants. I took walks with him sometimes in different botanical gardens around the world. And *God*, it was like it was almost an orgasm for him. Looking and seeing some plant he had never seen before, or a tree that he knew there were only twenty of in the world or something. And that was his get-off. By *far*, I think, more than anything else. Canned Heat had groupies. You know, there were girls, and if we ever saw Alan walking off with a girl, it was like — everybody just fell down."

According to some of his closer friends, Wilson did actually want a romantic relationship, but didn't quite seem to know how to go about it. "He was extremely lonely even after he was successful," says Barry Hansen. "He had a hard time handling relationships in general, women especially. I never knew him to have a girlfriend, but he certainly wasn't gay; he just couldn't... he really had a hard time, dealing with anything romantic, and that was one of the things that made him so unhappy."

This dissatisfaction intensified into depression. When Wilson returned from being on the road with Canned Heat, friends like Hansen could see that things were getting worse. "During the time that I first got to know him and he slept on my floor, I did not think of Alan as a depressed person," he says. "I thought of him as somebody who was lonely, and took refuge in music, but that was just like me. I mean, I knew I was somewhat depressed but I never thought of myself as being clinically depressed. But I thought here Alan is very much like me, except he's a better musician. So we bonded pretty quickly."

On one occasion, Hansen paid a visit to Bob Hite and overheard a remark about Wilson's preferred activities. He remembers, "Bob made some kind of rude comment about how, when the rest of the band was partying and having fun, Alan would be out there staring at a tree. I mean, it's not that they minded; they just thought it was ... he did not behave like the rest of them, and the rest of them liked to smoke dope and maybe find some women, or, at the very least, go out and hear some music somewhere. Alan's favorite thing to do was to go off by himself and look at the local plant life. I think he would like to seek out places that were calm."

Wilson mentioned his activities of choice while on tour, as Hansen recalls: "He told me that the band would go to a place that he had never been before, and his favorite things to do was to go off by himself and look at the local plant life, which ... it's beautiful, but it's, you know, it's an odd life for a blues musician. It was his life. He was not like anybody else I knew."

In the midst of the sixties "counterculture" revolution, Wilson found himself caught up in a rock and roll lifestyle. He didn't seem to know quite what to make of it. Sometimes he was taken aback the groupies, and even by the way Canned Heat's audiences expressed themselves during shows.

Barry Hansen recalls, "He was kind of bemused by the scene. I remember him telling me a story about how he was taking a solo once, and he had his guitar cranked up pretty loud, doing the John Lee Hooker boogie. And a guy ran up onstage and plastered his head right against the Marshall amps. You know, hundreds of decibels. But, it's like staring at the sun. And I think Alan made that remark. But this guy was just so involved in the music, and probably whatever chemicals were in him, that he just had to get to the center of the music, with reckless disregard for his health. So, I didn't see this, but Alan came back from a tour and just told me about this, with wonderment."

Nature was Alan Wilson's retreat from the bizarre world of Canned Heat stardom. It seemed to be the only relief from the worries, anxieties, and depression that haunted him. What could he do, then, when his beloved Nature seemed to be as fragile as his own emotional state?

Sometime after moving to California, Wilson became aware of the plight of the coast redwoods, *Sequoia sempervirens*, which were being "harvested" for lumber mills at a terrifying rate. These redwoods, whose remaining groves consisted of old growth dating back hundreds, even thousands of years, became his love and obsession.

At some point, Wilson decided to use his income from the band for environmental work. He began saving and planning to establish his own non-profit foundation, hoping that with dedication, he could make a difference for the earth. In terms of his own well-being, however, this mission was not enough to sustain him.

During the last couple of years of Wilson's life, his own personal demons seem to have become entwined with his concern for the redwoods. No matter what he did — no matter how well he played his music, and no matter how much of himself he gave to Nature — things refused to get any better. He couldn't keep loggers from cutting down trees any more than he could find a woman to love him.

As obsessively as he had pursued the blues, Alan Wilson now memorized the names of trees and plants. With the same intensity he had once given to old records, he was now studying botany textbooks. Neither music nor Nature, however, could heal his depression.

In late 1968, Marina Bokelman noticed a difference in her friend Al. When he came over to her house, he didn't want to talk about music. He wanted to talk about the redwoods — and the end of the world. Bokelman believed that his fears were aggravated by a popular doomsday mentality, which went hand in hand with that era's continuing fear of nuclear war.

"There was a feeling of fear and doom," recalls Bokelman, "that the end of the world was imminent and that things were going to end any minute. I think Al really felt that deeply. That is one thing that I really remember him talking about, very animatedly and at length."

Apparently, Wilson's fondness for *Sequoia sempervirens* had developed into a personal theory of mystical ecology. Bokelman says, "He had pinned it all on the redwoods, that the redwoods were really the key to the ecosystem. And if the redwoods went, then it was all over for the world; there would be like a domino effect."

This profound feeling for the redwoods had become very spiritual. Though anxious about their fate, Wilson was also overcome with love for his favorite trees. One acquaintance recalled that when they took LSD together, Wilson revealed that he could "talk to the trees" and receive communication from them in kind. When he put his arms around a tree, this facilitated the process.

Marina Bokelman remembers hearing Wilson express his feelings: "It was truly a mystical thing. He would talk about that, and express at length such viewpoints. He had what I would describe as a mystical feeling about the redwoods, that they were the most noble and sentient of all trees — perhaps even all life forms."

Unsuccessful with women, Wilson had taken Nature as his lover, the recipient of the tenderness that he was unable to express to another human. Unfortunately, this opened him up to more pain. "I think there was this ... extremely tender and sensitive side that certainly came out towards the end, in the love of Nature," says Bokelman. "All the sensitivity came out there. But it was an undefended sensitivity. It was a vulnerability that didn't have any boundaries around it, so that the plight of the redwoods became his plight."

Wilson became openly emotional when he talked about the redwoods. "He would be extremely distressed, distraught even, about the trees," Bokelman remembers. "He would come in and it would be like, 'Do you realize!? This is what's happening! And they're becoming extinct at the rate of this, and do you realize what's happening?' There was a sense of urgency and despair, that this thing was happening and there was nothing he could do about it."

At some point, Wilson went to work as an ecological consultant for a governmental agency, possibly the National Forest Service. Unfortunately, proper records pertaining to these activities could not be located. Information comes mostly from Canned Heat manager Skip Taylor, who has shared his recollections of this work Wilson was doing.

According to Taylor, Wilson was appointed to perform a study on how rising levels of pollution would affect plant life on the earth. As part of the study, he was to determine which species would survive if pollution levels continued to rise at then-current rates. By the time he finished the study, Wilson's conclusion was dire: *nothing* could survive the pollution that threatened the natural world.

Skip Taylor says, "I'm not even sure how, but at some level he was credited with the discovery of two new species of trees in the Northwest. I think that led him to where he was doing a study on plant life and vegetation, and how it would cope with environmental problems such as pollution, DDT, and things of that nature, and what species would continue to exist through that. And he came up with an answer: *Nothing* would. And that really depressed him. ... This is a guy who took his sleeping bag and lived outdoors. He would go to Yosemite or Yellowstone, or go to any park he could, on any vacation or off period that the band had."

Wilson's depression, deeply rooted in his own personal issues, had become entwined with his despair over the environment. The result was an obsession that, despite the joy he found in the natural world, did not seem to help his overall mental state. Skip Taylor says, "His whole outlook on society and the environment, pollution and growth of cities, things like that — that's what was really getting to him," says Skip Taylor. "I think he had just locked himself into a kind of tunnel vision, that things were, excuse the word, fucked. And that there was nothing he or anybody else was going to be able to do about it, and he didn't want to be around to see it all. I think that was driving him at that point in his life."

Marina Bokelman recalls, "The sixties was a time when there was a huge collective awakening of environmental awareness. Al felt this very deeply and personally, as if the pain of nature was his own pain. His greatest pain was that the redwoods were becoming extinct, and that this would somehow mean the end of everything. I believe this sense of impending tragedy contributed to his depression and even his death."

14 LIVING THE BLUES

Canned Heat released their third album, *Living the Blues*, in October 1968. Its title was also emblazoned on Henry Vestine's left arm as a tattoo. The album's cover photo was reversed, as one can see by observing Wilson's hair. On the cover, it appears to be parted on the right side, whereas in life he always kept it parted on the left.

The back cover features a photograph of Vestine, in which he appears as a peaceful hippie with a rapturous gaze while the other band members gaze up at him. Both front and back covers were overlaid with psychedelic colors.

The album cover also unfolded to reveal a depiction of the band members, naked, in a stand of trees and bushes. There is no full frontal nudity, as two negatives were overlaid to effectively "clothe" everyone in greenery. Wilson's back is turned to the camera, which he appears to be ignoring in favor of communion with the plants. Bob Hite's back is also turned, but he looks over his shoulder to cast a sly grin toward onlookers. He and Wilson provide the pictures most explicit nudity by turning their backs, thus making their naked buttocks visible to viewers.

The work contained in the album was marked by originality and an increasing willingness to go beyond traditionally accepted blues structures. Another increasingly apparent aspect was the sharp divergence between Wilson's musical vision and the work of the other band members.

Living the Blues was a double album, with the entire second record composed of one extended boogie recorded at a Kaleidoscope club show. Operated by Skip Taylor and John Hartmann as a side project, this club featured Canned Heat as the house band during 1967 and much of 1968. The band had wanted the album to be sold for the price of one record, providing buyers with "forty minutes of free boogie music". The record company balked at this, however, and it ended up being sold for around the standard double album price.

The first record's material consisted entirely of studio work. The songs containing Bob Hite vocals, including "Pony Blues", "Sandy's Blues", "Walking By Myself", and "One Kind Favor", were generally faithful to the band's established sound. "Boogie Music", previously issued as a single, was also included on the album. To the knowledgeable blues fan, the band's traditional sources were fairly obvious. However, their blues were performed in a fresh and invigorated style as opposed to the slavish imitations that characterized some "revivalist" recordings.

"Pony Blues" opened the album. It included elements from diverse prewar blues items; only the lyrics were directly related to Charley Patton's famous song of the same title. Wilson's guitar part was more heavily influenced by two or three obscure songs heard on an Origin Jazz Library album *Alabama Country Blues*. The artists, obscure even in hard-core blues circles, are listed as Ed Bell or "Barefoot Bill".

"Walking By Myself" was a straightforward version of a 1957 hit by Chicago bluesman Jimmy Rogers, and is notable largely for Alan Wilson's harmonica playing. "Sandy's Blues" was based primarily on Elmore James's "It Hurts Me Too", and includes bottleneck guitar by Wilson.

"One Kind Favor" has been recorded by various artists, but is generally associated with Blind Lemon Jefferson (under the name "See That My Grave Is Kept Clean"). This version focuses on Wilson's bottleneck guitar playing, which is dark and intense. When it was time to record the vocal track, Bob Hite turned to his friend Claude McKee for last-minute help.

McKee recalled, "There was one time that they called me up. Canned Heat was in the recording studio, recording a record at three o'clock in the morning. Bob wanted me to go downstairs, dig out a copy of my old 1927 Paramount Blind Lemon Jefferson recording of 'See That My Grave Is Kept Clean', play it, and give them the words over the phone so they could do the part."

Wilson sang two items on *Living the Blues*, as well as providing backup vocals for Bob Hite on "Boogie Music". The first item featuring his voice is "My Mistake", an original song. Like "An Owl Song", it represents a conscious effort by Wilson to use his own vocabulary and manner of speaking while writing lyrics. He would continue to utilize selected blues phrases and lyrics, but did not rely on them solely, and his comments suggest that such lyrics were limited to those that resonated with him personally.

"My Mistake" contains a rather enigmatic storyline. Wilson describes how he thought he had been fooled in some way by a girlfriend, and it made him depressed. Then he realized that she had not actually done anything to let him down. The story becomes vague, as he says that now everything is fine between them, but does not explain how or why he came to understand this.

The song ends on a somewhat positive note, as Wilson says he will cry no more. The song as a whole, however, cannot be said to have an overall feeling of happiness. Rather, it deals with conflicting emotional states. As the title indicates, the main point would seem to be that Wilson recognized his mistake in misjudging the woman. However, more than half of the song concentrates on his state of unhappiness, which is described as a nightmare of listlessness and heartache.

The second Wilson-sung piece of *Living the Blues* is "Going Up the Country". It is totally unique among Wilson's songs, containing an overriding feeling of happiness that is not heard anywhere else in his extant work. Wilson's voice sounds inviting and almost joyous as he sings about leaving the city to go where he's never been before. This was his love of nature, finally expressed through his other love, music.

The music for "Going Up the Country" was based on "Bull Doze Blues", recorded by the Texas songster Henry Thomas in 1928. Thomas had accompanied himself on the guitar and panpipes. In "Going Up the Country", Wilson utilized a flute to achieve a similar effect.

"Bull Doze Blues", the Henry Thomas song, and "Going Up the Country", sound very similar during a cursory listen. Indeed, some commentators have accused Wilson of lifting the Thomas song "note for note". However, the two songs are distinct from one another.

Both songs share a lyrical theme of travel, but use completely different words. They also diverge in that a great deal of Thomas's song is taken up with the panpipes (a total of eight panpipe choruses are played: one as an introduction and one after each verse), while Wilson's use of the flute is much more sparing, including only four flute solo parts. This ended up placing the listener's attention primarily on his unique vocals.

Two different studio versions of "Going Up the Country" exist, varying only in the flute accompaniment. The original flute part had been recorded by Edgar Synigal. However, the sound ended up offending Wilson's sensitive ears. Richard explained, "The flute is slightly out of tune on the original track, the *hit* track. Alan had perfect pitch, and it used to drive him crazy. So he finally got to go in and have the flute part redone."

This time, Wilson contacted multi-instrumentalist Jim Horn, whose experience included tours with Duane Eddy. His extensive studio experience included contributions to sessions with Tina Turner, The Righteous Brothers, and the Mamas and the Papas, as well as flute and saxophone parts for the Beach Boys' acclaimed *Pet Sounds* album.

In addition to replacing the original flute with a more properly tuned instrument, Wilson also wanted to add multiple tracks. Flautist Jim Horn recalls, "Alan asked me to put one flute on, and when I finished I started to put it in my case, and he said, 'Put one more on please.'"

This seemed a little unusual. Horn says, "I was surprised that he was putting more than one flute on the song! Than he asked me to put one more flute on, and I said, 'Are you sure you want three flutes on this song?' He said, 'Yes, I'm going to mix them right, center, and left.'"

Afterward, the original version of "Going Up the Country" became something of a rarity. The version most commonly heard today contains Jim Horn's three flute tracks, which are typically mistaken for a single instrument by radio listeners. With headphones, it becomes easier to discern the three flutes mixed throughout left, right, and center channels as devised by Wilson.

Horn remembers his excitement when "Going Up the Country" became Canned Heat's biggest hit. "I was driving down the freeway a few months later, and heard the flute come on 'Going Up the Country" and really got excited!" he says. "That was my first big hit to play on. I've recorded that song quite a few times on my own records. I'm proud of that song and what it's meant to my career. I was fortunate enough to get to work with Alan 'Blind Owl' Wilson. He had a cool voice!"

Though he didn't spend enough time around Canned Heat to get to know the band members very well, Horn was impressed with Wilson's self-assuredness when it came to music. He comments, "Alan was a very nice guy who knew what he wanted on his songs. He left this earth way too soon."

On *Living the Blues*, most of the second side of the first record was taken up with "Parthenogenesis". This long suite marks the point where the album diverges from the blues forms and instrumental lineups that the band had more or less adhered to on all their work up to this time. It was made up of nine separately executed parts, each with its own title.

The word "parthenogenesis" refers to asexual reproduction, typically of creatures such as bees, ants, and wasps, or, more rarely, some vertebrates. It is unclear what the band members meant to signify with such a title. Perhaps its strangeness represents the peculiarity of the music.

Al of "Parthenogenesis", save for the "Bear Wires" section, is instrumental. "Bear Wires" featured Bob Hite's singing accompanied by an uncredited pianist, actually John Mayall. Other non-Wilson pieces include "Snooky Flowers", a drum solo, and "Sunflower Power", a psychedelic display from Henry Vestine featuring five overdubbed guitars.

However, over half of "Parthenogenesis" consists of pieces composed and performed by Wilson. Most of these were deliberate, coherent non-blues compositions, very different from anything Canned Heat had ever recorded. Four of five could be categorized as ragas. Their progressive nature displayed his independence from the blues-rock idiom.

The inclusion of these items on *Living the Blues* was a bold expansion of the sounds to be heard on Canned Heat's records. However, it wasn't really an expansion of Canned Heat's music or style. Wilson's instrumentals on "Parthenogenesis" were mostly his own, more independently conceived and executed than "On the Road Again" had been.

Four of Wilson's instrumentals on "Parthenogenesis" can be traced back to 1966, when John Fahey had been making promising noises about releasing Wilson's music on his Takoma label. Therefore, these particular pieces had been conceived and recorded prior to Canned Heat's dominance of Wilson's career. From a musicological standpoint they cannot be considered part of the band's work, despite being released on a Canned Heat album. These include "Nebulosity", "Rollin' and Tumblin'" (*not* the same as the blues song already recorded by Canned Heat), "Childhood's End", and "Raga Kafi".

Wilson's only "Parthenogenesis" segment featuring other members of Canned Heat is "Five Owls". This is a harmonica showcase, including the rhythm section along with Wilson multi-tracking four harmonica tracks and one guitar. The harmonica used here was retuned in the same manner as the "On the Road Again" harmonica.

"Nebulosity", "Rollin' and Tumblin'", and "Childhood's End" were performed by Wilson on a jaw-harp whose sound was run through an echo chamber. This relatively ignored instrument is rarely used in blues or rock, and when it is heard, it is generally used as something of a "sound effect" to lend a twangy accent to a song. Wilson, however, uses the jaw-harp as a real instrument. He was likely inspired by classical Indian music, where twanginess is better utilized and the jaw-harp has a long history of serious use.

"Raga Kafi" is a raga performed on the chromatic harmonica. (There are actually two multi-tracked harmonica parts; one consists simply of a one-note drone.) It too was recorded for John Fahey in 1966, and the piece appearing on *Living the Blues* is but a portion of the entire raga. More can be heard as "Fear & Loathing at 4th & Butternut", released on John Fahey's 1992 album *Old Girl Friends and Other Horrible Memories*. On this album, Fahey does not credit Wilson for the song, but excused himself by saying, "I didn't think Wilson would mind."

"Raga Kafi" is the only example of Wilson's chromatic harmonica playing on any Canned Heat record. While he did play it in a blues context in their live shows, he appears to have stopped doing so for the most part after 1967, and never played it on any known Canned Heat studio recordings. Wilson's expertise on this instrument is, then, sadly under-documented. His utilization of it on blues items was, of course, quite good, but his chromatic harmonica ragas were unusual and therefore musically exciting.

The second record of the *Living the Blues* double album was recorded live, during a show at the Kaleidoscope club in Los Angeles. Alan Wilson had wanted to record live for some time. He felt that their studio sound, which now involved a great deal of overdubbing, was so different from their live sound that the band's entire personality would not be captured on album until they recorded live.

Somewhat dramatically, Wilson said, "I think we're going to become a dual-level schizophrenic band. Our live and record [styles] are going to become increasingly divergent. Unless we go all the way, and record live."

The other band members were also interested in recording live. Henry Vestine said, "Playing live is much better than recording. I guess there's no band that you really hear what they sound like on record, unless that's what they happen to be into. With a band where there's a lot of improvisation, it doesn't happen that way in the studio. It's much better to hear the band live somewhere, and it's more fun for the musicians, too. There you are in the studio with, you know, the lights and really a lot of pressure. It's really a bad scene."

Prior to the release of *Living the Blues*, bassist Larry Taylor commented on performing live versus recording: "Well, I like both of it; just two different things. I think as far as recording goes, this band has yet to get what it wants in the studio. But we will get it. ... I guess everybody's just got to get used to recording and playing in the studio because it's a whole different feeling when you go in there."

At last, Canned Heat's live personality would come through on *Living the Blues*. The live recording, "Refried Boogie", was one prolonged song which took up both sides of the second record. The band members had originally wanted to call the piece "Live: The Real Shit", according to Richard Hite; however, this met with some resistance from the record company.

"Refried Boogie" included some conventional song parts with vocals by Bob Hite, but it was composed primarily of long solos from the other members of the band. Such free-form jamming has sometimes been called self-indulgent, but on the other hand, many listeners have admired it. At the time Canned Heat recorded this long boogie in 1968, such extension of songs into solo showcases was a relatively new phenomenon in rock and roll. Eventually, this kind of thing became commercially successful through bands such as the Allman Brothers Band, the Grateful Dead and their many offshoots (most notably Furthur and Ratdog), as well as legions of other "jam bands" as they are now called.

Vestine's solo on "Refried Boogie" is exciting, but in live performance, there was an issue for some listeners: the music was so very loud. In 1968, Vestine admitted, "I'm really as much into playing the amp now as playing the guitar."

Recently, the band had been sponsored by an amplifier company, encouraging them to crank up the volume even more. Richard Hite remembers, "For a while there, the band was real, *real* loud. Henry used to play just *so* loud. At one point, he had eight speaker cabinets with two fifteen-inch speakers per cabinet. ... I remember a gig that they played that my parents and I came to see. I don't know how my parents made it through it. My ears, two days, were just completely ... I don't know how my parents sat through it."

Skip Taylor says, "Henry got into what they call playing the amplifier. Playing the speakers, where he could hit a note, turn around toward the speaker and get it to feed back, and then just sustain and play it, bending the string more, moving the guitar to get it to change frequencies. He would go and do solos like that for ten or fifteen minutes. The psychedelic era — that's what it was all about. Guitar players playing their feedback."

Wilson didn't like the volume necessary to produce Vestine's style. He was extremely worried about his hearing, and was still wearing earplugs as protection against the onslaught of sound. Originally, he had been attracted to Vestine's Telecaster style which was not as loud or psychedelic. This new tendency to "freak out" with ear-shattering, chaotic solos had Wilson rather bemused, but he wanted to support Vestine's artistic direction, and commented in April 1968, "We freak out generally once a set. This is various impulses within the band. Particularly Henry has urges that he did not have a year ago, in this direction. So, everybody's accommodated."

Not all Canned Heat fans enjoyed the psychedelic sound. Mainstream rock fans usually appreciated it, but the blues enthusiasts who had been the band's original audience often didn't find it as appealing. One of these was Roger Handy, who had been listening since the early days. "At the Ash Grove, really what they had in the audience was a lot of purists, who liked the electric sound but not like the Who or something," he said. "I remember the audience back then was really wishing that Vestine wouldn't have done all that [psychedelic] stuff. I heard comments ranging from 'selling out', to that it was just kind of hackneyed — kind of an attempt to sort of wow or coo the audience that was being brought along by Hendrix and everybody else. ... That Vestine kind of stuff always threw me, and I really did not like it at all, actually."

Vestine, for his part, didn't think there was any conflict with his playing and the more traditional blues-rock style typical of Canned Heat. And while Wilson did not find prolonged, disorderly solos to be in keeping with his personal musical inclinations, he did not tend to criticize Vestine's choice of musical expression.

Wilson came close to overt criticism of the psychedelic style in one conversation with Marina Bokelman, commenting, "I like a freakout of it has some tie to the song's framework. I think the Cream's version of 'Rollin' and Tumblin'' does not qualify there. They play the thirty-three measure thing a few times and then just stop, and start droning, and roaring. And then at the end they come back. So that doesn't sound too integrated to me. It sounds like two different songs."

"Refried Boogie" features two guitar solos from Alan Wilson; one serves as the lengthy introduction to the boogie. These are typical Wilson solos, in that his guitar style was somewhat primitive and was not based upon the single-string lead guitar style exemplified by B. B. King and blended with psychedelia by Henry Vestine, Eric Clapton, and the like. Wilson's non-bottleneck style was based upon the darkly profound technique of John Lee Hooker, but was far more intricate and agile.

Bob Hite commented on Wilson's guitar playing: "He definitely gets his roots out of Mississippi. Alan reads, eats, and thinks Mississippi. It just sticks out all over him when he plays guitar."

While Wilson's playing was inspired by the work of older bluesmen, he used the style in an original way, by virtue of its integration into the Canned Heat lineup. "I correspond on rhythm guitar to the old stuff only in the sense that's where I get my stuff from," he explained. "We [Henry and Wilson] correspond to like, different delineations from other generations. Just different delineations."

WIlson's favorite electric guitar was a 1954 Gibson Les Paul. He preferred to play in open tuning, and when he worked in standard tuning nearly always altered it to suit his own tastes. Richard Hite said, "He couldn't play in standard tuning very well. He always preferred open tuning. 'Big Road Blues' is actually in standard tuning, but the low E string is dropped down to a D. That's about as close to standard tuning as he ever got."

Wilson's favorite tuning was open G. "That was the same tuning as, like, John Lee Hooker and things like that," said Richard Hite. "That was the key he seemed to like the most. He would capo, quite a bit. ... He usually used a glass bottle slide. I saw him use chrome too. He used to always make his own capos though. It was funny; he would take a pencil and rubber bands; that's how he'd make a capo. He wouldn't use one of those newfangled things." (Actually, Wilson was documented using a commercially made capo while onstage, presumably for greater ease in changing its position on the guitar between songs.)

Wilson didn't resort to posturing with feedback and bizarre sound effects, nor did he play a large number of notes. Instead, he chose to play in his distinctive, archaic manner, which, although not notable as a style of lead guitar playing, was refreshing in the face of the hysterical electronic shrieks and squeals that consumed so many guitarists of his day.

In fall 1968, Alan Wilson visited Mike Perlowin, who had been Canned Heat's first lead guitarist for a brief period. This would be the last time the two saw each other.

Perlowin had noted the surprising popularity of "On the Road Again", and found it ironic that Wilson had the band's big hit when Bob Hite was the usual lead singer. He remembers, "I expressed some concern about, how does Bob feel, as the lead singer, not to be on the hit record? I thought that was a pretty strange thing. And Alan agreed. He said, 'Bob's taking it pretty well.' And then he said, 'I'm singing on the *next* one, too!' And I thought, 'Oh God, poor Bob.'

Basically we were talking about Bob's feeling about not having been on the hit record."

By "the next one", Wilson was referring to "Going Up the Country", which was released as a single in September (backed with "One Kind Favor"). It was an even bigger hit than "On the Road Again", and quickly became *the* song associated with Canned Heat. Nowadays, it is still their best known work. It has been licensed by a wide variety of corporations for commercial uses, and utilized in movie soundtracks, throughout the years; it is still popular for these purposes today.

"Going Up the Country" stayed on the *Billboard* singles charts for eleven weeks, peaking at #11. Its popularity might have been partly due to the lyrics, which were composed partially of traditional blues phrases, but also seemed to reflect the "back-to-nature" attitude that so many young Americans were adopting at the time. Since Wilson himself was an ardent devotee of nature, it seems appropriate that his most famous song expressed this.

The bulk of the band's material was, of course, sung by Bob Hite. Onstage, he was clearly the main man. Singles buyers and radio listeners, however, heard Alan Wilson as the voice of Canned Heat. There was clearly a slight incongruity, if not an outright conflict, between the popular recorded sound of the band as perceived through Wilson's hit songs, and the band's live image, which was based largely on Hite's friendly, outgoing presence.

Hite usually had little or nothing to do with the creation of Wilson's songs. He didn't even like the Henry Thomas record that Wilson had used as the musical base for "Going Up the Country". His friend Claude McKee reveals, "The 'Going Up the Country' thing, Bob didn't like that tune. It was actually a Ragtime Henry Thomas tune. And I played the original record for Alan and Bob didn't like it; he thought it was a piece of shit. But Alan wanted to record it. And consequently we all know what happened to 'Going Up the Country'."

Alan Wilson was more of an artist, whereas Bob Hite was more of an entertainer. His old friend David Evans contrasts his behavior with the extroversion of other music stars: "You had guys like Jim Morrison, very flamboyant people out there. Or Bob Hite in Canned Heat — he was just opposite of Al. Those were the people that had success with the [live] audiences. Al, I think significantly, had success through *recordings*. You'd hear him and you'd have no idea what he looked like or what he was like onstage... and then when he did get onstage, you had the group to sort of diffuse his, ah, lack of charisma."

Indeed, somebody in the band had to put on a show, for Wilson certainly wasn't going to. He usually appeared very serious onstage, and wasn't about to project a media- or audience-friendly image. To him, that would have seemed artificial and contrived. Therefore, a great deal of Canned Heat's success was due to the presence of Bob Hite. He enjoyed being onstage, creating a party atmosphere for the show just as he did at home for friends around the record player.

Wilson was so shy that he rarely acknowledged the audience while onstage. Usually, he stood almost perfectly still, often keeping his eyes closed against the glare of the spotlights and the stare of the audience. While performing, he typically directed eye contact only at Hite, Vestine, or the rhythm section as part of a musical cue. Occasionally he can be seen on film directing brief glances in the direction of the audience; however, these would likely have been blurred and out of focus from his perspective, as he seldom wore corrective eyeglasses onstage.

Wilson's onstage introversion contrasted starkly with the other members of Canned Heat. Barry Hansen, who saw a variety of Canned Heat performances throughout the years, comments, "Bob was very dynamic; he would stomp around on the stage and holler and flail his arms while he sang, and he was a big man. Henry could be quite animated when he played; he'd kind of bend over at the waist and bend up and down and look real involved, in a physical and dynamic way, with what he was playing. Larry Taylor moved around quite a bit. But Alan, whatever he was doing, he stood stock still. He hardly moved a muscle, except what it took to sing or play. It was just like, he was just there in his world. It was not in his makeup to move around in the way that rock musicians are expected to."

Wilson simply did not consider himself a performer; rather, he approached his art more as a classical composer might. No doubt he wished that his audiences would quiet down and learn to listen with "respect and discipline", as sitar master Ravi Shankar once suggested. We may presume that Wilson did not care for the noise and rowdiness of rock audiences, and might have felt more at home playing for classical listeners. Wilson's perception of himself as a serious composer went so far that, while planning arrangements, he often referred to Canned Heat as "the orchestra".

Alan Wilson was a musical genius, but as with many artists, his brilliance did not extend to marketing. Without promotion and publicity, and a good dose of the "hype" usually required to hook record buyers, his music would have been relegated to the cult-following status of someone like John Fahey or Leo Kottke.

Canned Heat's commercial success relied on the team of Alan Wilson and Bob Hite, who contributed different abilities to the group. Skip Taylor was at the helm, steering them through the world of rock with his management and promotion skills. He remembers, "I think Alan, in his own quiet way, realized that without him there wouldn't be Canned Heat. And yet, in my management business mind, without Bob there wasn't Canned heat. Even though I knew Alan was the creative force of the band, for the most part, Bob was still capable of coming up with old blues songs and redoing them or finding some kind of a hook in something that would work in today's market. And he was the front guy and was looked upon as Canned Heat. But the two of them together was Canned Heat."

Wilson provided Canned Heat with precision and expertise. Bob Hite was the showman. David Evans recalls, "Bob Hite did most of the singing, partly because he was aggressive and wanted to. He was a big guy with a big voice. Bob was very competitive, but I think he knew he needed Alan. It was really Alan's concept, talent, and ability to play that music. And Bob could not sing in that style. Bob would sort of bellow. I think he respected Alan as a musician, and knew that Alan was unique and crucial, and probably also knew that Alan needed somebody like himself, to get out there and bellow and move around to put on something of an act. Alan would have been hopeless in that role. But without Alan, Bob would have been just some bellowing guy."

Another Canned Heat single issued around this time was the quirky "Chipmunk Song", backed with "Christmas Blues". These were recorded with fellow Liberty Records artists "The Chipmunks". Though some modern references cite this single's release date as 1969, *Billboard* magazine lists it among the "Best Bets for Christmas" in their December 1968 charts.

Originally created in 1958 by Ross Bagdasarian, Sr., the Chipmunks were actually a fictional, animated singing group whose singing consisted of electronically sped-up vocals. This was designed to resemble the chattering of chipmunks. The group would be featured in comic books and cartoons, as well as on records. The main characters were named "Alvin, Simon, and Theodore", after three Liberty Records executives.

Canned Heat's work with the Chipmunks has often been dismissed as a novelty seasonal item. However, according to his friend Barry Hansen, Alan Wilson found the production process quite fascinating. Hansen would later report that Wilson telephoned him after the session, excited and wanting to share the experience.

Specifically, Wilson was intrigued by the way that Chipmunks creator Bagdasarian produced the high-pitched "chipmunk" vocal effect. This was done by initially recording the characters' voices at a normal speed, with subtle alterations to certain vowels and consonants so they would remain intelligible. The vocals were then sped up to the high-pitched "chipmunk" sound.

Though the idea of the Chipmunks now seems silly to some music fans who consider themselves too mature for fictional pop bands, Wilson appreciated the concept. Through this novelty, he perceived the effective use of recording technology. This, along with his interest in the ability to overdub different instruments, would surely have led to fascinating new sounds of his own, had he been given more time and the luxury to further explore the resources of the recording studio.

In February 1969, Liberty released one of Alan Wilson's new songs, "Time Was", as a single. It was backed with "Low Down", sung by Bob Hite. This single's reception would not even approach the success of "On the Road Again" or "Going Up the Country". It peaked at #67 in the *Billboard* singles charts, and was Wilson's last single to appear on the Hot 100 list.

Why "Time Was" didn't follow in the popular footsteps of Wilson's previous singles is uncertain; it is every bit as fine as his other songs. It was, however (and perhaps notably) the first of his singles to fall within the musical framework of Canned Heat itself. It was the first to feature Henry Vestine's lead guitar work, which is quite outstanding here. Free of psychedelic trappings, it is sensitive and beautiful, leading luminaries such as John Fahey to cite "Time Was" as a favorite Canned Heat song.

The lyrics of "Time Was" deal with conflicting emotional states. At first listen, Wilson's words, which discuss a once happy relationship now troubled by conflicts, might appear to be about some romantic situation. It is, however, equally possible that he was referring to disagreements within Canned Heat.

Wilson's words reveal simultaneous disappointment and optimism, or at least hope. The message as a whole is enigmatic, and the exact reason for his hope or optimism is never revealed. His words do not exclude the possibility that he was considering leaving Canned Heat.

After Alan Wilson's death, Bob Hite confided in John Fahey about some of the band's internal issues. Among other things, he revealed that Wilson had been wanting to leave Canned Heat for some time. This led Fahey to hear "Time Was" with a new perspective. In later years, he would theorize that the song was a premonition on Wilson's part, referring to the band's career after his death and the long-term public embrace of his songs that would occur. This, however, was pure speculation from Fahey. While interesting, it may or may not have any relation to Wilson's original meaning behind the song.

15 BLIND OWL BEHIND THE WHEEL

In 1969, Alan Wilson reached a turning point in his adult life. In high school, he hadn't experienced the traditional milestone of getting a driver's license, and never bothered to do so in his early twenties. However, the idea of being able to drive places on his own was becoming more appealing. Around the age of 26, he got a license from the state of California, in a step that would change his life.

The end goal of having the driver's license was so that Wilson could drive his new van, which would double as his home. His van — or more accurately, vans, as we shall learn — became a major factor in his lifestyle, and the tales that grew up around his adventures in the van are an integral part of his legend. (Neither of Wilson's two vans should be confused with the so-called "Canned Heat Boogie Bus", a communally owned Volkswagen used for touring in the band's early days.)

The first van was a white Volkswagen, and was said to have some kind of expandable top, containing a bed and possibly even a stove. Barry Hansen remembers the vehicle: "A Volkswagen; it was definitely new. It had something built at the top to make it taller. I remember seeing that. Like some customized thing you could get that made it taller, and made a space at the top."

Bob Hite reportedly gave Wilson this van for his birthday, probably in 1969. According to John Fahey, "Bob told me that he bought it for Al, and gave it to him on Al's birthday." This seems a thoughtful gift, perfectly suited to Wilson's love of nature, as it would provide transportation as well as shelter for camping expeditions.

There was just one problem. Hite didn't realize that Alan had no idea how to operate this new gift. Fahey remembered, "Wilson said, 'Well, I don't even know how to drive; what did you get me that for?' And Hite said, 'Well, I'll teach you how to drive, Al.'"

With help from Hite and the other members of Canned Heat, Wilson soon learned to drive — or, more accurately, to get the van down the road in one piece. He was not a particularly good driver, but managed to pass the state test and obtain his driver's license.

With this, Wilson began enjoying a newfound mobility. Now he could drive to the forest at every opportunity, and camp whenever the band's schedule allowed. His leaf and pinecone collections grew as he took more expeditions into the wild.

At this point, Wilson moved permanently out of the house in Venice that he had shared with Mike Turner. "When he moved out of the house that we lived in, he bought this van," says Turner. "He just lived in his van, basically, and had all his stuff in there. I kind of still kept in touch with him through 1969. I forget the name of the studio where they recorded; it was right there on Santa Monica Boulevard. He'd record and then he'd come down and park his van at my house and stay."

When he had time to get away from Los Angeles, Wilson usually went camping. He always had botany books with him, and carefully identified the flora he saw. Collecting samples, he organized his treasures in plastic bags and labeled each bag with the scientific name of its contents. "I went camping with him to Yosemite a couple of times," says Turner. "With his tree book, he was totally self-taught. He'd just try to do it by going up to each tree and finding out what it was by the pictures in the book."

On one occasion, winter was approaching, but it didn't stop Wilson from going alone to the Sequoia National Forest. When he drove down a dirt road that was too much for his van to handle, he got stuck, and remained stranded until a ranger stopped by and rescued him.

Turner remembers hearing about this adventure: "He went up there by himself once to Sequoia and almost got stuck up there. I guess he took his van on the back road and got stuck. The only ranger that happened by wasn't supposed to be out there, but he was making his last patrol before the winter started."

No matter what season it was, Wilson always wanted to go camping, and the van gave him a freedom he had never experienced before. He had no interest in buying a house or otherwise "settling down" with his newfound means. "He never had a home, not while I was around," recalled band manager Skip Taylor. "He just didn't want to; he didn't care about it. Whenever he wasn't on the road, he would jump in the van and go. Go to some woods, mountains, somewhere. And when we were in L.A., rehearsing or recording, then he would stay behind Bob's house, up on the hill."

Alan Wilson's van was a fine home for him — when it wasn't moving. When he was driving it down the road, the situation occasionally became dangerous.

Wilson's driving skills had been acquired from a few informal lessons with Bob Hite and the other members of Canned Heat. The value of such lessons could likely be debated. It's easy to imagine a half-blind, spaced-out Wilson at the wheel and the rest of the band hanging out in the rear, enjoying a party led by Hite as was wont to happen. Such a situation wouldn't have led to maximal capabilities on Wilson's part.

Tales of Wilson's driving lessons would be retold in various guises. The most spectacular, amounting to quite possibly the strangest Alan Wilson legend ever, claims that Wilson attempted to kill himself and the rest of the band using the van. He is said to have done this by trying to drive the van over a cliff while they were all inside. The other band members supposedly gained control of the wheel before it went over, thus averting the attempt.

This version of the story was told to Mike Perlowin by Bob Hite. "I only know what Bob told me," explained Perlowin. "Bob told me that he tried to take the whole band with him. When he tried to kill the whole band, he was driving, and he attempted to drive over a cliff. They wrestled the wheel away from him, according to Bob, and forced him back on the road."

This particular story can be traced only to Mike Perlowin; if Bob told such a story to anyone else, it has not come to light. This author has been unable to locate any living associate of Wilson who claims to have been in the van at the time. Drummer Adolfo de la Parra does not document any such incident in his published memoirs, though he has recalled being told of a crash that happened while Wilson was driving alone.

The tale told to Mike Perlowin seems most unfitting, for it is quite difficult to imagine that a compassionate person such as Alan Wilson would have wanted to murder his fellow band members as part of a suicide. He is never remembered as being physically violent or malicious in any way. Ergo, this story is quite bizarre and does not fit with what we know about Wilson.

It is, however, certainly easy to imagine Wilson crashing accidentally in his van, especially during driving lessons when his skills were minimal. His visual impairment combined with absentmindedness made him a poor driver, and he might have found it difficult to concentrate on the road. He could have become preoccupied with musical thoughts, or perhaps a bit of attractive vegetation by the roadside.

"He [Wilson] was blind as a bat," Perlowin admits. "One of the things that struck me was that he couldn't drive when I knew him, and I was very surprised when Bob told he he'd tried to kill the band by driving the van, because I hadn't known he was able to drive. He wore really thick glasses."

It is possible that a near-miss happened due to Wilson's lack of skill, later to be joked about by Bob Hite. Hite apparently said something to the effect that Wilson had been trying to kill them all;; however, it is possible that this was in jest. Such a joke might have been taken seriously by Perlowin, whose misconception was never corrected by Hite. It is also possible that Perlowin, of whom Hite was not fond, had been deliberately misled as a prank.

Bill Givens, a friend from earlier days, remembers a story about Wilson's bad driving being repeated publicly to great amusement. Interestingly, this story did not involve a suicide attempt, but focused more on the humor involved in Wilson's driving lessons. Givens recalled, "It was told in front of a lot of people at the old Jazz Man record center, which was a hangout for many people. I got it second-hand, and the people were cracking up even though they heard the story second-hand."

A more frequently heard variation on this story is that Wilson wrecked his van deliberately while driving alone. This seems a less unlikely story, although it is also strange, given that suicide by auto would not be a very reliable mechanism to ensure one's death. Wilson could not have been certain of his death in an auto wreck unless he had driven over a tall cliff, say, or directly into the path of an oncoming vehicle at high speed. Even then, he could have faced the disagreeable possibility of becoming maimed or paralyzed in such an attempt.

Wilson was intelligent enough to consider such factors, even if his mind was addled by depression. If any van wreck was indeed a suicide attempt, one must therefore question Wilson's sincerity, or perhaps his lucidity. It is also possible that Wilson wrecked his van through accident or carelessness, then passed the incident off as a suicide attempt in a "cry for help" — or as a last-ditch effort to get out of his responsibilities with Canned Heat.

John Fahey remembers hearing this story from Bob Hite. He said, "Hite told me he [Wilson] tried running his camper off the side of the road and stuff like that."

Richard Hite was told a similar story by his brother. He recalled that Wilson had two van accidents, both while he was driving alone, one of which was said to be a suicide attempt.

In his 2000 autobiography, *Living the Blues*, Canned Heat drummer Adolfo de la Parra wrote about Wilson's van wreck. He recalls that Canned Heat manager Skip Taylor informed the other band members that Wilson had crashed deliberately, and was subsequently incarcerated in a mental hospital. However, Wilson himself apparently did not make any statement of his intent to his band mates.

The confusion only mounts further, as Skip Taylor's personal recollection varies from the account given in de la Parra's memoir. In a 1997 interview with this author, Taylor did not remember Wilson's van wreck as a suicide attempt. "I don't recall that at all," said Taylor. "I remember him having an accident in the van; I don't remember him doing it purposely. I remember him getting it fixed. He was not a good driver. The fact that he got a driver's license was *amazing*. Because of his eyesight, and he was just a spacey guy. ... I think he was too smart to try to commit suicide that way. I don't think that would be the way he would choose at all. I have no recollection of that ever being a suicide attempt."

Skip Taylor also commented, "Him getting a driver's license was an event. I helped him get his license but I didn't want to be on the road once he got it! He was not the greatest driver. He had his corrective lenses and all, but he still *was* the Blind Owl. And he also was very spacey. To the point that his mind was on anything but driving. I mean, when he was driving he was the only one on the road, as far as he was concerned!"

It is entirely possible that Wilson told one story to some people and another story to others, perhaps wavering in his claim that the van incident had been a suicide attempt. It is ultimately impossible to determine what actually caused him to crash, and whether or not it was purposeful. It is well established, however, that he did have at least one wreck in his van, and it is possible that there were two separate wrecks.

Richard Hite said, "I believe the first time he wrecked the van, he was trying to commit suicide or whatever like that, and didn't make it. And then there was a second accident — I think. I'm not really sure on that."

At some point, probably in early 1970, Alan Wilson would acquire a second van (presumably dispensing of his first one, or perhaps trading it in). The second van was a 1970 green Ford

Econoline. It may have also been equipped for camping like his first vehicle, and was, likewise, a home for Wilson. Richard Hite had a vague recollection of Alan being in a wreck with this van, and having it repaired or replaced. This, then, might have been the second of two wrecks Wilson experienced with his vans.

Wilson didn't die on the road in his van, but he was injured in one of the wrecks, perhaps more than anyone realized at first. Bob Hite's best friend, Claude McKee, saw Wilson around the Hite household frequently. He reports that Wilson had actually rolled the van, and that afterward, he was troubled by severe, chronic headaches. According to McKee, this also affected Wilson's drug usage.

"Basically, Alan was mainly into pot," said McKee. "Until, it was after he rolled the van in Topanga Canyon that he actually started using uppers and downers and things of that nature. After he rolled the van over the side of the embankment in Topanga Canyon, he was bothered by extremely bad headaches."

Unfortunately, Claude McKee died before he could be interviewed extensively, and Wilson was apparently silent for the most part about the increasing physical pain in his life. "Alan didn't talk much about it," said McKee.

Wilson apparently also chose not to seek medical attention for his headaches, but chose instead to treat his symptoms with illicitly obtained barbiturates. It was a decision that might have ended up costing him his life.

Alan Wilson had been unable, or perhaps not entirely willing, to end his life in an auto wreck. There were other ways to take his own life, however, and Wilson was exploring such options during the summer of 1969.

To resolve his insomnia, and now to kill the pain of what might have been a concussion, Wilson had begun using barbiturates or "reds" as they were casually known. Now, he began buying extra stashes, hoarding them as a possible means of suicide.

Skip Taylor has recalled that Wilson twice attempted to kill himself by ingesting a combination of barbiturates and alcohol, specifically gin. He was said to have done this in Bob Hite's backyard, and was discovered unconscious but still alive by Bob or his wife Verlie. Richard Hite has also recalled hearing of such an incident.

Taylor says, "He had two other overdoses before he died. Barbiturates and alcohol combo. At that point we actually helped him get into a hospital ... I think he was in the hospital twice or three times. I think some of it was voluntary ... I remember going to court, but I don't remember what had to be done. We did go to court; Bob and I went to court. I can't tell you really now what happened. But I do know that it wasn't totally voluntary. And yet it wasn't taking him away in the white jacket and cuffs or anything either. There was some middle ground there."

To Taylor, Wilson never actually stated that he intended to take his own life. "In Alan's kind of way," Taylor recalls, "it was sort of like, 'Well, I just wanted to see how far I could go,' or, 'I just wanted to lose myself.' He wouldn't say he wanted to kill himself. He never said that."

In his published memoirs, however, Canned Heat drummer Adolfo de la Parra says that Wilson did confess suicide plans to his fellow band members. According to de la Parra, Wilson said that he had been hoarding barbiturates to kill himself, but lost them in a stoned or drunk fugue, much to his annoyance.

Whether or not he would admit to attempting suicide, Wilson realized to some extent that he was mentally unwell. Skip Taylor says, "I think he knew he needed help, and he would go through different periods where he was willing to get help, and then he wasn't. And that's why I think we finally went, 'Well, you're going to get help.' That's when the court was needed to step in. It kind of fell on either Bob or myself's shoulders. I can't tell you how it all came down — I don't remember."

According to Taylor's remaining memories, Wilson didn't try to escape or actively resist commitment, yet he wasn't totally agreeable. "We had him committed," says Taylor. "We signed papers, like two or three of us together, and took him. He wasn't fighting it; he sort of knew he needed it. You know, and thought maybe it could help, or else he was playing a game as a lot of people do at that point in their life. If once you've got to that stage it's a matter of, 'Well, I'll go along with the program, but ... I can con my way out of this too.' So, I mean, he didn't go willingly. Let's say that. I mean, we did have to in fact, in quotes, commit him."

Richard Hite commented, "You'd have just said to Alan that this was what he had to do, and it's for your own good. He probably would have gone along with it. He was a follower. I don't think it was against his will; I think after the first attempted suicide, maybe it was something he was willing to try to get help for."

Little is known of Wilson's experiences in the hospital during the summer of 1969, except that he spent some time composing a song about his latest natural fascination, the moon. Apparently he was cooperative with whatever mental health program he was required to undergo, as he was soon scheduled for release.

Richard Hite has recalled that according to be released, Wilson had to be put in somebody's care. Apparently he had at some level been deemed incompetent due to a confession of suicidal feelings. Upon his release, he was turned over to Bob Hite, who signed papers promising to look after him. Wilson was now in Hite's custody.

According to Richard Hite, the legal custody agreement, which was apparently temporary, didn't really change much about his brother's relationship with Wilson. In practice, it meant that Wilson would continue to sleep in Bob's backyard, and Bob would continue reminding him when it was time to take a bath or wash his clothes.

Richard remembered, "He would live, hang out, at my brother's house, basically. When you say take care of him, it's basically, 'Alan, you know, how about a bath? Are your clothes clean? You know, *wash*.' I mean, all that kind of stuff. You basically had to lead him around."

Though Wilson was around the Hite household a lot, he spoke little about his problems, or his hospital experience. "He never said anything to me about it," said Richard. "He just seemed like Alan afterwards. There was no difference, no big marked change or anything. Just Alan. ... He was pretty withdrawn, though, in that period."

It is uncertain what, if any, effect his hospital stay had on Wilson's mental health. "I do know he seemed better," recalled Skip Taylor, "and I do know that it appeared not only to me but to the doctors and other people that had control of the issue that he was well enough to be released. So that there was thought to have been progress. Otherwise they wouldn't have released him."

Wilson's introversion, however, made it hard to tell if he was depressed or just quiet. "It was hard to get Alan to smile or laugh," said Taylor. "Very serious *all* the time. So you didn't know whether it was just him being serious or being depressed. It was a fine line there. And I think it was even similar after he got out. But by all clinical criteria, they thought he was well enough to be out."

In the hospital, Alan Wilson had written a new song, entitled "Poor Moon". It was recorded on July 2, 1969. One report suggests that Wilson was actually still committed at the time, and had been temporarily released from the hospital for a daytime recording session.

As with "On the Road Again", "Poor Moon" is not a musical reflection of Canned Heat proper. It is, rather, a highly individualistic expression from Alan Wilson. Henry Vestine is entirely absent, and it is likely that the rhythm section was directed by Wilson in their arrangement, as with "On the Road Again". The music was heavily influenced by Charley Patton's 1929 recording of "Jesus Is A Dying-Bed Maker", which included Patton's wife Bertha Lee on backing vocals.

"Poor Moon" is unique among Wilson's songs because it features multi-tracked vocals. Wilson sings lead as well as multiple background parts, which are primarily wordless syllables. The only actual words sung in the backing vocal parts consist of the phrase "oh well", placed between some of the lead vocal lines.

"Poor Moon" illustrates Wilson's growing awareness of himself as a singer. Had he lacked confidence in his role as a vocalist, he surely never would have recorded this song which makes his unusual voice so conspicuous. The multiple vocal parts provide the feeling of being surrounded by his voice, an eerie effect. His singing is the focus of the song; there are no instrumental solos, no flashy guitar or harmonica parts. None are needed.

The subject of "Poor Moon" is, as the title suggests, the moon. Wilson had developed fears that the moon, like the earth, would be defaced and polluted by humankind's industrial activities. He was extremely disturbed by thoughts of the upcoming moon landing, fearing that the moon's beauty would be lost forever to "progress" and technological tampering.

Wilson's attachment to the moon was intense. One acquaintance recalled his distress after viewing a well-known Georges Méliès image from 1902, featuring the moon with a fanciful face and a rocket ship embedded in one eye. This image, part of the silent science fiction film "A Trip to the Moon", might have escalated Wilson's distress as he faced the prospect of an actual moon landing in 1969. "Poor Moon" became his expression for these feelings.

Interestingly, Wilson uses the word "moon" only in the song's title; it never appears in the actual lyrics. Instead, he gives the song a startling perspective by addressing the moon itself with his words, wondering when "your face" will be destroyed. The personification in this song conveys passionate feelings about the moon, with words of evocative power.

"Poor Moon" was released as a single, backed with "Sic 'Em Pigs" from the *Hallelujah* album. It hit record stores on July 15, the day before the launch of the first manned American space rocket to the moon. On July 20, astronauts walked on the lunar surface, much to Wilson's horror.

Nobody around him could quite understand why Wilson was so upset about the moon. Record buyers suffered form the same lack of comprehension, with the unusual sound and subject matter of "Poor Moon" proving too much for the average fan. The single never even made *Billboard*'s Hot 100. This was no doubt disappointing to Wilson, who put much of himself into the song. The failure of "Time Was", followed by this, might have also marked a turning point in his relationship with the band.

A few enlightened listeners appreciated "Poor Moon". Barry Hansen remembers the development of Alan Wilson's songs: "The fact that he had the first hit, 'On the Road Again', meant that he was given pretty free rein in doing more concepts with the band, at least for a while. I mean, he had crafted that hit virtually on his own. And that had been the biggest thing the band ever had, so of course when he thought, 'Let's do this,' people listened. So, after 'On the Road Again' and 'Going Up the Country', the next one after that was called 'Time Was', and that didn't do as well. And then, Alan wrote a song called 'Poor Moon'. That went absolutely nowhere. Radio was not ready to play that record. And I loved it. It ties in with an ecological concern. ... I hadn't seen him for a little while before that, and the record just came out and I bought it, and just went, 'Wow. That's far out.'"

Skip Taylor remembers, "During the stay in the hospital, he wrote 'Poor Moon'. And we brought him out; he came out of the hospital to record that. His whole thing was just, you know, what will they do to the moon someday? It was so off the wall, I actually thought it could have been a hit. The record company looked at me like I was stone crazy. But I liked the combination; the beat was totally weird. And just the phrasing and stuff. I thought it was a neat record; I really did. And a really great commentary on the state of affairs of the world. He was looking at L.A. in those days, when he was coming out of the hospital — it was like under a smog alert. ... I think it's so distinctive, and really is such a culmination of the way he evolved, and his style, his writing and thinking. It's just a really pertinent kind of song."

Many years after Alan Wilson's death, "Poor Moon" would finally start receiving some popular recognition. The band Blues 'N' Trouble would record a cover version, and name their CD after it, in 1995. In 2008, musicians Christian Wargo, Casey Wescott, and brothers Ian and Peter Murray formed a band named Poor Moon after the song. Based in Seattle, they currently record for Sub Pop Records and perform frequently. Another band, Hiss Golden Messenger, named a 2011 album *Poor Moon* after Wilson's song.

Shortly after getting out of the hospital, Alan Wilson decided to make some changes. His possessions, mostly consisting of leaves, pinecones, books, and records, were outgrowing the storage space in his van, and it was time to find a new place to keep these items.

Wilson had also collected a number of stuffed owls; some were children's toys made of plush and others were actual owls that had been stuffed and mounted. One favorite, a great horned owl with wings outstretched, had been acquired from record collector Steve LaVere. For months, Wilson had seen the owl on display at LaVere's house, and frequently pestered LaVere about the possibility of acquiring it for his own collection. Finally, LaVere gave him the owl on "permanent loan".

With his botanical items neatly labeled and organized in boxes, Wilson was ready to find long-term storage space. He made an inquiry with Richard Hite, who was about seventeen at the time and still living with his parents.

Richard said, "Alan asked if he could keep all his stuff at my parents' house. Pine cones and books and guitars and records — everything. I thought it was pretty strange that he would choose me to store all his stuff. I just thought it was pretty weird, but in my brother's band, of course you can store your stuff here."

Alan Wilson's possessions stored at the Hite family home also included some records, though his collection was paltry compared to Bob's. He collected specific items, such as John Lee Hooker records, but was not very interested in acquisition for its own sake. In 1968, he commented, "I'll pick up a record on rarity if I can get it for a quarter or less. If I happen to stumble across it on a field trip. But I would never bid for that kind of item on an auction, where I'd have to pay five or six dollars for it. ... But I do have some collector spirit, nonetheless. Some of these [record] labels are so off-the-wall that it's pretty interesting to have some of that stuff."

By 1969, however, records were holding less interest for Wilson. After all, in the woods, he wasn't able to listen to them anyway. So to the Hite household they went, with the younger Hite as guardian.

Richard would never completely understand why Alan Wilson chose him as the steward of his possessions. In later years, he mused, "I thought it was pretty strange that he would choose me to store all his stuff there, at my house. I mean, *everything*. Records and feathers and leaves and all that kind of stuff. It seemed weird to me at the time. I mean, that's *really* weird, now, thinking about it. Because I had everything. I didn't have clothes. But every book, every record, pinecones and leaves and all that stuff. His owls. I had all his guitars, too. He had a couple of Martins and a National, a couple of little Gibsons, and ... a lot of pinecones. I mean, *big* boxes. Oh yeah, each one in a plastic bag with the real [scientific] name."

Wilson never came over to listen to his records, make additions to his nature collections, or play his guitars. Eventually, the records got mixed in with Richard's own growing collection. "It was just sort of a storage place," he explained. "And they all got really integrated, you know, with my collection that I had in my parents' house. We had a three-bedroom house, and I had my bedroom and my record room. So everything just got sort of mixed in there. I mean, I got his concrete bricks and his shelving units for the records!"

One wonders if Wilson might have informally bequeathed his possessions to Richard Hite out of fondness. As Richard would later recall, the two had a good relationship, enjoying each others' company despite the age gap of nearly a decade. Richard said, "You see, my relationship with him was so different, just because — I was a young kid, you know. Alan was like a playmate in some ways. I didn't question his mental abilities or anything. I mean, he was an incredible musician, just incredible. I wish I would've paid more attention. When you're thirteen years old, you don't care much about most of that stuff."

Richard also remembered that his brother Bob, while a kind and generous soul, was also somewhat of a bully at times while they were growing up. Wilson's quiet and gentle ways were no doubt refreshing to the younger Hite. "Alan was always really genteel," Richard said. "He was like a playmate ... and talked to me at my level. And a friend, actually."

The possessions at the Hite household were never retrieved. After Wilson's death, Richard remained the custodian of most of his possessions for several years. Reports vary as to the disposition of the leaves, pinecones, and other natural keepsakes. Richard once claimed that most of these were returned to Wilson's family, but some family members were apparently not privy to this exchange and contend otherwise.

Some of Wilson's possessions revealed his absent-mindedness. "He was forgetful," said Richard. "When I was going through his books and stuff like that after he died, there'd be checks that had never been cashed, stuff like that. Yeah, he just, he wasn't all there; you basically had to keep your eye on him."

Richard Hite held onto Wilson's records until the last few years of his life. During the late 1990s, he began selling items to fellow collectors, and occasionally gifted selected collectibles to those he thought would appreciate Wilson memorabilia. This appeared to be part of a larger unloading of his own lifelong collection, in preparation for impending death, as Richard suffered from a variety of health issues. After his passing from cancer in 2001, the disposition of any items remaining from the Wilson collection is unknown.

Wilson's possessions left with Richard Hite included, among others, the following LP records:

- *Africa — Music of the Malinke' and Baoule*, Counterpoint Grand Prix du Disque 529
- *African Highlife*, Fontana MGF 27519
- *The Blues Roll On*, Atlantic 1352
- *Bunk Johnson and His Superior Jazz Band*, Good Time Jazz M12048
- *Chicago Mob Scene — A Folk Music Jam Session*

- Jean de Vres and His Afro Drums, *Exciting Voodoo*
- *Folk Songs and Dances of North India*, SPL 1614
- John Lee Hooker, *Driftin' the Blues*, United UM710
- John Lee Hooker, *The Great Blues Sounds of John Lee Hooker*, United US7731
- Ali Akbar Khan, *Sound of the Sarod*, World Pacific WP-1435
- *Koto and Flute — The Music of Kinichi Nakanoshima*, World Pacific WP-1443
- Odetta, *At Carnegie Hall*, Vanguard
- Odetta, *Folk Song and Minstrelsy*, Vanguard
- Ravi Shankar and Ali Akbar-Khan [sic], *The Master Musicians of India*, Prestige PR1078

Of Wilson's collection, Richard Hite recalled, "There was stuff like George Lewis and Bunk Johnson. Early traditional New Orleans stuff. And Louis Armstrong, stuff like that. Bessie Smith reissues. Folk music ... Oscar Brand, he had a lot of Oscar Brand."

16 HALLELUJAH

During the first five months of 1969, Canned Heat recorded their fourth album, which would be entitled *Hallelujah*. "Time Was" was included on the album, as well as three more of Wilson's songs.

Increasingly, Wilson's lyrics were becoming enigmatic, with his thoughts expressed in multiple layers of meaning. He apparently made little or no attempt to make the subjects of his songs comprehensible to listeners.

In 1968, Wilson explained his approach in reference to "An Owl Song". When asked if he tried to make his words in any given song revolve around a "general theme", he replied: "Well, yeah. Me. Me, yeah. Not obvious ones [themes]. See, the main thing of the words is that the singer wants to sing them; it doesn't matter so much if they're completely intelligible. Like that "Owl" thing, see, they're all words I wanted to sing. The message is not really too intelligible, but it's okay. Because it's all around a theme."

Unlike some singer/songwriters, Wilson did not make up stories, affect fictitious attitudes or feelings, preach "general truths" or philosophy, or create striking imagery merely for the sake of lyrical interest in his songs. Each one of his lines, in every song, had some profound personal meaning to him.

Bob Hite took a different approach to songwriting. He could often be found writing lyrics in the studio as the band recorded a song, occasionally with assistance from Skip Taylor or the rhythm section. As a singer, he was much more spontaneous. Wilson's lyrics were independently composed in a much more deliberate manner.

Skip Taylor remembers, "Alan would come in with the lyrics totally prepared, and would rehearse with the lyric intact. And any changes to a lyric would be already completed by the time we got to the studio. Whereas with Bob's songs, a lot of times he'd come to the studio, we'd get the track all done and I'd go, 'Well, can I see the lyrics to this?' He'd say, 'There isn't one!' The idea would be there for this song, and a couple of phrases or lines, but there wouldn't be a lyric!"

On the *Hallelujah* album, Wilson's most readily comprehensible song is "Change My Ways". Here, in a straightforward expression of loneliness, he laments that he is tired of sleeping alone, and offers to love "some woman" more than he loves himself. Given his choice of words, it sounds as if he is hungry for any relationship, and did not have a specific woman in mind. He then describes going down to the ocean and sitting on the shore, unsuccessfully seeking consolation in the waves and the water. This song is also notable as the only recorded example of Wilson's whistling.

Any easy comprehensibility vanished from Wilson's *Hallelujah* songs with the last notes of "Change My Ways". "Time Was", which has already been discussed, took a lyrical turn toward the enigmatic, and "Do Not Enter" is equally if not more abstruse.

Musically, "Do Not Enter" has an unusually torrid feeling of forcefulness and urgency. Continuing the theme of lack of fulfillment, the lyrics appear to be about a woman who is afraid to have a relationship with Wilson, or is simply leading him on. The actual words are a little difficult to understand in a few lines, and Wilson's diction is unclear, as are his feelings. In the final line, he tells the subject of the song to reject her "father's rule". This might be a representation of moral objections to having sex, though the entire song seems so textually muddled that one cannot conclude this with any certainty.

Finally, there is "Get Off My Back". Of all Wilson's songs, it contains the most developed usage of lyrical symbolism. Various layers of meaning appear to be encoded in this song, some suggested in symbol, some given in a more straightforward manner, and others suggested by instrumental variations. The song is divided into several distinct musical and lyrical sections, all apparently pertaining to the same topic but giving only oblique hints of the actual issues.

In the first section, Wilson describes how an unnamed "man" has been harassing him, telling him what to do, say, and smoke. The "man" reads his letters to his girlfriend, listens when they talk on the telephone, and listens to them having sex. He says that the man has held him down too long, and he wishes the man would get off his back.

The song is then divided by a wild guitar solo from Henry Vestine, morphing through several rhythmic and tempo changes before returning to the original musical theme. Perhaps Vestine's playing represented Wilson's frustrated anger at his unnamed oppressor, anger being an emotion that Wilson himself did not tend to express. This has been pointed out by the late John Fahey among others.

Wilson then enters the most lyrically fascinating section of the song. He describes a childhood dream, which takes place in some kind of cold, icy realm near the ocean. Wilson remembers the dream with feelings of love, according to the song, and believes that the location in the dream is inaccessible to "the man". Most shocking of all, he states his intention to return there.

There are two primary issues in question regarding this song. The first is the identity of the unnamed man; the second is the significance of Wilson's dream, and his stated intention to return to "that place".

Newcomers to Wilson's music, or those who did not know him well, typically interpret "the man" as a police figure, or the government itself as an authority figure. "The man" was a popular counterculture term of the time, referring to governmental staff or entities. It seems unlikely, however, that this was Wilson's meaning.

He is not remembered as being particularly obsessed with politics or the government, and while "Get Off My Back" quite frankly reeks of paranoia, none of his friends or colleagues remember him as having paranoia related to the government or police. It seems more likely that the paranoia involved some other power figure, and that Wilson adopted the term "the man" simply to mean an oppressive figure.

Manager Skip Taylor suggests that "Get Off My Back" was directed at Canned Heat. "Well, that was directed toward the band, for sure," says Taylor. "To get off my back, like, leave me alone, guys, and I'm doing my thing."

In recent years, one of Wilson's family members has suggested that "Get Off My Back" was directed specifically at Bob Hite. The same relative suggests that Wilson had expressed, via written correspondence, that Bob was somehow threatening or oppressing him. However, such correspondence has not actually been revealed to researchers, and this kind of claim cannot be verified in any way.

Wilson's friend John Fahey had a different perspective, and suggested that this song could relate to psychological issues between Wilson and his father. Comments from the likes of Fahey and David Evans confirm that the Wilson father-son relationship was indeed troubled at times. Therefore, it is possible that Alan could have perceived his father's influence as a continuing psychological oppression in his life.

Such a theory seems particularly plausible given Wilson's description of the dream, which he says he had as a boy. This involves the childhood phase of life which would relate to the father-son relationship, but could not possibly involve his band mates, whom he had not known as a boy. In his memoir *Living the Blues*, Canned Heat drummer Adolfo de la Parra also suggests that "Get Off My Back" was a reference to Wilson's family, though he does not provide any supporting statements indicating why he believes this to be the case.

The location of the dream is uncertain, but Wilson apparently viewed it as more than just a dream. If his final words are to be taken seriously, he believed that the dream's location is an actual place to which he can return. He does not explain how he will get there.

Some, such as John Fahey, have suggested that this was a foreshadowing of Wilson's own death and/or a reference to a suicide attempt. Perhaps he thought that, in death, he could return to this dream world where he felt safe. However, this is pure speculation.

Alternately, Wilson could be referring to some sort of meditative practice in which one "travels" to a mentally conjured location of one's choosing. This is sometimes done in forms of counseling which advise that the patient go to an "inner place" to help achieve mental peace. It is entirely possible that when Wilson sang "I'm going," he meant that he was going to a mental space of inner peace, where thoughts of oppressive authority figures, family issues, and/or troublesome band mates would no longer bother him. This too, however, is speculation, and "Get Off My Back" remains one of the most enigmatic songs in Wilson's catalog.

Hallelujah was not as commercially successful as *Living the Blues*, which was unfortunate, as it contained some of Alan Wilson's most creative work. His songs were his own musical statements from beginning to end, still based in part on blues, but decidedly surpassing the idiom in overall sound and originality.

The band's first album, while well executed, had a relatively basic electric blues sound, made up of traditional songs and arrangements. Save for Wilson's unusual singing on "Help Me", it broke no new ground for the blues. The musical arrangements had become more innovative on *Boogie With Canned Heat*, and on *Living the Blues*, his versatility had been displayed with Eastern-influenced compositions. All are fine musical works and important milestones in Canned Heat's career.

On this new album, however, Wilson's musical genius had become truly stunning. His songs were now distinguished by lyrical inventiveness that his first songs, good as they were, had never contained. His singing grew in expressive power as his words became more original. These new songs, in their complexity and depth of feeling, were incredibly potent creations. Alan Wilson was taking his listeners to some exciting new places, and seemed to be at an artistic height.

17 THE SNAKE SLIPS IN

In the summer of 1969, disaster struck Canned Heat. Guitarist Henry Vestine's drug habits, always extreme, had gotten progressively worse. This often resulted in inappropriate behavior both offstage and on, and was now at an intolerable point.

On July 29, the band played at the Fillmore West in San Francisco. Vestine was so addled that he couldn't even tune his guitar, and played a long, aimless solo that was in the wrong song key. This infuriated bassist Larry Taylor, who took his art seriously and had little patience for Vestine's drug-addled stupor.

Manager Skip Taylor recalls, "It basically got to a point where the solo was so long, and so out of it, that Larry Taylor said, 'I'll never go onstage with him again.' That was the bottom line. Henry said, 'Well, fuck you too, and I'm not gonna play with you either,' and he didn't."

In disgust, Vestine quit the band that night at the Fillmore. This was devastating to Wilson, for in his mind, the lead guitarist was irreplaceable. He had carefully arranged the band's sound around Vestine's style, and in 1968, stated, "The group is the group. If Henry isn't in the group, it ain't the group."

There wasn't time for Wilson to ruminate about this now, however, much less to formulate a new concept for his "orchestra". The Sunflower had been plucked from their midst before anyone could do much to address Canned Heat's growing internal strife. Now they needed a new lead guitarist, and quickly, for they had a second night booked at the Fillmore West. The following week, they were scheduled to start a national tour.

The next night at the Fillmore, Michael Bloomfield sat in on lead guitar during the first set. Bloomfield's resume included work with the Paul Butterfield Blues Band, and more recently, the horn-laden Electric Flag; his ability as a blues guitarist was widely renowned. Though he wasn't familiar with all of Canned Heat's songs, he kept up with them onstage, to everyone's delight.

During intermission, Hite and the other band members asked Bloomfield to become a member of Canned Heat. However, the guitarist declined, as he was weary of touring and didn't want to go on the road again. Like Alan Wilson, he suffered from insomnia that was apparently aggravated by the pressures of the music industry.

At the Fillmore that night was another guitarist, Harvey Mandel. He had backed up Charlie Musselwhite on the *Stand Back!* album, and kicked off his own solo career with the *Cristo Redentor* album. That evening, Mandel played with Canned Heat during their second Fillmore set. It sounded impressive enough for the band members to agree that he would fit in with them as full time lead guitarist.

Skip Taylor recalls, "I said, 'What do you guys think?' They said, 'Go ask Harvey if he wants to go back East with us.' I went, 'Oookay,' so I went and asked him. He said okay, and back he came!" Just like that, the band had been transformed.

The playing of Harvey Mandel has a unique sound. Its evolution had begun in Chicago, where he played with harmonica master Charlie Musselwhite. He then relocated to San Francisco, where he played at the Matrix club and spent time jamming with locals like Jerry Garcia and Elvin Bishop. In 1968, he released the *Cristo Redentor* album, which was almost entirely instrumental and whose title track was a jazz classic.

Mandel's guitar style contains elements of blues, rock, and jazz. His playing is marked by a progressive sound with heavy — and effective — use of sustain effects. In later years, he would play with John Mayall, the Rolling Stones, and other luminaries. In 1969, his style was already well developed. It in no way resembled the sound of Henry Vestine, and would change the sound of Canned Heat entirely.

There were just a few days before the Canned Heat tour started. Wilson found time to go music shopping, and ran into his friend David Evans. It would be the last time they ever saw each other.

"It was at a record shop, or maybe a guitar store," remembers Evans. "He said he was depressed. He'd been touring and all that. ... We didn't have much time to really talk, but he said something to the effect that there were just a lot of bad things going on in the world, things that were bothering him. Especially about the environment, cutting down the redwoods. I remember him saying he was depressed."

Then Wilson was gone. As he was on the road that August and September, Evans was moving to Orange County, California, and starting a new teaching job. He and Marina Bokelman had broken up, and it was the end of an era for all of them.

Within days of the Fillmore gig, Canned Heat began a North American tour with their new lead guitarist. As they flew toward the first gig in Atlantic City, New Jersey, Harvey Mandel spent some time on the plane studying the set list and familiarizing himself with the songs he would be playing. As part of the band, he would be known as "The Snake", a nickname given to him by keyboardist Barry Goldberg years ago in Chicago.

The fourth show on this tour was a festival that would become known around the world simply as Woodstock. This three-day event was immortalized on film, with a subsequent movie release featuring the studio version of "Going Up the Country". That helped to cement the public association of Canned Heat's biggest hit with the counterculture, hippies, and the sixties in general.

Decades later, "Going Up the Country" would maintain its strong association with the Woodstock festival. In 1994, a second

"Woodstock" festival was held to commemorate the event's 25th anniversary. This time, it involved a nationwide marketing blitz and extensive commercialization — and no Canned Heat in the band lineup.

Back in 1969, the members of Canned Heat didn't realize the scope of the festival until they arrived in a helicopter and saw the size of the crowd. While waiting backstage, the band members, along with Skip Taylor, dropped some LSD while listening to the Incredible String Band's performance.

By the time Canned Heat took the stage, the psychedelics had kicked in. Skip Taylor felt that this caused Wilson's performance to suffer, recalling, "He was very much heavily on acid. We all took acid right before that show. He was out there; all you have to do is listen to that song. It was not the normal Alan. I helped put the first Woodstock album together, but I didn't want to put that live version on it, because it was just horrible. But eventually it surfaced."

Despite the band's chemically influenced state, their set was well received. Today, Wilson's live performance of "Going Up the Country" can be seen through online sources as well as on DVD compilations of festival footage. Most fans seem to feel that his vocals, though somewhat raw compared to the studio version, are by no means "horrible".

Canned Heat's set took place around sunset, to dramatic effect. Skip Taylor says, "Probably in the entire Canned Heat experience, that was the most magical moment for me. We followed the Incredible String Band, an Irish kind of trio that was very low key, and not made for an outdoor concert in front of four hundred thousand people! So when we went on, the crowd was just at a low ebb point. Alan went out to do his little introduction to 'Going Up the Country', and it was like the sermon on the mountain. The crowd just came off the ground, like four hundred thousand people. It just sent chills up and down your spine. It was phenomenal."

From Woodstock, the band continued on an extensive North American tour, playing at locations including British Columbia, Dallas, New Orleans, Detroit, New York City, and Miami. This kept them busy for the remainder of 1969. On the radio, "Going Up the Country" ended up reaching #1 on the singles charts in twenty-five foreign countries.

Wilson, however, was far from happy. Not only was he suffering from his usual depressive tendencies, he had taken the departure of Henry Vestine hard. In his mind, Vestine had been the perfect lead guitarist for Canned Heat, as well as a friend. According to Adolfo de la Parra's memoirs, Wilson was so fond of Vestine that Bob Hite occasionally accused him of having romantic feelings for the guitarist.

On and off, Wilson had been considering quitting Canned Heat. Occasionally he expressed this to Bob Hite, pondering different options such as recording with Canned Heat but not touring with them. In late 1969, he quit entirely for a few days. According to Richard Hite, Wilson wanted to play with Henry Vestine, who was forming a band called Sunn.

Skip Taylor remembers, "I think he [Wilson] grew to like Harvey and Harvey's playing, but it was still not the same. That was definitely a major rift in the band right there. One of many to follow. ... It was like, 'If you guys kick Henry out, then I'm out.' He was always on Henry's side."

Richard Hite recalls the Sunn endeavor: "He [Wilson] actually quit Canned Heat. It came down to, there was a problem in the band; it came down to between Larry Taylor and Henry. It was like, Larry says, 'If you want to keep me, get rid of Henry.' So they got rid of Henry. And Alan was *really*, really upset about that. And, in fact, Henry then, for a while, formed a band called Sunn. S-U-N-N, like the amplifier. ... And, for a very brief period Alan had actually quit Canned Heat, to play with Henry. And then came back."

Henry Vestine's drug use had increased to frightening proportions. His life had degenerated in other ways as well, becoming fueled by amphetamines and filled with grungy, drug-peddling bikers who could be found hanging around his house at odd hours. He had also begun complementing the speed with heroin, much to Wilson's horror. The effects on Vestine's musicianship were, of course, equally horrific.

This drug abuse worsened throughout Vestine's life, and in the decades after Wilson's death, he became a notorious addict. Sometimes he became violent when intoxicated. In the seventies, Richard Hite performed with him, and remembered, "Henry was crazy. We were playing a club one time. They had a small, suspended type ceiling, and when we got to the gig, there was a big neon sign out there says 'Jack Daniels 25 cents a shot'. Henry saw that, and ... instead of going to the dressing room, Henry makes it down to the bar, and by the time he made it up to the second floor dressing room, he'd probably had very many quarters of Jack Daniels, and was real wasted. Couldn't tune his guitar. Got real pissed off. Took his guitar, broke out one of the panes of the window in the dressing room."

The scene got even more lurid. "Then," Richard recalled, "we went down to play. And ... this is a little sad. We were doing the boogie, and there was a girl dancing onstage. So, it was getting time for Henry's solo. Henry decided that she was going to have a solo. And, we're playing, we stopped, and Henry's trying to motion her for her solo. She has no idea what's going on here but Henry thinks it's a good idea, for a solo. And she didn't quite get it. Then he got pissed off, and then started taking his guitar and knocking out the acoustical ceiling. And it's crumbling down all over the stage. Henry — some craziness!"

Back in 1969, Alan Wilson could probably tell that Vestine's drug problems wouldn't make for success with a new band. He ended up not enlisting in Sunn, and instead, returned to Canned Heat.

Although joining Vestine was not a good option, it was clear that Wilson's heart was no longer fully in Canned Heat. Throughout the remainder of his life, he continued to toy with the idea of leaving the band. According to John Fahey, Wilson once asked Bob Hite for "permission" not to tour with the group. Hite gave his consent, as he later related to Fahey, but Wilson felt guilty and decided to go on tour anyway.

Shortly before Henry Vestine's 1969 departure from Canned Heat, he had been trying to persuade the group to record a new song entitled "Let's Work Together". It had recently been a hit for rhythm and blues singer Wilbert Harrison. Not wanting to steal Harrison's thunder, the band stalled, waiting until his original had peaked on the singles charts before recording their own version. By that time, it was December 1969, and Vestine had been gone for months.

Canned Heat's version of "Let's Work Together", sung by Bob Hite, was first released in Europe. It quickly became a hit single, and the band booked a month-long European tour beginning shortly after the New Year.

Wilson's habits were immediately disrupted, because it was too cold for him to sleep outside. One postcard, from Wilson to David Evans, described their experience in Sweden where the temperature was but 18 degrees Fahrenheit in the middle of the day. Upon nightfall it was, of course, even colder. Wilson with his sleeping bag couldn't endure it, and was forced to spend his nights in motel rooms throughout the tour. This did not make him very happy, especially when any attempts to find company for his evenings seemed doomed to failure.

To others, it seemed strange that anyone in Wilson's position could fail to get laid. Groupies, it seemed, could be had for the taking, enticed easily by most musicians with a come-hither motion of a guitar or drumstick. The other members of Canned Heat had no trouble. In an unreleased solo tape, Wilson once sang that it took "one big dog and three shaggy hounds" to find help him find women when out of town, presumably a reference to his band mates and being on tour.

"There was something wrong," said Richard Hite, recalling Wilson's misery when even his musical genius and Canned Heat's stardom didn't resolve his difficulties with the opposite sex. "He could play music, but something wasn't working. He couldn't get laid. He couldn't have a relationship with a woman, and that was very frustrating to him. That was his big thing, trying to have a relationship; it was real difficult."

During this 1970 tour of Europe, Alan Wilson began performing "London Blues", an original song set to a John Lee Hooker-style guitar part. The lyrics were composed about a bad experience he had with a woman on a previous Canned Heat tour. The woman was apparently a groupie he felt attracted to, and asked on a date. According to "London Blues", she led Wilson on, raising his hopes and making him think that she had feelings for him.

According to drummer Adolfo de la Parra's memoir, Wilson was very excited about his planned date with the woman. He reportedly spent hours getting washed and dressed for the occasion, even asking de la Parra for advice on clothing. Though he wanted to select something fashionable, Wilson had no idea what he should wear.

When the girl arrived at the motel to meet him, Wilson was disappointed. She had brought several friends with her, and obviously had no interest in being alone with him. He proceeded with the date anyway, putting up with the presence of her uninvited guests and even paying for their dinners.

After Wilson had taken them all to a show, the woman invited the entire crowd back to her home, implying to Wilson that her friends would soon leave. For the rest of the evening, however, she avoided him, bantering and socializing with her friends instead. Frustrated, he left, reporting back to de la Parra at the motel that he had spent over three hundred pounds and didn't even receive a goodnight kiss.

Reports of this failed date vary, with Fito de la Parra and others suggesting that it caused Wilson great distress. Bob Hite apparently had the same impression; he would later recount the incident to his brother Richard Hite as being a severe trauma for Wilson.

However, Henry Vestine — who was in the band at the time of the actual incident, as opposed to Wilson's later recounting of it in song — had a different perspective on the matter. In a letter to a friend, which was made public online years later, Vestine wrote that he did not feel this episode had a significant effect on Wilson.

Though we can never know for sure, it is possible that Wilson felt more frustrated by this incident than hurt.

On the other hand, it's possible that Wilson was putting on a "brave face" for Hite and Vestine, and was more hurt than he let on. If Vestine's letter discussing the incident is authentic, helping us to clarify the chronology of this incident, it seems that the actual encounter occurred in September 1968 when the band appeared in London. However, there is no documentation of Wilson performing "London Blues" until early 1970. There are two possible implications for this large gap of time between the incident and the performance of the song.

It is possible that Wilson was reminded of the woman at some point when she contacted him via phone, as detailed in the song, and requested free admission to the band's next London show. This reminder could have inspired him to composed "London Blues" as a kind of catharsis. However, it is also possible that he had been secretly nursing hurt feelings about the incident over the last year or so, and that his 1970 performances of "London Blues" were indicative that he had indeed been traumatized by the incident as some acquaintances seemed to feel.

In the end, it is impossible to know Wilson's true feelings about the incident except through "London Blues". Therein, he expresses what sounds like anger at the groupie in London, to whom the lyrics are directly addressed. When she telephones and asks to get into the Heat's next London show, he suggests that she come to the hotel first and visit him. If she fails to do so, he sings, she can go to hell. This sort of bitterness is without parallel in any of Wilson's other recordings.

In the studio version of the song, recorded later in 1970, the final line is altered so that instead of telling the woman to go to hell, Wilson instead sings "fare thee well". Whether this represented a softening of his feelings toward her, or whether he simply did not feel comfortable expressing that kind of animosity on a studio album, is uncertain.

In the absence of female companionship on the Europe 1970 tour, Wilson's quest for happiness in nature was beginning to take on a rather desperate quality. Frequently, he caused the rest of the band to put things on hold while he investigated trees that caught his interest. At times, the road crew had to track him down and retrieve him from local woods, parks, or swamps, in order to get him to shows or to travel with the band in a timely manner.

The band's new guitarist, Harvey Mandel, noticed Wilson's inactivity in the romance department. "He was the loner of the group socially, off by himself," Mandel remembered. "He was very introverted and weird. While the other guys in the band would be chasing women and stuff, he'd be off sitting under a tree or something."

Sometimes Wilson even interrupted the band's travel when they were already underway. "It happened all the time," said Mandel. "We'd be driving through all kinds of weird country; he'd see a certain tree and say, 'Stop the car!' and go over to it. He knew every kind of tree there was — he was a tree expert."

Some of the live shows from this tour were preserved on film and on tape. When viewing films of the band from around this time, WIlson's increasing isolation is obvious. At times, he had taken to standing apart from his band mates, occasionally hiding behind rows of amplifiers during the show. He told Skip Taylor and Bob Hite that this was for aural reasons, however, claiming that it was difficult to hear his own instrument through the volume of the lead guitar on the main stage area.

Ironically, even while Wilson seemed to be drowning in a sea of his own melancholy, he was capable of singing and playing as brilliantly as ever. A portion of the tour was recorded for the creation of Canned Heat's first proper live album.

Entitled *Live in Europe*, this album would be released later in 1970. It is an excellent representation of Canned Heat's sound at the time, including versions of "Let's Work Together" and "London Blues". It also features a cover of Sonny Boy Williamson's "Bring It On Home", which had not been recorded previously by Canned Heat, and is notable here for Wilson's excellent harmonica playing.

"The live album in Europe was recorded in like five or six places and then I came back and put all that together," says Skip Taylor. "He [Wilson] played really good on that. I think of that era, that's a pretty innovative album, too, in that I took shows from everywhere and tried to make the album sound like one concert. I just took the best of all the recordings and tried to make a set of them all, and put it together, kind of got the applause and response to kind of coincide with one another, so that you actually felt that you were sitting down for a live show. Even though it was many shows."

Live in Europe also features Wilson's lachrymose "Pulling Hair Blues". It is perhaps the saddest song ever recorded by Alan Wilson, whose entire catalog is suffused with shades of emotional despair. Here, the subdued musical setting and slow tempo create a dark atmosphere. Wilson's voice is filled with an aching loneliness, completely vulnerable as he expresses the hopelessness that must have overcome him after a long and restless night.

Featuring Wilson on harmonica and vocals, accompanied only by Larry Taylor's stunning bass work, "Pulling Hair Blues" is an example of the kind of performance Wilson sometimes gave at the end of a set, as the rest of the band left the stage. On the record, the song is positioned at the conclusion of the first side, giving the feeling of a subsequent intermission as the listener turns the record over to the second side.

Bob Hite's friend Claude McKee recalls other, similar performances: "I've seen Alan literally move an audience, captivate it. The band would take a break and ... when they first started out Alan would be left onstage. Just Alan and his harmonica, and hold a whole audience captivated."

In this powerfully understated setting, with no band and no elaborate musical accompaniment, Wilson exposes the most personal kind of feelings. On "Pulling Hair Blues", he sings that he has been compulsively overeating and pulling his hair out. He cannot sleep at night because he can't be outside. He doesn't like the long train rides on the tour, and it rains all the time. In the final line, as he sings that there is no relief for his troubled mind, he seems to be resigned to his depression.

At one point, Wilson sings that not only is he prevented from sleeping outside, but he can't even "get laid". On the *Live in Europe* album, at this point we hear the curious sound of titters from the audience, the nervous kind of giggle that some produce when faced with something embarrassing. These die down almost immediately, as Wilson repeats the line and his voice almost breaks with emotion. His raw, naked pain was just too much for an audience that had come to hear a rock show. Just as his strange personal habits tended to make women uncomfortable, his open vulnerability had made this audience a little uneasy, when perhaps they were expecting a carefree ditty like "Going Up the Country".

18 FUTURE BLUES

Canned Heat returned to the United States in February 1970. With Harvey Mandel, the group ended up recording an entire album of new music that would eventually be released as *Future Blues* (though it did not hit stores until August 1970, after Mandel had left the band).

Some of this material included "Let's Work Together", "Sugar Bee", "That's All Right Mama", "So Sad (World's In a Tangle)", and "Future Blues", all of which were sung by Bob Hite. "Sugar Bee" featured Wilson's harmonica playing, and was based on a Cleveland Crochet zydeco tune. "That's All Right Mama" was an Arthur Crudup song that had also been recorded by Elvis Presley.

"So Sad (World's In a Tangle)" had been written by the band. It features guitar solos from both Wilson and Harvey Mandel, and contains lyrics addressing the problem of environmental pollution. This probably represents Wilson's influence on the song.

"Future Blues" was based in part on the 1930 Willie Brown recording of the same title, but was reworked considerably. Wilson's guitar is not featured in the arrangement, and the song was largely a showcase for Harvey Mandel's playing.

The *Future Blues* album also contained Wilson's "London Blues", a studio version with some noteworthy differences from the *Live in Europe* rendition. In the live version, Wilson explicitly tells the offending woman to go to hell; whereas in the studio this is softened to "fare thee well". The studio version is also interesting for Wilson's extended exploration of his high tenor's upper register, with vocals unlike those on any other Canned Heat record.

Wilson also sings "Shake It and Break It", a variation on a traditional barrelhouse theme. It had previously been recorded by Charley Patton, with different interpretations and related songs performed by Son House, Geechie Wiley, and pianist Louise Johnson. One can also hear versions performed by New Orleans-style jazz bands. Wilson's version is unique in the song's longtime tradition, and it is one of his most fascinating works.

It is somewhat surprising that Wilson chose to record this kind of song. After all, the versions of "Shake It and Break It" that he had heard were, for the most part, bawdy barrelhouse songs. The song is also associated with ragtime, of which Wilson, by all accounts, had a horror. However, John Fahey once suggested that Wilson did not actually despise the ragtime form itself, but rather felt that it was improperly utilized by most musicians.

The subject of "Shake It and Break It" is sex, a pleasure that Wilson was rarely afforded. This does not mean that he was uninterested, however, and though the sexual metaphors in the traditional lyrics were clouded, Wilson was surely aware of their meanings. As David Evans indicated earlier, Wilson usually did not care for hokum or double entendre songs. Fittingly, his rendition of "Shake It and Break It" is not particularly humorous, but does contain sexual innuendos.

Louise Johnson's version of "Shake It and Break It", entitled "On the Wall", regales the listener with tales of sex in the barrelhouse, and promises to show other women how to effectively "cock it on the wall" — that is, have sex standing up. This presumably took place in the back of the barrelhouse, or perhaps out back. Most other versions of this song do not use the word "cock", but as with standard blues phrases like "shake that thing" and "jelly roll", the sexual connotations are apparent to the initiated listener.

Musicologist and friend David Evans commented on Wilson's song and the earlier Patton recording on which it is primarily based: "Alan has taken the Patton melody (more or less) and guitar part ... and a somewhat misinterpreted and reinterpreted version of the lyrics of Patton's refrain and added new verses. ... The 'it' of Patton's song is clearly his 'jelly roll'. All the violent things that are done to 'it' may have to do with literal jelly roll, i.e., bread, making this an extended double entendre. Of course, it can also be assumed that Patton is singing about a woman's 'booty', so that the things that are done to the 'jelly roll' could also describe sexual activities."

Wilson's lyrics primarily appear to be about uncertainty combined with a desire for intimacy. It is possible that, in his mind, the traditional lyrics served as a reference to his own intimacy issues. Some of his verses and phrases appear in early songs by the likes of Henry Thomas, William Harris, Kid Bailey, and Willie Brown.

David Evans commented on Wilson's "Shake It and Break It" lyrics, which included some verses borrowed from earlier singers: "It's possible that in the first verse he has sublimated the sexual meaning to one of 'dance', almost as if he is some sort of voyeur of a women doing an erotic dance. The 'cigarette-smoke' verse he probably associated with marijuana, as we all did, hoping that William Harris was also endorsing marijuana use as early as 1927. The 'I don't want it, mama, if it falls' line may well refer to impotence in some way. So the song might be Al's fantasy of what would turn him on sexually, as was evidently Patton's version for himself."

Future Blues also featured "My Time Ain't Long", written and sung by Wilson. His most significant influence is Charley Patton's "Oh Death", a religious selection recorded in 1934 as a duet with his wife Bertha Lee.

Wilson's lyrical text is relatively short. In the first verse, he describes the beauty of the moon and a tree, and the sound of the ocean. In the second verse, this peace is disrupted as he wonders what he will do if "the Bear" disturbs him. This is, of course, undoubtedly a reference to Bob Hite.

Wilson then sings that he would like to stay "here", but knows his time is not long. The song ends with a separate musical coda featuring a Harvey Mandel guitar solo.

It seems possible that this could be a recounting of a Wilson suicide attempt, during which he might have been aware of natural phenomena such as the moon, trees, and ocean. He sings of a concern of discovery by Bob Hite, which would be undesirable if his goal was to die peacefully, merging with the elements of nature. When he sings that he would like to stay "here", this could refer to his reverie, or perhaps it even means that place where "the man ain't found", as he sang about in "Get Off My Back" the year before.

Skip Taylor has suggested that by "My Time Ain't Long", Wilson referred not to his physical life, but to his time in Canned Heat. Taylor said, "I don't know if he meant it in real chronological terms, but I think that was 'My time ain't long,' as far as continuing to play in Canned Heat. At that point."

It is possible that by stating he would like to stay "here", Wilson was referring to California, and that his reference to the Bear disturbing him meant that Bob was about to bring the unwelcome news that it was time to leave for a band tour or performance.

On the *Future Blues* album sequence, immediately following "My Time Ain't Long" is Wilson's "Skat". For this, one of Wilson's most interesting vocal works. the band is augmented with a horn section. As the title implies, the singing is performed in the wordless "scat" style, which consists of assorted nonsense syllables. The style is associated with jazz, and this recording represents the first overt surfacing of Wilson's jazz background.

Musically, "Skat" is one of Wilson's most upbeat songs, providing a strange contrast with the preceding song which had contained rather ominous elements. While the syllables may appear to be nonsense, one suspects that Wilson's precise, analytical mind would have carefully selected each sound for maximum effect. In particular, his repetition of the phrase "shoobie doobie" might have been a subtle tribute to one of his favorite plants — marijuana — which could be smoked in the form of a "doobie" or hand rolled cigarette.

On the front cover of *Future Blues*, the band is shown acting out a parody of the 1969 moon landing, conflated with a parody of the famous 1945 Iwo Jima flag-raising photograph. However, in this case, the members of Canned Heat gather on the lunar surface to raise an inverted American flag. The picture shows a smoggy, polluted Earth in the background, representing Alan Wilson's fears about ecology and the health of the planet. Due to the inversion of the flag, some retailers around the United States refused to carry the album.

Inside, the unfolding album cover contains a message written by Wilson. In an essay entitled "Grim Harvest", he describes the beauty of the coastal redwoods and deplores their ongoing devastation by humans. It was also a plea to the public, an appeal for help in saving the groves that he loved so much.

Wilson had recently decided to use his rock star money to save as many redwoods as he could. The checks from his work with Canned Heat had gone largely uncashed. In later years, Richard Hite would find many of them scattered among his books, stuffed between the pages as place markers.

Now, however, Wilson hoped to use his money to buy acres of old-growth forest. John Fahey recalls being told by Bob Hite that Wilson had eighty thousand dollars in the bank for this purpose, but this report cannot be confirmed. At any rate, further financial backing would be needed, and Wilson decided to form an organization for this purpose. Thus, the inner cover of *Future Blues* contained a message encouraging record buyers to send donations to "Music Mountain", an organization working for the benefit of the North Coast groves.

Wilson had conceived Music Mountain with assistance from manager Skip Taylor. The tree-hugging Wilson had big dreams, but no skill in accounting or fundraising. Indeed, as his check-bookmarks would later reveal, he had no real money management skills, though he certainly knew how to live frugally. He left the administration of Music Mountain largely to Taylor.

The Music Mountain project remained incomplete at the time of Wilson's September 1970 death, and no redwoods had yet been purchased through the organization. According to one report appearing in the *Boston Globe* on September 11, 1970, Canned Heat had pledged to raise two million dollars through Music Mountain. This would go toward a six million dollar purchase price for an undefined acreage of redwood forest.

In a letter also dated September 11, 1970, Skip Taylor wrote to the Wilson family on a Canned Heat letterhead: "And it is with the thought of Alan's steadfast commitment ... that we make our donation in his name and in his memory to the Music Mountain Save-The-Redwoods project which he was instrumental in beginning and which we shall carry forward to its successful realization."

In the September 11, 1970 article, the *Boston Globe* also reported that the Ford Foundation and the State of California had each pledged to match the Music Mountain contribution. Other reports after Wilson's death have cited the Skunk Cabbage Creek area in Northern California as the location that had been earmarked for purchase.

Unfortunately, research has not unearthed any official records pertaining to the Music Mountain foundation. Its financial status could not be determined, nor could the amount of Canned Heat's actual donation, if any, be confirmed. Donations from other organizations, if any, could not be traced. The Skunk Cabbage Creek area remains somewhat intact today, featuring a nature trail for hikers, but there is no evidence that it was preserved through the efforts of Music Mountain.

19 HOOKER AND HEAT

In spring 1970, Larry Taylor left Canned Heat, exhausted by the band's rigorous touring schedule. Harvey Mandel followed him, and the two subsequently joined John Mayall's Bluesbreakers band. The loss of Larry Taylor, and his phenomenal talent on electric bass, was a hurdle for Canned Heat.

Henry Vestine's Sunn band had not worked out, so he was ready to return. The band accepted him back, initiating a pattern of frequent comings and goings that would last for decades after Wilson's death. Vestine had not changed his habits; he was more addicted to drugs than ever. Nonetheless, he seemed like the best option for Canned Heat, especially in Alan Wilson's mind.

To fill the role of bassist, the band turned to a friend of drummer Adolfo de la Parra. Antonio de la Barreda had played with de la Parra years ago in Mexico, and more recently had worked for Sam and the Goodtimers, a Los Angeles rhythm and blues outfit. His playing didn't compare to Larry Taylor's work, but was solid enough for Canned Heat.

Around this time, Wilson entered the psychiatric ward again. Canned Heat was scheduled to record an album in late May with John Lee Hooker, who was a musical idol to them all, particularly Wilson. Now they had to deal with the band's musical director being hospitalized. But, as his band mates had learned, there wasn't much they could do to help Wilson with his problems. The best they could do was learn to work around them.

"When we did the *Hooker n' Heat* album, the hospital was right around the corner from the studio," remembers Skip Taylor. "That's why we chose the studio we did to make that album. They'd let him out, and he did that record. ... He was inspired. He played fabulous for that, and he was excited about that. That was something that we thought would bring him around because it would give him something ... I mean, there he was, playing with an idol."

Richard Hite, who got to witness some early Canned Heat recording sessions, remembers, "Alan's biggest thrill was to record with John Lee Hooker. And John Lee Hooker, at one point, couldn't believe Alan! Hooker is very hard to follow, because he changes chords when he wants to change. And Alan could follow him, and Hooker was amazed that this boy here could do that. It was second nature to Alan. It really was."

Besides being an artistic accomplishment, *Hooker 'n Heat* is representative of a particular musical era and a sociological phenomenon that had begun several years ago. This was the so-called blues revival, which Wilson himself had helped to instigate when he interacted with Booker White and Son House. The "revival" was a sort of musical crossroads in the fabric of time, music, and culture, where older bluesmen came together with young fans who were from vastly different backgrounds.

Many legendary blues performers took part in collaborative projects with the young, generally white blues revival artists of the 1960s and early 1970s. This concept proved popular and was continued; to this day, releases from older artists are often garnished with "special guest" appearances from rock stars and pop idols. Sadly, many of these seem to be based more on business and sales figures than on genuine affinity between the artists involved.

When young white longhairs sat down with elderly bluesmen, culture clash could also be a problem. Wilson's recordings with Son House are a prime example of how the situation could be quite successful, with music as a unifying factor overcoming any sociological issues. However, not all musicians had Wilson's talent that enabled him to establish a productive rapport, and not all collaborative blues recordings are as artistically successful as his work with House.

Perhaps the best-known example from Wilson's era is that of Sonny Boy Williamson, also known as Rice Miller. Williamson was very popular in Great Britain and Europe, and toured there to great acclaim in the 1960s. He performed and recorded with the Yardbirds, which at that time included Eric Clapton on guitar. However, he wasn't impressed by the band or the budding "guitar god". Later, Williamson reported to American friends that English musicians wanted to play the blues "so bad", and did indeed play the music very badly!

No such difficulties plagued Canned Heat and John Lee Hooker. Not only was Wilson a musical genius, the entire band idolized Hooker and would do anything to avoid stealing the spotlight from him. They took care to feature his style on this album, devoting the first six tracks to Hooker alone with his guitar and stomping feet. They wanted little more than to back him up and present his classic blues style to their fans, and the result is a magnificent album. The high caliber of their musicianship, and their ability to connect intuitively with Hooker, makes this a milestone among blues recordings — not just from the blues revival, but in all blues history.

John Lee Hooker himself, however, didn't seem quite sure what to make of the experience. Wilson's minimalist approach seemed, at first, a bit archaic and curious. It was not what Hooker had come to expect from the younger generation of musicians.

In 1997, a few years before the death of John Lee Hooker, Richard Hite recalled the recording sessions: "That was a very difficult album to make, because Hooker wanted the whole band to play. If you listen to John's early work compared to the last fifteen years, it's like a night and day difference. They wanted him to play that great guitar like he used to play, but, you know, the times were changing, and in the middle fifties he started being in a band and stuff like that. You're a modern musician, you play in a band, so that's what Hooker wanted to do. And they had a really hard time trying to get him to play by himself. Finally it worked out that way and they would slowly add things."

Hooker n' Heat ended up being a double album. The first six tracks feature Hooker alone, and he does all the singing throughout both discs. Bob Hite is not entirely silent, however; he does provide chatter and vocal interjections between songs.

On "You Talk Too Much", "Burning Hell", and "Drifter", Wilson plays harmonica, interweaving with Hooker's voice and guitar to excellent effect. The following two songs, "Bottle Up and Go" and "The World Today", are interesting because they mark the only time Wilson's piano playing would appear on a Canned Heat record.

After this, the rest of the band finally appears. Wilson plays rhythm guitar on some tracks and harmonica on others. His guitar is extremely subdued throughout, probably because his non-bottleneck playing was based so much on Hooker's style that to display it here would have been tasteless. Wilson would not have wanted to step on Hooker's musical style in the presence of the Boogie Man himself.

Once again, Wilson had used his abilities to complement the talent of a blues legend. Although his own music had gone beyond pure blues a long time ago, this album confirmed his and Canned Heat's commitment to the preservation of traditional blues. Their eagerness to record with Hooker was due in part to their awareness that they could introduce him to new, lucrative audiences. They wanted him to share in their success.

Later in Hooker's career, this continued to be a reality. In 1989, Hooker broke through again into mainstream success with *The Healer* album, and once again Canned Heat was involved. Decades after the passing of Alan Wilson, the band recorded a track with Hooker for *The Healer*, led by drummer Adolfo de la Parra who continues to steward the band to this day.

Shortly after the *Hooker n' Heat* recording session, Alan Wilson checked out of the hospital. He then left with Canned Heat for a handful of U.S. shows, then to Europe and the U.K. for a few appearances, including a BBC television show.

On June 30, the group was in London again. Son House was also in the area, playing a gig at a local club that evening. Wilson went to see him, and ended up sitting in on harmonica for a couple of songs. The two played together much as they had in 1965. The performance was later issued on a record album, and in later decades, in digital format.

Canned Heat returned from Europe in July. During their recording sessions that summer, Wilson recorded a song called "Human Condition", which appears to be written about an encounter with his psychiatrist. Presumably this was the same doctor he had consulted throughout the preceding few years, about whom "An Owl Song" had been written.

In "Human Condition", Wilson sings about visiting the doctor and sitting on her bed; this might have been a reference to his recent hospital stay. He says he is feeling sad, weak, and weary, but is told by the doctor that this is simply a "human condition". He is also told that many people have experienced feelings of sadness and dissatisfaction. Wilson then stands up from the bed and walks away from the doctor, searching for a "brighter day". This song could be interpreted in various ways and it is impossible to determine whether it was a lament of ubiquitous misery, or a message of healthy acceptance and hope.

In 1970, "Human Condition" went unreleased. In 1978, Canned Heat would record a different version of the song for John Fahey's Takoma label. Bassist Richard Hite claimed that he was largely responsible for the arrangement, and that it was his way of paying tribute to his friend and mentor Alan Wilson. The original Wilson-sung version would not be released until 1994, when it was included in a Canned Heat compact disc collection.

As the summer of 1970 progressed, Wilson was again looking for an escape from Canned Heat. The stresses of rock stardom and the rigors of the road were hard on him, but he didn't want to stop playing music.

In a seemingly desperate move, Wilson called Frank Cook, the former Canned Heat drummer who was now working with a band called Pacific Gas and Electric. "He came to me, and wanted to join Pacific Gas and Electric," recalls Cook. "He asked me, 'Would you be open to that idea?' I said, 'I of course would be open to that idea, but I'll have to talk to the rest of the guys in the band."

The other members, for whatever reason, were reluctant to change their band's lineup by adding Wilson. The idea never went anywhere, and Wilson stayed in Canned Heat.

According to John Fahey, Wilson decided to take a "vacation" from the band in August, and told Bob Hite that he would be retreating to the forest for an undefined period of time. Hite apparently had no problem with this, but Wilson couldn't stick with his decision. He ended up returning, humbly asking the other band members if they still wanted his services. Of course, he was welcomed back to Canned Heat. (This may be the same incident recalled by Adolfo de la Parra in his memoirs, in which Wilson quit the band for an approximate two-week period.)

On September 2, Canned Heat was scheduled to leave for a tour of Europe. Everyone in the band was expecting Wilson to join them.

20 THE BLIND OWL'S FINAL ROOSTING PLACE

On August 22, 1970, Canned Heat performed at the Forum in Inglewood, California. Also on the bill were the Iron Butterfly and Herbie Hancock. In early September, the band was scheduled for a tour of Europe, starting in Berlin.

During the last week in August, Alan Wilson attended several shows at the Ash Grove in Los Angeles. Over the last year or so, he hadn't had much time to visit the club, but now seemed to want to reconnect.

Owner Ed Pearl noticed that Wilson seemed depressed, and became concerned. "Up to 1970, I hadn't seen Al for maybe a year," he now recalls. "And for like a week, he started coming into the Ash Grove a lot. I knew that something was wrong; I just knew that he was in trouble. ... I didn't know what to ask him. I hadn't seen him for a while, and I wasn't sure of anything."

Throughout the years, Pearl had noticed Wilson's lack of success in romantic relationships. "I always wondered, you know, why he never got married," Pearl comments. "I never saw him with a girlfriend or anything. There were a lot of gay people around, but I didn't have any sense that he was gay. I didn't have any sense that he wasn't. I just knew that he ... seemed very alone. He was alone. He came in alone, and, you know, watched the show and so on."

According to Pearl's recollection, Wilson's last visit to the Ash Grove was most likely on September 1, 1970. He wanted to reach out to Wilson, but was uncertain of how to approach him. "So on that last night, I just kept thinking, I really should talk to him," says Pearl. "But I didn't know what to say. I didn't know what to do, exactly. Every time I was about to start asking him to come in, sit down and talk to me in my office, something else would happen at the club where I had to do something."

It was the last time they would see each other. Pearl says, "I just really loved his spirit and his generosity and his kindness and his musicianship, and his devotion. Here was a person with so much love to give, and nobody to give it to, I think."

During the first couple of days in September 1970, Alan Wilson also went to visit John Fahey at his home. In later years, Fahey would recall that this last visit took place on the evening of Alan Wilson's death, though of course at the time he didn't realize the significance of the night.

When pressed regarding his certainty of the date, Fahey admitted, "No, I'm not sure of that. It seems to me like a few days later, I heard that he had done it [died] that night. But I'm not absolutely certain that that is true. But I'm absolutely certain that I did *hear* that he'd done it that night." As shall be seen, this is not the only confusing element in the chronology of Wilson's last few days.

"It was about seven p.m., seven-thirty p.m. in the evening or something like that," Fahey recalled. "He came by my house and told me that he had been sick. But that he was all right now, and everything was gonna be all right. And I said, 'Gee, Al, I didn't know you were in the hospital; why didn't you call me? I would've come down.' He said, 'No, no, I've been crazy, but I'm all right now.' He stayed about a half an hour."

Looking back on the evening after Wilson's death, Fahey felt that the visit had some deeper, veiled purpose. He said, "He didn't stay very long but he stayed long enough to establish kind of ... something I would remember, say magnetism, communication, or, you know, something that we would both know that ... I mean, it wasn't a brief thing that I could forget. We actually kind of came together one last time."

Sometime on September 2, 1970, Alan Wilson drove his van to Bob Hite's house for the last time. The band had already left for Europe earlier that day, and presumed that he would be joining them. He had been late in the past, had missed flights before, and had always showed up in the end. Perhaps, his band mates thought, Wilson was doing his laundry in preparation for the tour.

It is uncertain who last saw Wilson alive. At the time, Verlie Hite thought that she was the last to say goodnight to him before he made his way up the hillside, as documented by the press shortly afterward. However, another member of the household also bid Wilson a late goodnight. Ed Marrow, fifteen years old in 1970, was Verlie's son from a previous relationship. He now recalls, "I think I was the last to say goodnight before he went up on the hill. ... When I said goodnight to him, he said the same back, nothing seemed out of place."

Exactly what Wilson did on the hillside before his death is unclear, as are his intentions. It appears that he had prepared for bed, unrolling his sleeping bag on the hillside where he often slept. In his pocket, he had carried with him a small plastic bag filled with an indeterminate number of barbiturate pills. These were the "reds" he had been taking since 1968 or 1969 to help him sleep.

Wilson took some of these pills, the number of which was not determined. Four pills remained in the bag; this was placed back into the pocket of his jeans. Wilson removed his clothes, placed them in a pile next to his sleeping bag, and crawled in, apparently going to bed.

At about two o'clock in the early morning of September 3, 1970, Verlie Hite was awakened by the telephone, as she would later report to police investigators. On the line was Skip Taylor. The rest of the band, accustomed to Wilson's habit of missing airplane flights, had left for Germany the previous day to begin the tour. Taylor wanted to know if Wilson was coming, and asked Verlie if she had seen him recently. She had not, but upon rising the next morning, someone noticed that his van was parked in the yard.

Verlie went outside to look for Wilson, enlisting the help of her son Ed and four other members of the household. One of these was a friend named Craig Hoppe. The group began searching the hillside.

Sometime between ten o'clock and ten-thirty in the morning, Hoppe found Wilson's body. Later press reports claimed that Verlie had found the body; however, the original police documentation indicates that it was actually Hoppe, who could not be located for comment.

By one-thirty, the police had arrived and pronounced Wilson dead. According to their notes given to the coroner's office, Wilson was found laying on his back, in his sleeping bag on the ground, naked. The notes record: "White froth at corner of decedent's mouth. A bloody purge emiting [sic] from decedent's nose. ... 4 tabs wrapped in plastic bag found in pants pocket of decedent. All clothing found on ground, outside of sleeping bag, next to decedent."

According to these notes, the hillside was fifty feet west of the Hite residence and fifty feet higher in elevation. Woods and brush surrounded the area. The hillside was very steep, and as Ed Marrow recalls, it proved difficult to remove Wilson's body.

The next day, September 4, an autopsy was performed. Alan Wilson's cause of death was listed as accidental acute barbiturate intoxication.

The full text of the official documentation of Wilson's death scene, written by an "E. Smith", reads as follows:

Decedent last seen alive 9-1-70 at midnite, at residence of decedent, by Verlie Hite same address. Decedent was a member of a rock music group. The other members left for Germany on 9-2-70. Manager of music group telephoned residence of decedent asking for whereabouts of decedent, at 0200 hrs, this date. Decedents 1970 Ford Econoline truck parked in front of residence. Other members of residence (total number of 6) went looking for decedent. Decedent found 1030 hrs., 9-3-70, by Craig Hoppe same address, 50 feet west of residence, also 50 feet higher in elevation. Relative to residence, on back, on ground, in sleeping bag, naked, in a wooded and brush area. White froth at corner of decedent's mouth. A bloody purge emiting from decedent's nose. 3 A.S. photos. 4 red tabs wrapped in plastic bag found in pants pocket of decedent. All clothing found on ground, outside of sleeping bag, next to decedent. A red stain or coloring on inside or palm of L hand. Sleeping bag not over face or head of decedent when found. No app. or visual evidence of foul play.

On September 5, Wilson's body was cremated. His ashes were sent to Woodlawn Cemetery in Everett, Massachusetts; hence some sources have erroneously listed Woodlawn Cemetery as his final resting place. However, the cemetery turned the remains over to stepmother Barbara Wilson. Feeling that Alan should be scattered among the redwoods, she sent his remains to Bob Hite.

The Wilson family held a memorial service for Alan on Sunday, September 13. The other members of Canned Heat were on tour and did not attend. However, they encouraged grieving fans to send donations to the Music Mountain foundation in Wilson's memory. (Whether any such donations were made, and what became of the money, is unclear.)

Alan Wilson's memorial service was held at Menotomy Rocks Park in Arlington, a place he had enjoyed in life. Barbara Wilson once recalled walking there with him as he told her about the different kinds of trees, including one whose leaves were shaped like "little mittens", as he said. Reverend Wilbur Canaday, minister of the Park Avenue Congregational Church, led the service. Readings included the Holy Bible's Psalm 150, along with a passage from Henry David Thoreau's *Walden*. Alan Wilson's old musical partner David Maxwell was among the speakers, and a letter from Dick Waterman was read aloud.

As for the surviving members of Canned Heat, they couldn't quite let go of Alan. In his own dysfunctional way, Bob Hite was grieving for his lost musical partner, and put off scattering the ashes. Richard Hite remembers, "There's one weird thing. Alan had been cremated and Alan's wish was to be scattered over the redwoods. My brother had custody of the remains, and ... everybody would get high and stuff like that and every once in a while it'd be time to get the box out and check Alan out. And so, they were in Topanga Canyon one time and Alan was the center of attention, the box ... Fahey comes walking in, took one look, and goes, 'Gee Alan, you've changed.'"

John Fahey recalled that Bob became so obsessed with Wilson's ashes that he started carrying the box to Canned Heat's concerts, "so Alan can see the show". This reportedly infuriated Henry Vestine, who saw it as less than respectful, and he insisted that Hite leave the box at home. It was placed under the kitchen sink, remaining there until Verlie Hite made a special trip to the forest, laying Wilson's earthly remains among the moss and ferns where he had found his only real peace in life.

Had the story ended there, Alan Wilson's legend might have been quite different. His lifelong struggle with depression had occasionally brought him to the brink of suicide; however, according to official reports there was no real evidence at the scene of his death to prove that he had taken his own life in the end. There was no note, and according to toxicology reports, Wilson had not taken a particularly massive overdose. Nor is there any evidence of alcohol reported in the toxicology results from his body.

Furthermore, the presence of the four pills remaining in his pocket would be difficult to explain in a suicide scenario. It would not have been logical for Wilson to save four pills if he thought he would be dead soon. Had he overdosed deliberately, he would have taken all of his pills, in the most logical of scenarios, and likely would have consumed large quantities of alcohol as well. However, this is not indicated by the autopsy laboratory reports.

Wilson had, however, attempted suicide in the past. His recent mental state was enough to cause some to suspect that he had purposely overdosed to take his own life. Speculations and rumors were passed like so many joints among Wilson's colleagues, friends, and fans. He had taken over three hundred pills, one story went. Another story suggested that the street drugs Wilson took had been tainted with strychnine, which poisoned him. Both of these are contradicted by autopsy and toxicology results, but Wilson's grieving friends and band mates didn't seek out such documents. Many simply believed whatever they had happened to hear first. Others reserved judgment, but nursed secret hopes that his death had been a mere accident, a miscalculation of dosage that had been simply intended to help him get to sleep.

For some, however, an Alan Wilson suicide was not just a possibility, but a reality. Canned Heat manager Skip Taylor has his own story of Alan Wilson's death, and it is somewhat different from the account documented by the police and coroner.

Skip Taylor's story, as told in 1997, opens with a strange prophecy the night before Canned Heat left for Europe. He said, "The night before we were going to leave for Europe, my wife woke up right in the middle of the night and said, 'Alan's dead.' Just woke up right out of a dead sleep and said that. ... I thought she was stone crazy."

The next morning, Skip tried to go about his business as usual, to no avail. "I got to the airport the next morning to leave for Europe," he said. "Alan never showed up. My wife knew, psychic as she was, she had that thought ... that's what I remember. And then everybody was at the airport ready to go and he wasn't there. I knew that she had been right. I said, 'Well, I'll stay behind and go get Alan. But I knew, I wasn't getting Alan. I knew what I was gonna do."

Then, as Taylor recalls, he went to Bob Hite's house, knowing what would await him. "Then I went up and knew where to find him," Taylor says. "He slept up behind Bob Hite's house in Topanga Canyon. ... And, went up and I found him there, asleep with an empty bottle of gin and an empty bottle of reds. And, the biggest smile you've ever seen. Just laying there dead as a doornail smiling like a Cheshire cat. It was so weird. And, it was the first time in my life, too, that I became a true believer in life after death, spirit or whatever, because I could feel Alan there and see him there and whatever."

The timeline and other details of Skip Taylor's account vary from the coroner's report, informed by the sheriff's department which had sent officers to the scene. Taylor remembers September 3, the day of Wilson's body being found, as the same day that Canned Heat was scheduled to leave for Europe. His story has him going directly from the airport to Bob Hite's house. The coroner's report, however, claims that the band left on September 2. This would mean that Canned Heat had already been gone for a day by the time Wilson was found.

The police/coroner report states that Wilson's body was found by Craig Hoppe. The only place Skip Taylor is mentioned is at 2 a.m. on September 3, when he telephoned the Hite household to inquire after Wilson. This is, however, incompatible with Taylor's claim that he came directly from the airport to Hite's house, knowing that Wilson's body would be there.

Skip Taylor's account is also contradicted in part by the memory of Verlie Hite's son Ed Marrow, who was also present that morning. He says, "Skip did not find him, Craig did. Was Skip there, I don't remember if he showed up or not; he usually travelled with the band which had left one or two days before thinking Alan would just show up."

Adolfo de la Parra's published memoirs support Skip Taylor's side of the story, at least that part of it which has Taylor staying behind in Los Angeles. According to de la Parra, Taylor did not accompany them on the plane, instead remaining to search for Wilson. This does not, however, resolve the discrepancy of dates, as the police report clearly indicates that Canned Heat left for Europe an entire day before Wilson's body was found. It also has Skip Taylor telephoning to seek Wilson, not stopping by.

In de la Parra's book, he also indicates that, according to the information he was given (which, as he makes clear, is provided by

Taylor), Taylor found Wilson's body in mid-afternoon. This conflicts with the police report which has Wilson's body discovered in mid-morning, and the police arriving at the property in the afternoon.

The specifics of Wilson's death scene, and the items present, also vary greatly in the two different accounts. The police report has Wilson naked in his sleeping bag, his nostrils bloodstained and traces of foamy saliva around his mouth. His clothes were in a pile next to him, and a plastic bag containing four pills was in his pants pocket. No other items were present at the scene. Taylor's story, however, has Wilson smiling and fully clothed, lying atop the sleeping bag with empty gin and pill bottles. Neither of these items appear anywhere in the police report; nor does the toxicology report suggest that Wilson had combined his barbiturates with gin.

There is also an irreconcilable variation in the two reports when it comes to Wilson's body positioning, clothing or lack thereof, and facial expression. Skip Taylor's account makes a suicide theory seem more plausible, suggesting that Alan was smiling with happiness because he had successfully ended his life. However, there are technical issues with this, primarily the fact that a barbiturate death would cause bodily muscles to relax and make it difficult, if not impossible, for a smile to remain on the face of the corpse.

As for the matter of clothing and bodily positioning, the two reports again conflict completely. There is no way to conflate Skip Taylor's account with that of the police.

Unfortunately, these strange discrepancies between the documented report and the Skip Taylor account cannot be easily explained away. Skip Taylor has declined to discuss these discrepancies in detail, and could not offer any explanation as to why the police report varies so drastically from his own story. When asked for comment, he declined to discuss Wilson's death further. As for the attending police officers, they could not be located to provide any remarks beyond the original documentation.

Skip Taylor believes that he saw Wilson's death coming, citing his wife's prophetic dream as an omen of warning. Richard Hite, however, recalled that nobody panicked when Wilson turned up missing. It had become a frequent occurrence. Richard said, "When he died, they really thought that maybe he was washing his clothes or something like that, because they couldn't find him. So they got the news when they arrived in Germany." For most of Wilson's friends and colleagues, the news of his death was a horrifying shock.

Early reports given to the press do not tend to support Skip Taylor's version of events. In such reports, Verlie Hite is typically cited as the person who found Wilson's body. At least one account, published by the Calgary Herald on September 8, 1970, confirms the police report of remaining pills found in a plastic bag — as opposed to Taylor's version, which features an empty bottle, not a bag, and no remaining pills.

The Calgary Herald story, based on an Associated Press report out of Los Angeles, was entitled "Rock Group Member's Death Investigated". Therein, the story includes the statements, "Wilson's body was discovered Thursday in a sleeping bag in the backyard of a Topanga Canyon home by Verlie Hite. ... A plastic bag of sleeping pills was found near the body, they said." Similar stories, all seemingly based on the same Associated Press version, are found in a variety of newspapers published in the week following Wilson's death. Nowhere in any of these stories is Skip Taylor mentioned as being on the scene.

The reason, if any, for Craig Hoppe not being mentioned in press accounts immediately following Wilson's death is unknown. However, his finding of the body is confirmed by Ed Marrow as well as by the documented police report.

With these many variations in memory and historical documentation, and few provable means of sorting facts from misinformation, Wilson's death becomes even more of a mystery. Over the years, various discrepant reports have generated confusion and controversy. It could be easy to believe that Wilson intended to kill himself, given his intense depression and history of suicidal tendencies. However, the specifics of his death scene (along with the autopsy and toxicology) really do not support this. There remains a significant possibility that he was simply trying to get some sleep, particularly given that he had a history of insomnia — and, later, headaches — that he treated with street barbiturates.

The attending coroner, Deputy Medical Examiner Luis Quan, officially recorded Wilson's death as "acute barbiturate intoxication, due to ingestion of overdose". The death certificate attributes this overdose to "accident". Nowhere in the official record is Wilson's death listed as a suicide.

In the autopsy report, one more mystery comes to light. The coroner records an apparent head injury, stating, "The scalp shows an area of superficial abrasion measuring 1.2 x 2.8 cm. ... It is located on the vertex of the scalp."

About the condition of Wilson's brain, Quan notes: "The vessels on the surface of the brain are moderately congested. In the parietal region of the cerebral hemisphere is a small amount of bright red blood." He also records "slight to moderate congestion" of the brain's surface, stem, and cerebellum.

Quan found Wilson's apparent head trauma worth noting, but did not cite it as a cause of his death. The cause of the "superficial abrasion", and any relationship to the condition, was not explored.

According to the late Claude McKee, Wilson had been suffering from "extremely bad" headaches for some time prior to his death, perhaps as a result of an automobile crash injury. This might have been some symptom of a more serious brain injury. Furthermore, it is possible that Wilson could have been suffering from one of these headaches on the night of his death, perhaps impairing his judgment or even affecting his physiological reactions to the drugs he took. As for the area of "superficial abrasion" on the top of his head, one can only wonder as to the cause.

Unfortunately, the ultimate truth about the circumstances of Wilson's death will likely remain hidden. No matter which account one chooses to believe regarding the scene of his death, and no matter how one interprets the pathological evidence, we can never truly know Wilson's mind. His deepest thoughts and feelings, and his real intentions as he climbed the hill to unroll his sleeping bag for the last time, remain a mystery. Friends, family, and colleagues of

Wilson, as well as those who admired him from afar, will have to content themselves with the many rich artistic truths of his life.

APPENDIX

September 3, 1970

Documented notes on how and where the body of Alan Wilson was found on September 3, 1970. From the Los Angeles County coroner's office report.

COUNTY OF LOS ANGELES
DEPARTMENT OF CHIEF MEDICAL EXAMINER — CORONER
MEDICAL REPORT

Name: *ALAN C. WILSON*   Case No. *70-9292*
Date: *9-3-70*   Dr.

CONTINUATION SHEET

DECEDENT LAST SEEN ALIVE 9-1-70 AT MIDNITE, AT RESIDENCE OF DECEDENT, BY VERLIE HITE SAME ADDRESS. DECEDENT WAS A MEMBER OF A ROCK MUSIC GROUP. THE OTHER MEMBERS LEFT FOR GERMANY ON 9-2-70. MANAGER OF MUSIC GROUP TELEPHONED RESIDENCE OF DECEDENT ASKING FOR WHERE-ABOUTS OF DECEDENT, AT 0200 HRS, THIS DATE. DECEDENTS 1970 FORD ECONOLINE TRUCK PARKED IN FRONT OF RESIDENCE. OTHER MEMBERS OF RESIDENCE (TOTAL NUMBER OF 6) WENT LOOKING FOR DECEDENT. DECEDENT FOUND 1030 HRS., 9-3-70, BY CRAIG HOPPE SAME ADDRESS, 50 FEET WEST OF RESIDENCE, ALSO 50 FEET HIGHER IN ELEVATION - RELATIVE TO RESIDENCE, ON BACK, ON GROUND, IN SLEEPING BAG, NAKED, IN A WOODED AND BRUSH AREA. WHITE FROTH AT CORNER OF DECEDENTS MOUTH. A BLOODY PURGE EMITING FROM DECEDENTS NOSE. 3 A.S. PHOTOS. 4 RED TABS WRAPPED IN PLASTIC BAG FOUND IN PANTS POCKET OF DECEDENT. ALL CLOTHING FOUND ON GROUND, OUTSIDE OF SLEEPING BAG, NEXT TO DECEDENT. A RED STAIN OR COLORING ON INSIDE OR PALM OF ① HAND. SLEEPING BAG NOT OVER FACE OR HEAD OF DECEDENT WHEN FOUND. No APP. OR VISUAL EVIDENCE OF FOUL PLAY.

E. Smith

Alan Wilson's death certificate, first page. Note that immediate cause of death is listed as "deferred". At the time the certificate was first filed, toxicology analyses had not yet been completed.

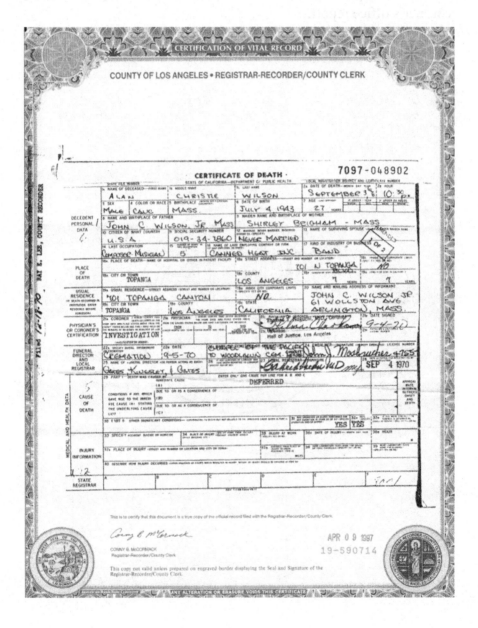

Alan Wilson's death certificate, second page. Filed in December 1970 after toxicology analyses were completed, this document declares Wilson's death accidental, with an immediate cause of acute barbiturate intoxication.

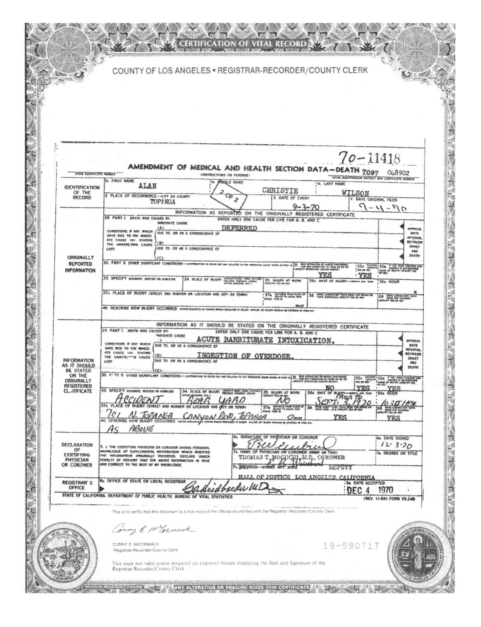

Letter of recommendation from John Fahey

In 1997, John Fahey endorsed the Blind Owl's biography with the following letter:

Al Wilson was one of my best friends, and ~~however~~ among the most signficant influences on my musicianship. He was saintlike, etc.

I am deeply saddened when I think of the unhappiness Al endured in life, and the lack of recognition which has been so ubiquitous throughout the years since his death brings me to a state of near depression. Al deserved better than what he received. It is time for him to be recognized as the genius he was, and his work must be appreciated for its immortal, spellbinding beauty. Only then can the music world rest with anything resembling a clear conscience.

I can think of no one better than Rebecca Davis to document and commemorate Al's life. In her extensive research as well as her musical analyses, she has relentlessly pursued the hidden truths about Al, and it is obvious to me that she understands him better than anyone else ever has or will. This must be due to her intense devotion, for she is, in effect, on a mission to unearth the facts about Al and relate them in an aura of dazzling glory. Her tireless crusade has been marked by tenacious determination, but also by an objectivity which allows her to see the inner workings of Al's personality.

I remember a time, shortly after I first met Rebecca, when I asked her why she liked Al so much. She tried to tell me during the course of our conversation that day, but her most eloquent explanation forms the pages of this book. It is a perfect description of Al's life, his music, and his inner brilliance. Rebecca has made things right for Al.

Signed, John Fahey:

Date :

BIBLIOGRAPHY AND RESOURCE LIST

Books

- Daniel E. Beaumont, *Preachin' the Blues: The Life and Times of Son House*, Oxford University Press, 2011.
- Stephen Calt, *I'd Rather Be the Devil: Skip James and the Blues*, Da Capo, 1994.
- Lawrence Cohn (ed.), *Nothing But the Blues*, Abbeville Press, 1993.
- Fito de la Parra, *Living the Blues: Canned Heat's Story of Music, Drugs, Death, Sex and Survival*, Canned Heat Music 2000.
- David Evans, *Tommy Johnson*, London: Studio Vista, 1970.
- David Evans, *Big Road Blues: Tradition and Creativity in the Folk Blues*, Berkeley: University of California Press, 1982.
- John Fahey, *Charley Patton*, London: Studio Vista, 1970.
- Gleason, Gosselin, Hodge, & Smith, *Clinical Toxicology of Commercial Products*, The Williams and Wilkins Company, 1969.
- Bob Groom, *The Blues Revival*, London: Studio Vista, 1971.
- Peggy Holroyde, *The Music of India*, Praeger Publishers, 1972.
- Laura Joplin, *Love, Janis*, HarperCollins, 2005
- David Kulczyk, *Death in California: The Bizarre, Freakish, and Just Curious Ways People Die in the Golden State*, Linden Publishing, 2009.
- Dave McAleer, *The All Music Book of Hit Singles*, Miller Freeman Books 1994.
- Robert Palmer, *Deep Blues*, Viking Penguin Inc., 1981.
- John Pareles and Patricia Romanowski, *The Rolling Stone Encyclopedia of Rock and Roll*, Rolling Stone Press, 1983.
- Mike Rowe, *Chicago Breakdown*, London: Eddison Press, 1973.
- Robert Santelli, *The Big Book of Blues*, Penguin Books, 1993.

- Charles Shaar Murray, *Boogie Man: The Adventures of John Lee Hooker in the American Twentieth Century*, Macmillan, 2002.
- Ravi Shankar, *My Music, My Life*, Simon & Shuster, 1968.
- Jeff Titon, *Early Downhome Blues: A Musical and Cultural Analysis*, University of Illinois Press, 1977.
- Eric Von Schmidt and Jim Rooney, *Baby Let Me Follow You Down*, Anchor Books, 1979.
- Edward Willett, *Janis Joplin: Take Another Little Piece of My Heart*, Enslow Publishers Inc., 2008

Magazines, periodicals, newspapers, and other article sources

- Newsweek, July 13, 1964, Son House and Skip James
- The Beat, January 13, 1968
- The Little Sandy Review, Volume 2, #4, 1968
- Daily Sun Dial, March 5, 1968
- Broadside, May 22-June 7, 1968, Volume VII #7
- Down Beat, Volume 35, Issue #12, June 13, 1968, "Look Back to the Future"
- New Musical Express, August 31, 1968
- Disc & Music Echo, September 14, 1968
- Melody Maker, September 14, 1968, "Canned Heat, the group that refused to be a jukebox and got fired"
- Los Angeles Times, December 8, 1968
- Go, December 20, 1968
- Billboard, December 21, 1968, "Best Bets for Christmas"
- Billboard, December 28, 1968, "Best Bets for Christmas"
- Chicago Sun Times, May 18, 1969
- The Day, September 4, 1970, "Deputies Probe Al Wilson Death"
- Los Angeles Herald Examiner, September 4, 1970, Alan Wilson obituary
- Los Angeles Times, September 4, 1970, Alan Wilson obituary
- The Milwaukee Journal, September 4, 1970, "Rock Group Member Dies"
- The Modesto Bee, September 4, 1970, "Rock Band Member is Found Dead"
- The Spokesman-Review, September 4, 1970, "Rock Singer Found Dead in California"
- Toledo Blade, September 4, 1970, "Rock Musician is Found Dead"
- Gettysburg Times, September 5, 1970, "Sheriff Checks Wilson's Death"
- Pittsburgh Post-Gazette, September 5, 1970, "Rock Composer is Found Dead"

- The Calgary Herald, September 8, 1970 "Rock Group Member's Death Investigated"
- Boston Globe, September 11, 1970, Alan Wilson obituary
- Rolling Stone, issue #68, October 29, 1970 "The People Leave Hyde Park Slowly"
- Rolling Stone, issue #76 February 18, 1971, Alan Wilson interview with Pete Welding: "Just Those Five Notes"
- Boston Sunday Globe, May 23, 1971, "Al Wilson: Musical Genius"
- Dark Star, July 1979, #21, Volume 4, Issue 3
- Goldmine, September 12, 1986, Cover story on Canned Heat
- Living Blues, Jan/Feb 1995, David Evans' letter to the editor
- Blues Revue, March/April 1995, David Evans' "Ramblin'" column, "Hypin' the Blues
- The Wire, August 1998, issue #174. "Blood on the Frets" by Edwin Pouncey. Later republished online by johnfahey.com.

Online Sources

Warning to readers and researchers: The Internet is not static, and pages may be changed or removed without notice. Therefore, this list is not to be considered a long term resource.

- AlanWilsonCannedHeat.com, a family-operated tribute and informational site, with contributions from Rebecca Davis.
- Ashgrovemusic.com, site commemorating and documenting the history of the Ash Grove club.
- Aleister Crowley quotes: Wikiquote.org/wiki/ Aleister_Crowley
- Billboard.com, historic Billboard chart information.
- Blindowl.net, a fan site dedicated to Alan Wilson.
- Calgary Herald, September 8, 1970 "Rock Group Member's Death Investigated" (AP): News.google.com/newspapers? id=2mpkAAAAIBAJ&sjid=33wNAAAAIBAJ&pg=2987,22 49031&dq=al-wilson&hl=en
- Cannedheatmusic.com, the Canned Heat website for the current lineup of the band.
- 45cat.com, extensive historical catalog of 45 rpm records as issued in a variety of countries.
- Chartstats.com, a compilation of chart listings worldwide.
- Chuck Hinson's recollections of an encounter with Canned Heat members: Open.salon.com/blog/mean_mr_mustard/ 2009/10/21/thoreau_blind_owl_and_the_bear
- Drdemento.com, Dr. Demento official website: Drdemento.com drdemento.com/members/blog/replies.html? id=92, "Christmas - continued", blog entry on the Chipmunks.
- Ed Marrow's profile and associated blog on MySpace: Myspace.com/edmarrow/blog
- Goldmine Magazine, Canned Heat profile by Peter Lindblad, April 21, 2010: Goldminemag.com/article/catch-fire-with-canned-heat-2
- Google Newspaper archive: news.google.com

- Google Books: books.google.com
- Jimhornmusic.com, Jim Horn's official website.
- Johnfahey.com
- Johnfahey.blogspot.com
- Letter from Skip Taylor regarding Music Mountain, appearing as a public ad in Billboard Magazine: Books.google.com/books? id=uSkEAAAAMBAJ&lpg=PA64&dq=alan %20wilson&pg=PA64#v=onepage&q=alan %20wilson&f=false
- John Fahey: Background and Brief Biography, from a thesis by Nick Schillace:_Nickschillace.com/thesis/Chapter_3.pdf
- Nashmusicians.wordpress.com, Nashville Musicians blog interview with Jim Horn: Nashmusicians.wordpress.com/ 2011/05/12/interview-with-jim-horn-legendary-reed-man/
- Paradiseartists.com, Paradise Artists representation, official Canned Heat bio: Paradiseartists.com/artists/canned_heat/ bio.pdf
- Rock Prosopography 102 blog by Bruno Ceriotti, a chronological list of live Canned Heat shows with band member lineup changes: Rockprosopography102.blogspot.com
- Tompkins Square label, "Max Ochs answers some questions from the producer": Tompkinssquare.com/max.html
- Travelingboy.com, Bob Hite interview by Tim Mattox: Travelingboy.com/tim/travel-tim-march08.html

The published writing of Alan Wilson

- "Bukka White: Master of the Blues Lyric", The Broadside of Boston, April 15, 1964.
- "Son House: An analysis of his music and a biography", first published in The Broadside of Boston, 1965. Republished as Blues Unlimited Collectors Classics 14 (Reprints Volume III), October 1966.
- Liner notes for John Fahey, The Transfiguration of Blind Joe Death
- Music reviews in The Little Sandy Review, 1966, including:
  The Mississippi Blues No. 2: the Delta, 1929-32, Origin OJL-11
  In the Spirit, volumes 1 and 2, Origin OJL-12, OJ-13
  Skip James, Today!, Vanguard VRS-9219
  Rare Blues of the Twenties, Historical Jazz 1, 2, 4
  "The Original" Sonny Boy Williamson, Blues Classics 9
  Big Joe Williams, *Classic Delta Blues*, Milestone 3001
  Otis Spann, *Nobody Knows My Troubles*
  Howlin' Wolf, *The Real Folk Blues* Chess LP-1502
  Sonny Boy Williamson, *The Real Folk Blues* Chess LP-1503
  John Lee Hooker, *It Serves You Right To Suffer* Impulse A-9103
  Contributions to Barry Hansen's review of The Mothers Of Invention, *Freak Out!*
- "Robert Pete Williams - his life and music, part 1", The Little Sandy Review, Volume 2, #1 - July 1966.
- "Robert Pete Williams - his life and music, part 2", The Little Sandy Review, volume 2, #2 - November 1966.
- Liner notes for Canned Heat, *Future Blues*, 1970 Liberty 11002
- Liner notes for John Lee Hooker, *Alone*, 1970 Specialty SPS 2125

<u>Other resources</u>

Correspondence, personal notes, and other miscellany:
- Personal correspondence from Alan Wilson to David Evans, July 26, 1964, August 2, 1966, and January 11, 1970, used courtesy of David Evans.
- Miscellaneous notes of Alan Wilson, from the personal collection of Richard Hite.
- School essay and notes by Alan Wilson, from photocopies from the Wilson family collection.
- Letter from the Town of Arlington to Boston University, September 1, 1961, regarding a scholarship for Alan Wilson.
- Personal correspondence from John Fahey to David Evans, July 25, 1966.

Documents:
- Commonwealth of Massachusetts: Birth certificate of Alan Wilson, public record.
- Los Angeles County: Death certificate of Alan Wilson, public record.
- Los Angeles County: Autopsy of Alan Wilson with attached documents including report of death scene, public record.

Interviews

Author interviews, conversations, and correspondence with the following people, not all of whom are quoted in "Blind Owl Blues":

- Mary Katherine Aldin
- Marina Bokelman
- Frank Cook
- David Evans
- John Fahey
- Heidi Galgowski
- Bill Givens
- Roger Handy
- Barry Hansen
- Jim Horn
- Richard Hite
- Tom Hoskins
- Lisa Konecny Lindenberg
- Harvey Mandel
- Ed Marrow
- David Maxwell
- Claude McKee
- Ed Pearl
- Mike Perlowin
- David Polacheck
- Skip Taylor
- Mike Turner
- Dick Waterman
- Barbara Wilson
- Jayne Wilson
- Martha Wynoff

DISCOGRAPHY

Commercially Available Recordings

Canned Heat recordings:

- *Uncanned* - CD, EMI 29165
- *Live at Topanga Corral* - LP, Wand 593
- *Vintage* - LP, Janus 3009
- *Canned Heat* - LP, Liberty 7526
- *Boogie With Canned Heat* - LP, Liberty 7541
- *Living the Blues* - LP, Liberty 27200
- *Hallelujah* - LP, Liberty 7618
- *Future Blues* - LP, Liberty 11002
- *Live In Europe* - LP, United Artists 5509
- *Best Of* - CD, EMI 48337
- *The Ties That Bind* - CD, Archive 80002
- *Hooker 'N Heat* (with John Lee Hooker) - CD, EMI 97896
- *Boogie House Tapes* - CD, Ruf 2000
- *Boogie House Tapes Volume 2* - Ruf 2004
- *Canned Heat Blues Band* - Ruf 1998
- *One More River to Cross* - Atlantic 1974
- *Hooker 'n Heat* Recorded Live at the Fox Venice Theater - Rhino, 1990
- *Boogie With Canned Heat: The Canned Heat Story*, DVD, Eagle Vision 2007
- *Canned Heat Live at Montreux 1973*, DVD, Eagle Rock Entertainment

Other artists:

The Beatles
- *Yesterday and Today*, Capitol ST2553
- *The Beatles*, Capitol SWBO-101
- *Revolver*, Capitol ST2576
- *Sgt. Pepper's Lonely Hearts Club Band*, Capitol SMAS-2653

The Paul Butterfield Blues Band
- *The Paul Butterfield Blues Band*, Elektra 7294-2
- *East-West*, Elektra
- *The Resurrection of Pigboy Crabshaw*, Elektra

Cream
- *Disraeli Gears*, Atco 33-232

Jean de Vres and his Afro Drums
- *Exciting Voodoo*

John Lee Hooker
- *The Ultimate Collection 1948-1990*, Rhino 70572
- *Original Folk Blues*, United 7746
- *John Lee Hooker Sings the Blues*, King
- *Driftin' the Blues*, United UM710
- *The Great Blues Sounds of John Lee Hooker*, United US7731

Son House
- *Son House and the Great Delta Blues Singers (1928-1930)*, Document 5002
- *The Complete Library of Congress Sessions 1941-1942*, Travelin Man CD02
- *Father of the Delta Blues*, Columbia 48867
- *Delta Blues and Spirituals*, Capitol 31830

Howlin' Wolf
- *Howlin' Wolf*, Chess 2ACMB201

Mississippi John Hurt
- *Avalon Blues: The Complete 1928 Okeh Recordings*, Columbia 64986

Elmore James
- *The Sky Is Crying*, Rhino 71190

Bunk Johnson
- *Bunk Johnson and his Superior Jazz Band*, Good Time Jazz M12048

Robert Johnson
- *The Complete Recordings*, Columbia 46222

Floyd Jones and Eddie Taylor
- *Masters of Modern Blues*, Testament 5001

Ali Akbar Khan
- *Sound of the Sarod*, World Pacific WP-1435

Little Walter
- *Best Of*, Chess 9192

Kinichi Nakanoshima
- *Koto and Flute - The Music of Kinichi Nakanoshima*, World Pacific WP-1443

Odetta
- *Folk Song and Minstrelsy*, Vanguard
- *At Carnegie Hall*, Vanguard

Charley Patton
- *Complete Recorded Works in Chronological Order Volume 1 (1929)*, Document 5009
- *Complete Recorded Works in Chronological Order Volume 2 (1929)*, Document 5010
- *Complete Recorded Works in Chronological Order Volume 3 (1929-1934)*, Document 5011

Ravi Shankar and Ali Akbar-Kahn [sic]
- *The Master Musicians of India*, Prestige PR1078

Henry Thomas
* *Texas Worried Blues*, Yazoo 1080/1

Various Artists
* *Africa - Music of the Malinke' and Baoule*, Counterpoint Grand Prix du Disque 529
* *African Highlife*, Fontana MGF 27519
* *Blues Masters, Volume 2: Postwar Chicago*, Rhino 71122
* *Blues Masters, Volume 5: Jump Blues Classics*, Rhino 71125
* *Blues Masters, Volume 8: Mississippi Delta Blues*, Rhino 71130
* *The Blues Roll On*, Atlantic 1352
* *Canned Heat Blues*, Bluebird 07863
* *Chicago Mob Scene - A Folk Music Jam Session*
* *The Country Blues 1966*, RBF Records
* *Folk Songs and Dances of North India*, SPL 1614
* *Mississippi Blues Volume 1 (1928-1937)*, Document 5157
* *The Monterey International Pop Festival*, Rhino 70596
* *The Rural Blues: A Study of the Vocal and Instrumental Resources*, RBF Records
* *Texas Pop Volume 12*
* *Woodstock: Music From the Original Soundtrack and More*, Atlantic T55NN-1
* *Woodstock Two*, Atlantic 400
* *Monterey Pop* - VHS
* *Woodstock* - VHS

Muddy Waters
* *The Real Folk Blues*, Chess 9274

Bukka White
* *The Complete Bukka White*, Sony
* *1963 Isn't 1962*, Genes GCD9903

Big Joe Williams
* *Piney Woods Blues*, Delmar 1602

Tapes from private collections

From the Marina Bokelman Collection at the Blues Archive, University of Mississippi. Recorded in Los Angeles by Marina Bokelman:

- Al Wilson, interviewed by Marina Bokelman, March 31, 1968.
- Al Wilson, interviewed by Marina Bokelman, April 5 and 16, 1968.
- Bob Hite, interviewed by Marina Bokelman, April 8 and May 6, 1968.
- Henry Vestine, interviewed by Marina Bokelman, April 21, 1968.
- Larry Taylor, interviewed by Marina Bokelman, May 9, 1968.
- Fito de la Parra, interviewed by Marina Bokelman, May 6, 1968.
- Canned Heat rehearsal tapes, April 9 and 10, 1968.
- Canned Heat live at the Whiskey A-Go-Go, April 21, 1968.

From the personal collection of Marina Bokelman

- Canned Heat Blues Band live at the Ash Grove, Los Angeles, January 8, 13, 14, and 20, 1967.
- Canned Heat Blues Band live at the Ash Grove, Los Angeles, March 29, 1967.

From the personal collection of Richard Hite:

- Films of Canned Heat in Europe, early 1970, including "Beat Club" show.
- Assorted Canned Heat tapes.
- Record of Alan Wilson, circa 1946, with family members.
- Assorted recordings of Alan Wilson accompanied by Richard Hite, circa 1965-1970, exact dates unknown.
- Assorted Alan Wilson solo recordings.

From the personal collection of David Evans:

- Alan Wilson, solo recordings with harmonica and guitar. April 30, 1964, Cambridge, Massachusetts.
- David Evans, accompanied by Al Wilson on harmonica. April 1964, Cambridge, Massachusetts.
- Son House, accompanied by Al Wilson on harmonica. Spring 1964, Cambridge, Massachusetts.
- Mississippi John Hurt, accompanied by Al Wilson on harmonica. February 11 and 15, 1964, Cambridge, Massachusetts.

ABOUT THE AUTHOR

Rebecca Davis was an author, consultant, and music historian. Her work included contributions to the family-operated Alan Wilson tribute website at AlanWilsonCannedHeat.com. As an independent media professional, she also contributed to a wide variety of newspapers, magazines, music-related publications, and multi-media projects.

Made in the USA
Coppell, TX
25 March 2024

30543925R10154